MEMOIRS

OF

LADY OTTOLINE

MORRELL

Lady Ottoline Morrell by Augustus John, 1909

MEMOIRS

OF

Lady OTTOLINE MORRELL

MORRELL

A Study in Friendship

1873-1915

Edited by Robert Gathorne-Hardy

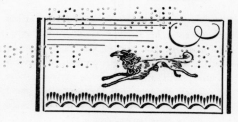

NEW YORK

Alfred · A · Knopf 1964

L. C. catalog card number: 64–12309

THIS IS A BORZOI BOOK,
PUBLISHED BY ALFRED A. KNOPF, INC.

Manufactured in the United States of America,
and distributed by Random House, Inc.

FIRST AMERICAN EDITION

Preface

For the larger part of her life Lady Ottoline regularly kept a journal. As will be discovered, she made great use of this in compiling her memoirs. The reading of her journal was far more to her than the sharpening of memory; she lived the past over again. Thus may be partly explained the life and vigour of her memoirs. Indeed, so complete was her return to the past that she seemed to become divested of the present. It would be difficult to conjecture from this book that in later years, and during the times when she was writing her memoirs, she was on terms of great devotion and sympathy with her brothers, frequently meeting and regularly corresponding: or that Lord Henry was to become known for opinions almost as radical as those of his sister: and that he left behind him a most sensitively chosen collection of fine contemporary paintings.

It must be allowed that her earliest memories, vivid as any, were recalled with no documentary aid. Small wonder that, with her journal for guide, she so surely and with such feeling retraced the ways of her old life. Other written resources, hardly less evocative to her, were the letters of friends. Some of these are already well known among the published letters of D. H. Lawrence and Katherine Mansfield.

While she was writing her memoirs, Lady Ottoline had succeeding stages of the work typed out. Copies of these parts she

v

sent round to a number of friends (Virginia Woolf was among them), for comment and criticism. In my own case, I confined myself to small matters of style; in every case she responded "Of course!" and made, with no reluctance at all, the proposed correction. At her death the work was unfinished, ending in the year 1918. She left a wish that I, who had known her so well, should be editor.

I originally conceived that my duty would be to prepare the book for publication at a somewhat remote date, perhaps in my extreme old age, should I ever attain such a state, or even after my own death. More and more requests came for earlier publication, until they were irresistible, and my problems were altered. The memoirs concern many people still alive, and as many not long dead. There are things about all of us which, however freely we might impart them to posterity, we wouldn't care to have known during our lifetime. This feeling is apparent in many posthumous autobiographies. There is nothing gravely objectionable left unpublished in these memoirs; yet there are passages which it would be unfeeling and uncharitable to make public at the present day.

Larger excisions have had to be made than those called for by consideration to others. The work, although essentially a fragment, is of enormous length. A complete printing would probably involve four volumes or more the size of this one. Large and painful cutting has often been necessary. Many important letters were introduced by her, and these have been discarded, in the hope that one day a collection of her correspondence will be published. Even with such cuts as have been made, it proved impossible to compress the memoirs, without crippling them, into a single, manageable volume. Accordingly it has been resolved to divide the work into two. A second volume will appear in due course.

One problem remained. During the late war, Philip Morrell occupied himself by preparing for publication a version short enough to be comprised in a single volume. Before starting, he asked Sturge Moore (a friend of Lady Ottoline's) for his opinion on the memoirs. The poet gave his opinion that the work was most interesting and of great value, but—that it should be entirely rewritten for publication (Sturge Moore, so R. C. Trevelyan once told me, had a curious habit of laboriously rewriting poems by great predecessors, like Wordsworth or Shelley). Philip Morrell did not go so far as this, but he attempted to add the elegance of his own method to the sometimes artless phrasing of his wife. And his cuts were huge. "She took," he said, in plausible justification, "any advice that was given to her about her writing."

This was true; but the strangely deadening effect of his well-intended polish has been a warning to me. The imposition of a different style might at times add clarity to the narrative; more often it would dull the fresh and passionate utterance of the writer.

I have felt free to alter her punctuation, which is often wayward. In less than a score of places I have made small changes in the text where the original was, at a first reading, ambiguous. These departures from principle can, I think, be justified. The turmoil of war-time movings, and packings and unpackings, led to the loss of the typescript which embodied her latest corrections and alterations. The version I have used is a text with manuscript corrections from which the lost copy was made. Most of the amended phrases may well have suffered from mechanical errors which would have been corrected in the lost typescript. (No manuscript could be found, and it is likely that, as soon as a typed copy was ready with duplicates, she threw the original away.) Although confident that she would have agreed to the changes, I have resisted every temptation to make what would have seemed to me a stylistic improvement. To his edited version, Philip Morrell added notes. These I have used, distinguishing them from my own by his initials P.M.

It remains only to thank Mrs. Igor Vinogradoff, Julian, the daughter of Lady Ottoline, for her help and advice and sympathy in the long labours of preparing this book for publication.

ROBERT GATHORNE-HARDY

Contents

List of Plates

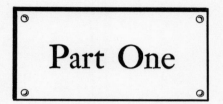

Part One

Childhood, Escape and Marriage

CHAPTER I

The Move to Welbeck

Le hasard est le plus grand de tous les artistes.

BALZAC: *Les Vieilles Filles*

My FATHER DIED in December 1877. His cousin, the fifth Duke of Portland whom my father, if he had survived, would have succeeded, died exactly two years later. If the order of these events had been reversed and my father had lived to become Duke of Portland, as he had always expected that he would, being much the younger man, it would naturally have made a great difference to my mother[1] and in many ways to us all. But events do not happen as mortals desire, and they must submit and accommodate themselves to them.

When my father died I was four and a half years old. I have a few charming recollections of him hidden away in the store-

[1] Afterwards created Lady Bolsover in her own right. She was born in 1834, her father being H. M. Browne, Dean of Lismore. In 1862 she married, as his second wife, Lt.-General Arthur Bentinck. His father was Lord Charles William Augustus, a son of the third duke. Ottoline's grandmother was Lord Charles's second wife, Anne Wellesley, a source of Irish blood in which she always delighted. When her brother became Duke of Portland, Ottoline and her brothers were raised to the rank of Duke's children.

house of my memory. In that private cinema of the past he appears as a tall large man, extremely handsome with a short, greyish beard and blue-grey eyes, which had a peculiarly enchanting expression, radiating kindness and good temper, and a loud but melodious voice. He was called, I have been told, Big Ben on account of it.

I remember his taking me out on long drives in a wagonette, with a pair of grey horses which he drove himself, I sitting on my nurse's knee at his side, through woods and soft silver-sanded roads on visits to neighbours—the Hankeys or the Walters—and also to a Military Review at Aldershot with crowds of carriages, clouds of dust and regiments marching past —one of them headed by a goat. Then in London in Hyde Park in the summer, where he would drive me in front of him, holding on to my broad pink sash. One day he put me over the railings to run on the grass among the flower-beds, and I was knocked over by a large black-and-white plum pudding dog which rushed by me, and he laughed as he picked me up amazed and indignant. One evening I find myself sitting on his lap, clinging to him in a fit of shyness with my head buried on his shoulder because some visitors had arrived, and he is saying with a gay laugh: "You see I cannot get up. I am not allowed to."

He died very suddenly at a hotel in London, where my mother had gone with him to consult a specialist.

My brother Charlie and I had been left in the country and when the news came to us we stood side by side at the nursery window and looked out on to the stable yard, feeling sad and solemn. "Papa is dead. That means that he will never come back again," and suddenly for the first time I became aware of my own separate existence—realizing perhaps that I also should one day die and go out into the unknown.

My mother's return from London, all dressed in black, her sadness and loneliness with no one to help her or support her, and my own pride, which even then I knew to be shameful, in a pair of black gloves and a black dress for going to church, are still vivid impressions; also her growing ill-health. Small as I was, I began even then to be her constant companion. I walked at her side holding her hand and can feel still the delicious warmth of holding my hand in hers in the deep pockets of an old coat which she used to wear trimmed with golden otter. At night I always slept in her room, my little hard bed at the side of hers.

Two years later when the old Duke died, we all went to London to Claridge's Hotel. Grapes and peaches came from Welbeck, wrapped in pink paper, in white wooden boxes. My brother Charlie and I were taken to Cremer's toyshop in Regent Street, where we were allowed to choose whatever toys we liked. After our comparative poverty this seemed like Fairyland, and I chose a doll dressed in spangled blue satin fixed on a handle that played music as you whirled it round. But none of these new luxuries gave us very much pleasure. They were all overcast by a sense of dullness and depression, which must have come, I suppose, from my mother's sadness at the absence of my father.

My eldest brother, who now became Duke of Portland, was nearly twenty-two years old. He was our half-brother, being my father's child by his first wife, who died a few days after he was born; but from the time of my father's marriage to my mother two or three years afterwards she had brought him up side by side with her own children, making no distinction between him and them, except perhaps that she spoilt him rather more.

Fundamentally he was always very kind-hearted, but in his

youth he was often moody, and had a curious power of alarming people. I think he would often have been glad to unbend
towards me, but did not know how best to do so. At any rate,
he remained unapproachable, and all through these earlier
years I was afraid and almost in terror of him.

But it would have been very difficult for any young man of
twenty-two to inherit great wealth and a Dukedom without
becoming rather conscious of his own importance. The world
rushed to lay itself at his feet; ladies of fashion smiled on him
and waylaid him; mothers schemed to get him for their daughters; pretty ladies beckoned to him; the turf offered him its
choicest openings; Lord Beaconsfield invited him to Hughenden
as the cousin of his old friend Lord George Bentinck and called
him "his young Duke."

Before the end of the year it was decided that we must all
go to Welbeck. My brother Charlie had lately been ill with
peritonitis, but it was felt that the entry into Welbeck must
not be delayed, and he was carried to the station wrapped in
blankets, looking very pale and feeble. The party was composed
of my mother, who was then forty-five years old and still very
beautiful, with thick raven-black hair; my eldest brother
Portland, who, as I have said, was nearly twenty-two; my
brother Henry, aged sixteen; Bill aged fourteen; Charlie aged
eleven; and I, who was the youngest of the family, just six and
a half, with my nurse Powell to look after me. We travelled in
a saloon carriage, arriving at Worksop on a dark, windy winter
evening. Outside the station there was a little crowd of people
waiting to see the young Duke arrive. Their white faces and
dark clothes caught the light of the dim oil lamps as they
pressed round the door of the old-fashioned carriage, while my
little brother Charlie was lifted carefully into a second carriage.
Then a long dreary drive to Welbeck, till at last we arrived be-

fore the house. The road in front was a grass-grown morass covered with builders' rubbish, and to allow the carriage to reach the front door they had had to put down temporary planks. The hall inside was without a floor and here also planks had been laid to allow us to enter.

Why the house had been allowed to get into this state I do not know, unless it was that the old Duke was so absorbed with his vast work of digging out and building underground rooms and tunnels that he was oblivious of everything else. He pursued this hobby at the cost of every human feeling, and without any idea of beauty, a lonely, self-isolated man. It was always thought that his love of tunnels was due to a dislike of being seen. Even round the garden of Harcourt House, where he lived in London, he erected high frosted-glass screens, so that he could not be overlooked; and when he travelled he never left his own carriage, but had it placed on a railway truck at the end of the train, keeping the green silk blinds closely drawn.

Naturally rumours spread that he was a leper or suffered from some other terrible disease, but I have talked to his old servants and they tell me that he had a delicate and lovely skin, and was an extremely handsome man, tall and thin, with a proud, aristocratic air. My mother had a bust of him made from a cast after his death, and from this he certainly appears to have been a remarkably handsome man, of a thin, clear-cut type, not very unlike the Duke of Wellington, but with a harder and more selfish face.

We were met at the front door by some of the heads of departments—McCallum, the Steward, a tall Scotsman; Tinker, the Clerk of the Works, and others—and shown up to the few rooms that were fit to live in. The late Duke had only inhabited four or five rooms opening into each other in the West Wing of the house. Here he lived, slept and ate; indeed, it was said

7

that he began his nights in one room, and if unable to sleep had a bath and went into another, keeping up fires in each room. To these rooms, which were scantily and almost poorly furnished, the little family party, all dressed in black, was solemnly ushered up, and my brother Charlie was put to bed.

Next day began the journey of discovery of the house. The suite of rooms that we were living in had double sets of brass letterboxes in the doors: one to push the letters in, and the other to push the letters out. Two of these rooms were quite charming: a large west room and a little room known as the north closet adjoining, which had been used by the second Duchess of Portland (Matthew Prior's noble, lovely little Peggy) who brought Welbeck into the family, and was a great collector of antiques and a highly cultivated woman. It was here that she and Mrs. Delany sat, embroidered and talked.[2] I remember the smell of these rooms now.

All the rest of the rooms in the house were absolutely bare and empty, except that almost every room had a water-closet in the corner, with water laid on and in good working order, but not enclosed or sheltered in any way. All the rooms were painted pink, and the large drawing-rooms decorated with gold; but no furniture or pictures were to be seen. At last, in a large hall, decorated rather beautifully in the manner of Strawberry Hill, was found a vast gathering of cabinets all more or less in a state of disrepair.

[2] Although Mrs. Delany did visit Welbeck, she and the duchess met most often at Bulstrode, not very far from London. A friend of Swift, and of many other great personages of the eighteenth century, Mrs. Delany is best remembered for her wonderful and celebrated representations of flowers, carried out in mosaics of coloured paper. The first, a geranium, was made on an impulse while she was staying with the duchess who, seeing her work, said, "What are you doing with that geranium?"

Then on by an underground passage and up through a trap-door into the building that had originally been the Duke of Newcastle's riding school and had been lined by the late Duke with mirrors and crystal chandeliers hanging from every point of the raftered roof, which was painted to represent the bright rosy hues of sunset; but the sudden mood of gaiety that had made him decorate it as a ballroom must have soon faded, leaving the mock sunset to shine on a lonely figure reflected a hundred times in the mirrors. For stacked here were all the pictures belonging to the house—pictures that had come down from generation to generation, but taken out of their frames and set up two or three deep against gaunt "wooden horses." The frames were afterwards found hidden away in a store-house.

In a similar building opposite this, which had been the stables of the Duke of Newcastle's famous horses, was the kitchen where the late Duke's perpetual chicken had been kept roasting on a spit, one chicken following another so that when-ever he should call for it one should be ready roasted and fit for eating. From this kitchen the food was lowered by a lift into a heated truck that ran on rails pushed by a man through a long underground passage to the house—a method of transit which I believe still continues. Another passage branching off from this one took us to three underground rooms, all very large, and one that seemed quite immense. These also were painted pink with parquet floors; heated by hot air, and lit from the top by mushroom lights level with the ground, so that in the daytime they were quite light and at night were lit by gas chandeliers. There was no beauty in them—they were just vast empty rooms, built down instead of up, and except for the top lighting you would not have been aware that they were

9

under the level of the ground. Along the side of them was a glass corridor intended for statues, but with no statues.

Then back we came to the house through more underground passages. Starting from these passages was the walking tunnel, about a mile long and wide enough for two or three people to walk abreast, that led from the house to the stables and gardens; and a little way off and parallel to it was another rather rougher one for the use of the gardeners and workmen; for the Duke did not wish to meet anyone walking in the same tunnel as himself. Then there was the great driving tunnel, more than a mile long, which was the only direct road to Worksop. It had been dug out under the old drive and was wide enough for two carriages to pass each other. In the daytime it was lit from the top by small mushroom windows which threw a ghostly light upon it, except where it dipped down under the lake, and there it was lit by jets of gas, as the whole tunnel was at night.

The collection of buildings, hunting stables, riding school, coach-houses, dairy, laundry and offices with a number of cottages and a covered tan gallop, about a quarter of a mile long, made a small town in themselves. They were all built in the same grey stone in dull heavy architecture, and stood without trees or flowers—flowers indeed were banished from the place—expressing only grandeur and pomp. The riding school was said to be the largest in the world. The vegetable gardens were on an equally huge scale—a series of square gardens, each surrounded by high walls, and of an average size of about eight acres.

The poor deluded owner seemed to assert his power and pride in making all the buildings as large and lonely as possible, banishing grace and beauty and human love and companionship, and leaving his fellow-beings in order to hide in tunnels.

He even cut down every tree within a considerable distance of the house.

He was kind to the hundreds of labourers who came from all the villages around to take part in these vast excavations, providing them with donkeys to carry them to and from their work, and with large silk umbrellas to shelter them from the rain. There was a large round donkey stable dug out near the house and paved with stone, where the donkeys stood and fed during the day while their riders worked.[3] He also provided a large skating-rink for the use of his household and others, with numbers of silver-mounted roller skates of every size and a man specially engaged to look after them; and we were told that if he ever came upon a housemaid sweeping in the corridor or on the stairs, he would send out the frightened girl to skate whether she wanted to or not. But these apparently were the only signs of kindness that he ever showed.[4]

At first this vast place, so denuded of all grace and beauty and life, cast a gloom over us all. My brother seemed to wish to shut it up and leave it, but my mother persuaded him that it was his duty to remain, and she began her long task of making it into a normal house, a home for him and for my other brothers. For many weeks the discoveries went on. One of the

[3] This curious underground stable, all built of stone, with its roof supported by a single stone pillar, giving it the appearance of a large and solid circus tent, was still standing when I first went to Welbeck soon after our marriage in 1902, but has since been pulled down and no trace left of it.   P.M.

[4] There is evidence to suggest that this judgment was mistaken. Records exist to show that tenants and servants at Welbeck were devoted to him; his political independence was commendable; and it has been said that his enormous works at Welbeck were carried out in order to employ poor people in lean times. It must be granted, however, that the particular work chosen indicated great eccentricity of character—a conclusion borne out by much of his behaviour.

rooms used by the late Duke was lined with cupboards reaching to the ceiling, filled with green boxes, and in these boxes was a huge number of dark brown wigs. In other cupboards were boxes and boxes of cream-coloured balbriggen socks, and white silk handkerchiefs, also fine nainsook ones each about a yard square, and all elaborately marked in fine cross-stitch with a coronet and the number of each lot, which was generally twelve dozen, and other mystic initials, describing the place where they were to be kept. There were also elaborate fine linen shirts with frills and high collars and sleeves of inordinate length.

In the storerooms and other parts of the house rare furniture and precious objects of all kinds were hidden away; high Coromandel screens and cabinets richly carved, a chest full of old red velvet robes, which had been first worn at the Coronation of King George I, and lovely pieces of rose-coloured Gobelins that emerged from long tin cases. How well I remember the smell of the pepper corns tumbling on the floor as these ornate rolls of tapestry were spread out before us.

One evening, I remember, when my brother was standing in the middle of a dark half-empty room, looking through the drawers of one of the cabinets, and was turning over snuff-boxes and watches and old miniatures, with someone holding a candle at his side, he came upon a little green silk quilted purse stuffed full of banknotes, which were taken out and counted and amounted to two thousand pounds. The little green purse —but without the notes—was given to me to keep, and still when I look at it I see myself again a small child peering up at those dim treasures lit by a solitary candle.

Day after day my mother worked incessantly, searching, investigating, directing and arranging for the furnishing of the house. But for her, who loved sympathy and good humour and wit, and above all kindness and companionship, it was often a weary task. If my father, to whom she had been very devoted, had been there to help and encourage her, it would have been all very different. But the thought of his absence made her feel more acutely the emptiness and loneliness of the great house. There were times when she almost lost heart, and I remember her one day sinking down exhausted and exclaiming to my old nurse—"Powell, I cannot go on." But she went on nevertheless as bravely as ever; and gradually something fine and beautiful came into existence.

In one portion of her task—the discovery and arrangement of the old pictures—she took a real interest and pleasure; and in this, young as I was, I felt that I could take part and even help her. All the pictures, as I have said, were stacked together in the old riding school, and my mother took endless trouble in sorting them out and investigating their history, inviting the best experts of that day to come down and give her their advice. My love of history, I think, was first stimulated by gazing at these old paintings, portraits of the courtiers of King James I's court, so elegant and lovely and sentimental, with pearls in their ears and long trailing lovelocks of golden hair hanging over their collars, and of the ladies whom they loved, with very low-cut dresses, showing pearly breasts, and embroidered skirts and exquisite shoes; portraits of the fighting Veres; portraits of the Countess of Essex, who had poisoned Overbury; of Louis XIV, a small dark olive-skinned boy of twelve, looking already vain and self-important; of Charles I, even younger, dressed in a green velvet doublet and skirt, with a sad pale face, his arms round a dog almost as large as himself, and a little toy gun in his hand; of his elder brother, Prince Henry, dressed in white; and of pale Arabella Stuart, who had been imprisoned nearby at Bolsover Castle. A small picture of Mary Queen of Scots,

13

who soon became my dearest friend—the exquisite face with a pearl drop on her forehead, and a fine gold cap over her small head—I used to visit very often. Whenever I see this picture now I still feel a thrill of my old emotion. There was also grim Bess of Hardwick, our old ancestress, dressed in black with a rope of pearls, who seemed to me nearly as important as Queen Elizabeth herself.

There was only one picture that was at all modern, and that was a full-length portrait of Fanny Kemble as Lady Macbeth, a tall, dark, handsome woman—a picture bought by the late Duke. She was supposed to be the one woman whom he had loved and wished to marry. It was said that old Tinker, eavesdropping outside a door, had once heard Lord John, as he then was, ask his father's permission to marry her—and that the old Duke's only answer was: "John, would you disgrace us?"; upon which the young man walked out of the room and never spoke of it again.

When once the spell of loneliness and isolation which the late Duke had cast over Welbeck had been broken, a new stream of life began to flow in. My brother's friends came for shooting parties. Young Guardsmen and hunting and racing friends and *"grandes dames"* of the most fashionable set, who came down to breakfast in velvet dresses with tight waists and lace fronts, and sat and gossiped all the morning, then drove out to lunch with the shooters in tweeds, had tea in pink satin tea-gowns from Paris, and dined in still more gorgeous brocades and velvets. I used to hide behind some embroidered curtains and peep at them as they swept into the drawing-room before dinner, composing themselves and giving their dresses a finishing pat before appearing. Now, as I look back on them, they seem almost as far away as the Knellers and Lelys hanging on the walls.

Once during these years the Prince of Wales came on a visit, with a retinue of attendants and friends and beautiful ladies and even his own little toy dogs. I remember amongst this party Lord Hartington and the Duchess of Manchester, whom he afterwards married, and Lady Lonsdale, who afterwards became Lady de Grey, with her magnificently handsome face and gleaming teeth, and odd high voice, like an Eastern empress. The late Duchess of Manchester seemed completely Elizabethan, a reincarnation of Queen Elizabeth or Bess of Hardwick. She and Lord Hartington were said to be already lovers, and I remember my mother telling us that she heard her as she sat at a writing-table near to Lord Hartington say, "Harty darling, stand me a stamp."

The first act of heroism in my life was asking the Prince to contribute something towards the Children's Hospital at Shadwell, for which I had a collecting box. My governess had suggested that I should do so. All the blood left my heart with an agony of nervousness at the thought of it, and a fierce struggle raged within me. At last duty won, and with a burning face I made my little curtsy and shook my collecting box before him, murmuring my timid prayer. Of course, he was charming and gave me a golden ten-shilling and a kiss. The memory of that kiss was to be revived over forty years later when I met Queen Alexandra at Welbeck in 1917. The first words she said to me were: "Ah, you were the little girl my husband kissed!" How she heard of this kiss or why she remembered it has often puzzled me. Did she keep a dossier of all his kisses?

Another kiss that made a great impression on me was given me by Lord Beaconsfield with his wrinkled Eastern mask. It was at our house in London, where he had been lunching with my

mother to whom he was always very kind. It was at his particular request that Queen Victoria had conferred on her the title
of Lady Bolsover which she bore for her life. I still see in my
mind his old, sad, experienced face bending down to confer his
kiss upon me.

My brother had a house at Melton in Leicestershire for
hunting, and another at Newmarket, and during his spells of
absence my mother would ask some of her old friends down to
Welbeck, and my other brothers would come there to spend
their holidays, when they were not hunting in Leicestershire.
But they were all much older than I was, and were very happy
together, hunting, shooting and fishing. To me they always
meant to be kind, but their kindness was so mixed with contempt that it could never make me happy or gay. I adored my
youngest brother and would have done anything for him, but
he was far too aloof to contemplate any return for my devotion.
In his eyes I was always a duffer. His pet name for me was
"Higgory Stiggins." Their attitude to me, I suppose, was very
much that of the ordinary British schoolboy to a shy younger
sister; but from my experience with them I could not believe
that it would ever be possible to talk with any freedom or frankness to a man.

The only real companion I ever had was one of my Irish
cousins, my mother's niece.[5] She was more than double my age,
but to her I poured out all my heart, and her visits were my
intense joy. My mother and I were nearly always together,
when I was not at my lessons, but I was naturally too young to
do more than adore her. She was intensely interested in politics
and history, and of course in all the business and affairs of Wel-

[5] Katherine Penelope Browne, daughter of the Rev. Henry Browne
(1856–1911), lord of the manor, and rector, of Bredon, in Worcestershire; he was a brother of Ottoline's mother.

beck, but a child of my age needed young companionship, and this was the one thing I never had except when Cattie came to stay with us. Other things were given me. On one of the first Christmas days at Welbeck I was taken up to the stables and there I found waiting for me a little phaeton with a minute pair of Shetland ponies all ready harnessed. A tiny groom in livery held them, and I was taught to drive by my mother and our old coachman, Ellis. When Cattie was with us I loved to take her out with the "mice," as we called them, through Sherwood Forest and into the woods, and when we wanted to go fast I made her clap her hands. Then they would gallop very swiftly, tails and manes swishing in the wind, through green drives, flying past the great gnarled oak trees. I would make Cattie tell me all about her life in Ireland, the ghosts that haunted their old home, the balls in Dublin and the wild doings of the family. We found some attics that had not been discovered before, and here we would sit crouched together until the darkness came on. One day we stole two red velvet robes from one of the chests, and trailed round in this pompous finery, twirling round and round and sinking on the floor with yards of rich velvet and gold tassels spread out. How heavenly it was, to laugh and play together! What long ill-written pages I wrote to Cattie after she left, in the dreary greyness that followed! Is there any intimacy so full and so warm and so abandoned as those early ones before experience has taught one the hundred subtle dangers of telling too much or of wearying others?

After my mother's death I saw but little of Cattie. I often begged her to come and see me at times when I was alone and so able to ask her, but she was shy of meeting strangers and would not come. Once or twice I went to stay with her at Bredon in Worcestershire, where my uncle was Rector.

17

Tragedy and loneliness closed in upon her; her father was hypochondriacal and selfish, keeping her to minister to his comforts and to assuage his loneliness. She was abnormally timid and would never leave her home, dreary as it was. The last time that I saw her was in 1911, after my marriage. I heard that her eyesight was affected and went to see her, and on November the 5th of that year I find written in my diary: "I went to see Cattie. Poor dear, how agonizing it is. There she was standing waiting and listening for me but quite sightless, so she could not see me at all. We sat and talked and held each other's hands and loved being together; but I feel so truly hopeless for her. Uncle H. is kind to her now. She goes and sits on his bed and he tells her little things of his life. I think he is more human with her than he used to be. I hope I shall never forget the sight of my darling Cattie, so that I may think of her and write to her. She stood a figure of loneliness, waving to me as I left."

Write to her I could not, for she very soon died. A little watch which I had given her was found in her bureau. Think of her—could I ever forget one woven like a golden thread into the pattern of my life? With her gaiety, her warm devotion and understanding? I see her now with her pale long face and beautiful eyes, with a blue scarf over her head, looking like a Guido Reni madonna, and then in a white tulle waterfall gown when my mother took her to balls in London, her blue-black hair parted in the middle and drawn down—a sylphide of the eighties. And then that last heart-rending scene—her standing outside the Rectory, her hair then a silvery grey and looking even more beautiful and distinguished, watching for me to arrive.

Many years later Philip and I went back to see the old church and Rectory at Bredon. I rang the bell, dreading the appearance of strangers. By some kind chance no one came, and we could wander at will in the garden that overlooked the Avon far below, and peer through the windows into the room that had always seemed so romantic and so sad. I could see my dear old grandfather and then my uncle as he grew old and bent, walking over to the church to take the service which he read so well in his melancholy sympathetic Irish voice. England, even Bredon with the silvery Avon flowing by, was not for them. English conventions galled and restricted them, making Cattie more and more timid. English county society suppressed in her all the gay wild life that would have flourished so happily if she had stayed in her own native land. I understood it with certainty as I walked that day in the garden, and I could still hear her singing "Dublin, fair city, where the girls are so pretty." Is it not perhaps the gay but melancholy Irish blood which ran in Cattie and still runs in her cousin that has made England and its people seem to her also marvellous indeed and beautiful, but a foreign land?

I do not remember myself ever feeling gay at Welbeck then or the sun ever shining brightly. The air, I feel sure, was always cold and dark and melancholy. The late Duke had cut off all the tops of the trees with the idea, it was said, that it would make them grow a better shape, and these poor decapitated trees seemed to me to express the inner bareness of the place. It seemed to be a place swept bare of all tenderness and mystery. He had also in a curious manner swept away the impression of any earlier time—it was a place denuded of romance. He had stamped it, one felt, for ever—with the impression of his pride and his mania for size, order and isolation. It made me long to find hidden and sequestered corners untouched by this ice-bound egoist. I curtained off a window recess in my schoolroom and put a little table there and a chair, and collected all my little treasures into that corner; a tiny bureau, my little collection of coins, china ornaments and a little picture of a pig that I bought with my own money. For me it had that magnetic quality which all good pictures have since had for me, and this my first picture possession holds its own even now. Here too stood the minute china hippopotamus which I stole when I was four years old on an afternoon visit with my mother to an old neighbour, Mrs. Vials. I loved it so much that I took it and hid it, pressing it tightly in my little hand during all the drive home. When it was discovered, I confessed what I had done, and was made to return it to kind Mrs. Vials, who said I was to keep it and I have kept it ever since.

One day when my governess was playing the piano, I started dancing unseen by her to my shadow on the wall, and I danced and danced, my bodily self mingling, waving and playing with the shadow self. Unfortunately, she and my mother discovered it, and would try to induce me to do it before visitors, and I shrank in despair, all my butterfly fancies shrivelled.

As the years went on, reading became my passion: historical novels, Bulwer Lytton and some old books on art that I found in the library. I had an excellent but sad and rather austerely religious governess, who found me, I fear, slow to learn and even slower to respond to her Bible teaching.

Parts of each year were spent in London in Grosvenor Place. I was sent to the usual dancing classes, where I met other girls, but I was far too unaccustomed to making friends to know how to do so. I shrank into a corner, self-conscious of myself and of my clothes, which were more fanciful and really far prettier than those worn by the others. I did not mind about the clothes. I only minded the whispers and sniggers of the others.

In London my eldest brother used to take me riding in the Park most mornings, but he always seemed to me to have so solemn and alarming an air that I do not remember these rides with pleasure. I believe he was really rather proud of me and of my riding, and I was secretly proud of my long and very thick golden red hair.

My mother took me out with her everywhere when in London; driving, shopping and visiting. Her friends would often remonstrate with her about it, saying that it would make me worldly, spoilt and blasé. How little they knew. Theatres were my great delight—the first play I ever was taken to was *The Corsican Brothers,* in which Irving was acting. I think I was six years old, but how vivid it is to me still! The lovely scene of the duel in the snow, before a pair of iron gates; with Irving taking off his overcoat, standing in his fine linen shirt-sleeves and throwing a long green silk purse to one of his attendants. Sarah Bernhardt I was also taken to see in *Frou-Frou,* and I still hear her far-away, languorous, melancholy, sing-song voice, and see her tall and slim in her high black silk dress with a frou-frou train. Of course we went to all the Gilbert and Sullivan operas. I think it must have been on the first night of *Patience* that we met Oscar Wilde, with a large sunflower in his buttonhole, rushing along quickly outside the boxes to reach Whistler, who was already sitting in the chief box near the stage, with white gloves and a cane and his white lock shining amidst his long, dark, curly hair. I also saw Whistler at an exhibition of his own work in Bond Street, and I still remember the delicious fairness of the room, so simple and yet beautiful, with pale lemon Chinese yellow on the walls, and a fine Japanese matting on the floor.

In the year 1889 when I was sixteen, there was a great upheaval in our lives. My brother Portland married[6]; and my

[6] His wife was Miss Winifred Dallas-Yorke, tall and very beautiful. P.M.

mother and I left Welbeck and went to St. Anne's Hill, Chertsey, as a country house, staying on in London at the house in Grosvenor Place. My mother's health now began to fail entirely, and a serious malady assailed her. She and I lived very quietly and happily at St. Anne's Hill, occasionally going abroad for her health. More and more the responsibility of our life and the management of the house and the farm now fell upon me, besides which I was my mother's nurse both night and day, for I always slept in her room and attended to her at night. My whole life and heart were given to her. Tired and worn out as I became, I never felt reluctant. Never was service more enthusiastically given. But my lessons, of course, became irregular and I probably looked very ill, for my former governess, Miss Craig, who came to see us, wrote secretly to my brothers and urged them to see that I was relieved. But I do not remember any alteration.

As I could not leave my mother during the day, I used to go out riding every morning before breakfast. She did not like me to go far by myself so I rode round and round a large field, our dear old coachman, Ellis, standing in a corner to see that no harm came to me. Our days went by very quickly. On most afternoons I drove my mother out with the phaeton and a pair of ponies for long drives through lovely Surrey lanes and woods into Virginia Water, to Windsor, to Chobham, Cobham and Guildford. Then in the evenings I would perhaps sit in the window with my feet on an old tapestry stool and do fine sewing, making her lovely chiffon jabots, hemmed with old Point d'Alençon lace, she sitting near talking of politics and history or the lives of great men or of her life in Ireland. It was only after her death, when I lived in other society, that

I realized how vigorous her mind had been and how free from all pettiness and frivolity.

On days when she was not able to drive I would push her in a wheeled chair about the charming eighteenth-century garden—a garden adorned by Charles James Fox (whose home it had once been) with an urn in memory of his faithful dog, and grottoes and a bosco to sit in and with little classical temples dedicated to friendship and other virtues, with poems to friendship or to the nightingales written on their walls.

It was a lonely and secluded life, but I did not question or criticize it. All I desired was never to leave my mother. The words of Ruth and Naomi were our mutual chant. How precious to me was praise from her! One day when I was bending over her, arranging her cushions, she looked up at me and said, "You have very dear eyes." I remember still the feeling of delicious surprise her words gave me. Those few years at St. Anne's Hill seem now to me years of extraordinary happiness and growth, wandering amongst the temples of friendship, shut in by the old eighteenth-century gates.

The devotion to my mother, at whose shrine I worshipped with so much passion and tenderness and pity, had only one rival, a passionate love of religion. How the seed of this tree began to grow in me I cannot tell—"The wind bloweth where it listeth." I was moved and impressed by my confirmation, but do not remember any other outside stimulus, nor do I remember how that terrible and beautiful book *The Imitation of Christ* came into my hands. I may have bought it myself or perhaps my mother gave it to me, but little did she or anyone else know what a scourging taskmaster Thomas à Kempis was to be to me. Every thought, word, action and motive was subjected to its fierce, burning light, none was kept back or hidden.

23

My young being was scrutinized, scourged and mercilessly pruned: all desire for food must be constrained, pleasant books put away, everything soft and pleasing renounced. Whenever I could leave my mother I crept away into an empty room and there would sit or kneel at a window, tearing out the meaning from this book:

> *Measure thy life by loss instead of gain,*
> *Not by the wine drunk, but by the wine poured forth,*
> *For love's strength shareth in love's sacrifice,*
> *And he who suffers most has most to give.*

The monkish writer never had a more willing and obedient disciple. In one thing alone I felt I could not follow him: in his command to avoid all human contact. Love and tenderness for humanity were an instinct too strong to be eradicated. But that was my only rebellion against him. This was the ideal of my life. For good or ill there was born in me then a new life, which has never died. It has indeed been reduced to order and reason by those other selves, that were then in their infancy. But these children, which have since grown up in me, have often seemed to me too divergent and ill-assorted a family for happiness or successful fulfilment.

I was always busy. In the morning my mother dictated her business letters to me, and I secretly did what good works I could find to do. I had one little charge, a gypsy child whom I had picked up somewhere in the lanes and had persuaded my mother to give work to in the garden. To her went all the good things that I denied myself. I also taught her to read and write. I wonder where she is now. She wrote to me for many years, and her first child was called after me.

I suppose all girls have sudden tempestuous attacks of despair and misery. These would overtake me and shake me so violently that I passionately longed for death. Generally some slight disagreement with my mother touched the lever that let loose these storms of despair. One of them I remember occurred at Pau, where we spent a winter, but this one had a more definite cause than many others. There was a dull little sporting Frenchman called Comte J. de M., a friend of Lady Howard de Walden, who was also staying in our hotel. This French count paid rather particular attention both to my mother and to me, and used to lend me horses to ride. One day my mother in a severe voice accused me of flirting with him. It was as if I had been accused of the most scandalous immorality, and I was overcome with misery. I knelt by my bed crying and crying and would not be comforted. The poor Count after that did not obtain many smiles from me.

In the summer of that year I came out, and went with my mother to my first dance in London. What a frightful ordeal it was! I can still see the cross faces of the dowagers sitting round the ballroom, eyeing the poor shy girls, and my mother and me taking our seats amongst them, and then at times standing out by myself in front, ready, as I thought, to be hired. Naturally I knew no one, but I must have had some dances, for I know I was led out into a highly decorated sitting-out room, with pink lights overhead, and taken to a basket chair by a young man. A feeling of intense shame overcame me. I felt degraded, sitting out in that strange room with a perfectly strange young man. Other balls followed, but my mother was not well enough to take me and I went with my eldest brother's wife. She was young and popular and very beautiful, and naturally enjoyed them very much. But all that I remember is a feeling of utter desolation, shyness and loneliness, for I felt myself quite apart from the smart world, and conscious of being out of it. I hardly ever found anyone whom I could talk to with pleasure. Sometimes the beauty of the great houses, such as Stafford House and Grosvenor House and Devonshire House, gave me some pleasure, but that was marred by the pomposity and display. The lovely scent of gardenias and stephanotis and white lilies is the only happy memory I have left. If only I could have been gay and light-hearted, what wonderful "seasons" I could have had; but great timidity bound up my spirit and my ideas. Underneath I rebelled with passionate disapproval.

In the winter of 1892 my mother and I went to San Remo, and I used to wander about in the old part of the town, peering into nooks and corners, and climbing up towers and staircases. Very soon we moved to Florence, stopping on the way at Genoa for a night. There I felt extremely ill, but successfully managed to hide it, as I generally did from my mother, and to please her went out in any icy wind to see palaces and pictures. When we arrived in Florence I sent for a doctor to see my mother, but he turned to me and I very soon found myself put to bed in high fever with nurses to look after me, and there remained as ill as it was possible to be and yet still alive. How long and how eventful each day of high fever is, so far removed from ordinary life. The small things that could not be noticed at other times become large and vitally important, and larger problems fade away. My brother Bill came out to be with my mother for a short time. I remember that he stood looking at me. I think it was he who told me that I had typhoid fever, which came to me as a shock, as I had not given any thought as to what my illness was. Oh! the weariness of those recurrent hours of burning and shivering and constant unquenchable thirst. A man who used to bring in wood for the fire was so disgusting and terrible that he became a nightmare to me. He would heave his wood down and come and stand near my bed, leering at me, and growling out horrible admiration. Was he Caliban in the flesh: or was he a phantom?

When I was convalescent I was invited by my aunt, Mrs. Scott,[7] to go and stay with her at the Villa Capponi just outside the town, and there I spent an enchanted fortnight. It was the first time I had ever met this aunt, or the two daughters who lived with her. She was the widow of my father's elder brother, and after his death she had married a Mr. Scott. She had had three daughters by her first husband: Cecilia, the eldest, who married Lord Glamis and is now Lady Strathmore,[8] and the twins, Violet and Hyacinth Bentinck, whom I was now to know and love. The Villa Capponi was a large old untouched Italian Medici villa, standing high up at Arcetri, tier upon tier of terraces with walls covered with roses and sweet-scented flowers. Underneath lay Florence, the great bell of the Duomo leading the ding-dong chorus of clamour as the Angelus floated up every evening. For the first time in my life I was spoilt and petted by these kind cousins, and for a fortnight I closed my eyes to duty and responsibility, and let myself drift in the loveliness of this new enchanting world.

But from this hill I had to descend to ordinary and anxious life in the hotel in Florence. This was not an easy task, naturally; I was weak and my nerves were very taut. My mother had grown worse during my illness. How we travelled to England I do not know—she always had to be wheeled along in an invalid chair, which we took with us, and to climb into the railway carriages abroad we had devised a little ladder which,

---

[7] Caroline Louisa Burnaby, the second wife of Ottoline's uncle, the Rev. Charles Bentinck. She married as her second husband H. W. Scott of Ancrum.

[8] The mother of the Queen (H.M. Elizabeth the Queen Mother). P.M.

together with air-cushions, a Viriginia nightingale and two pugs, was carried along the platforms.

One of the illnesses that my mother suffered from was that terrible disease, myxoedema. It was at this time that the cure of the thyroid gland was discovered, and her doctor in England, old Dr. Kidd, sent it out to her in Florence. "At last a discovery has been made that may cure you," he wrote. But alas! besides myxoedema she had other serious troubles that made the cure of the thyroid gland a dangerous remedy. Within a fortnight from beginning it she became quite slim and transparent-looking. But my anxious eyes saw a very haunting look in her face. As she stepped out of the train at Victoria Station we were met by two of my brothers, and it struck me with a poignant blow, "What will they think of her?"

On our way through Paris my mother had insisted on buying me some very lovely muslin dresses, and for some reason this had greatly upset me; also it was there that she bought for me a row of pearls at the sale of the French crown jewels; she liked to feel that I should wear a row of pearls that had been round the neck of Marie Antoinette. These gifts gave me acute pain. I felt really unhappy that she should spend money on me, and in my anxiety and distress they seemed a mockery. I must have already felt the chill and wind from the wings of death hovering near her. My old nurse Powell was with us in London, but the nursing was too severe for us to manage and we had to call in a professional nurse.

Silence, silence, seemed to reign. Her battle for life was done. She lay quite still, hardly speaking, looking and looking and following me round the room. Thinking to please her, and as a sort of penitence for my past ungraciousness, I put on one of the Paris muslin dresses with mauve and yellow ribbons, and stood where she could see it, and kissed that dear hand, which I had held and kissed so often. A smile rewarded me. But the eyes saw beyond that muslin dress now. What they saw made them infinitely sad and infinitely loving. They were the last looks of tender love that I was to look on for many years. As words failed her then, they fail me now, but those looks live on for ever.

I find these lines written in 1919:

"Here in my hands again lies this long tress of my mother's hair; raven black, and silver shining, and silken and soft, and still with the perfume of almonds that it always had. It has still upon it the tender love that it was touched with twenty years ago. I keep and touch it again and again, with the same undying passionate love."

CHAPTER II

From Scotland to Italy

I WAS NUMBED, and not consciously lonely or miserable. I only desired to give as little trouble as possible. In real life the producer does not wait for the young actor to learn his new part, but pushes him on the boards to play as best he can. I was told that I had better go and stay for a few days with my brother Henry and his wife in Sloane Street. My brother, I knew, was very unhappy at my mother's death, but my family never talked about or discussed anything that affected them deeply, particularly not a thing sad and melancholy. To speak of the death of one so loved would have almost shocked them, and would have had the tinge of morbidity. Then I was told I had better go up to Langwell, my eldest brother's place in Scotland, and so obediently I went, travelling up with Henry and his wife.

I arrived at Langwell and joined the shooting party that was already assembled there. I was perhaps peculiarly guileless and simple and affectionate, and no doubts had crossed my mind as to whether I should be welcome or not. My great desire was to avoid showing my feelings or to cast any gloom upon people, and I imagined I should mix quite naturally with them. But I came from a home where I had had work and responsibility, and had talked with a distinguished and sincere mind, a complete absence of artificial affection and talk of flattery. It was quite natural that the serious and romantic girl should be an irritation to the circle I joined. I knew my brothers and sisters-in-law wished to welcome me and to be kind to me. If I had been like them and made to their pattern, I should have had what is called "a glorious time." But the system of which they were part did not admit of thought or individuality, or indeed of liberty or cherishing any delicate ideas. Perhaps it is from a certain ancestral sense of *noblesse oblige* that these personal feelings have to sink out of sight, like a stone in water, while the current of life flows rapidly on obliterating them. But where does it flow? Why hurry and rush?

After a time I asked myself that question, but I could not find any answer. The day's performance must be carried through without a hitch. Each one must play his part, with agility and cheerfulness: the orchestra plays a quick march. Some are golfers, others shooters, the ladies would walk or fish, they talked and flattered, and in the evening the performance ended with the grand chorus of the letter game.[1] It is a perfect performance. To those who are beautiful and gay it is not difficult, the applause always complimentary and laudatory. Unfortunately, try as I might, I could never learn my proper part. I tried very hard; stage fright perhaps prevented me; but I

---

[1] Has the time come when this needs explanation? The game was played with squares of card, each with a letter on it; in the commonest form the letters, having been put face downwards, were turned up in turn by the players, and the first to claim a word in the ensuing jumble, took it; it was allowed, by changing with additions a word already taken, to claim it from another player. This game, "word-making and word-taking," was regularly played in country houses, at least until the end of the 1914–18 war—particularly on Sunday in the many homes where cards were not then allowed.

31

could never take the cue or enjoy the pleasure of the privilege of treading those polished boards. I longed for the happiness that comes from understanding and contact with life.

I was filled with admiration for the amount of good deeds and philanthropy that were done. And yet, even in this, I somehow could not find any part to play. During the first few months I was too simple to criticize; as I said before, I took it for granted that all members of a family were devoted to each other, and in my timid way I did my best to please them.

Some whisper must have come to me that they criticized me, for I remember vividly standing by my bedroom door as I was going out one day, and realizing it so vividly that I said aloud to myself: "They do not like me. My presence among them is unwelcome to them." It came upon me as a shock. I shut myself up in my room as much as I could after that. I became more and more religious. I spent all my mornings reading history and theological books. I read slowly and did not get on very well. I cracked my head over things and had no help, and I always felt ill. My reading annoyed my family very much, and they attributed to it all my ill-health. "If only you would come out and play games like other girls, you would be quite well." I did not then realize all they thought. I was numb to it, and oddly enough not even rebellious as I should be now. My whole soul was filled with thoughts of religion, and I used to creep out and go on long walks alone, and so get moments of wonderful religious ecstasy in woods or in lonely places: nature was divine to me then, it was a mother to me.

It was a pity I knew very little poetry; Shakespeare or Shelley even were unknown to me. Milton was the only poet I knew. George Macdonald's[2] verses and all his books were my great consolation.

[2] Poet and novelist. He was an intimate friend of Lady Byron's and

I really grew to live entirely in a mystic religious world. I did not care for dogma or High Church teaching—it always gave me a tight dreary feeling. At one time I had an agonizing struggle as to whether to submit to the strict Evangelical doctrine, which depressed me by its condemnation of many things I loved. It was while I was in this state of mind that I came across the writings of Thomas Erskine[3] of Linlathen (Carlyle's St. Thomas). I found it difficult to understand but at last after days I understood it, and it was a real enlightenment to me: it was the thing I sought, the mystic doctrine of the Vine and the Branch, God as the Father Full of Love.

When I think of all that side of my life, which was of course the whole of my real life then, I remember that I had an extraordinary spiritual, almost magical, happiness. I lived in a mystic haze:

"The corn was orient and immortal wheat, which never should be reaped, nor was ever sown. I thought it had stood from everlasting to everlasting. The dust and stones of the street were as precious as gold. . . . The green trees when I saw them first through one of the gates transported and ravished me, their

---

—so Ottoline told me—one of two people to whom she confided the story of Byron's incest (the other was Mrs. Beecher Stowe). He is probably best remembered now by his stories for children, in particular *The Princess and Curdie* and *The Princess and the Goblin*.

[3] Thomas Erskine of Linlathen, 1788–1870, came of an old Scotch family. A man of independent means, he was chiefly renowned for the amiability of his character, and for his writings on theology. He was liked and respected by many notable men, including Carlyle. He held the belief that all mankind would be saved, a proposition which, although probably permitted as a hope by the more formal churches, would undoubtedly be proscribed by them if preached as a certainty. His favourite reading was said to be the Bible, Shakespeare and the dialogues of Plato.

sweetness and unusual beauty made my heart to leap and almost mad with ecstasy, they were such strange and wonderful things. . . . Eternity was manifest in the Light of the Day, and something infinite behind everything appeared: which talked with my expectation and moved my desire."

These words of Thomas Traherne described my feelings at that time, and indeed those feelings have never left me.

I loved reading passionately, but I felt that it was self-indulgent, and that instead of reading I ought to be doing things for other people. The fire of asceticism still burnt me up and made all the things that my intelligence and artistic sense hungered for appear self-indulgence. I stripped the flowers and the tender branches off my life, and tore them from me, leaving only the stem. I became frenzied, every thought was examined, and those that were "worldly" stamped upon, crushed and thrown away. Mercifully, my temperament was tender, and love was the fulfilling of my ideal. Hard, selfish thoughts were replaced by love; at least, that was my desire—but love, though it developed sympathy and understanding, did not help one to develop intellect or freedom for my aesthetic instincts.

When I was in Scotland, I used to walk miles and miles, visiting the crofters and talking to them and giving them books. There was a little shooting lodge far away where I sometimes went to stay with my youngest brother, Charles. He was out shooting all day, and I was free to go where I liked. I loved these long days alone in the wild, lonely country, and I felt as if I were transported away and free from that dreary, cold, conventional world. I felt as if my spirit were carried up and up and had wings. Alas! I had to return to the evenings with my brother, for whom I felt a deep affection, although I never was able to get in touch with him. If I talked to him about his stalking, I was sure to ask the wrong thing, and I had not the nerve to start any of the other subjects.

It never entered my head that I should ever find people who would talk about the things that I cared for.

When we went to Welbeck things were very much the same: shooting parties, hunting, bazaar-openings. I lived with a continual shrinking in my soul, a continual sense of dreariness, and of knowing that I was flat and dull in their eyes.

The aim of my eldest brother was that his family should be a credit to him, but he never considered that there should be any intellectual or unconventional distinction. His carriages were to be the smartest in England, his shooting was to be the best shooting in England, his postillions were to be the best turned out—better even, he hoped, than Lord Lonsdale's. And was his sister equal to her part? Why did she wear such old dresses? And do her hair so untidily? And generally do such odd things? Once he saw me in the train at Retford or some station on the Worksop line in a very full third-class carriage. I knew by his face that I was in disgrace. That evening he came to my room and said he wished to speak to me. "I should be glad if you would travel first-class in future, because I should not like it said that my sister had not enough money to travel first-class." After that I used to change from a third to a first when I got near Worksop.

The loneliness I felt at Welbeck was never relaxed. The only person I could talk to was the nurse to my little nephew and niece, Sister Grace.[4] She had been a Nightingale sister, and

---

[4] An aunt of mine by marriage, who was related to the Bentincks, used to live in Windsor, and at her house I often met Sister Grace. She was a good, estimable old lady, and of strong character; once, when

matron of one of Dr. Barnardo's Homes for Babies. Then her health had broken down, and she had come as nurse to my sister-in-law. She was a kind, energetic, managing woman who liked me, and stood up for me against criticism. She felt, I think, sorry for me, when she saw how strange and out of sympathy I was with all that was round me. She was very evangelical—a disciple of Frances Ridley Havergal[5]—and suggested to me that I should have a Bible Class for the young men on the estate on Sunday evenings. My heart quailed. I could never do it. But believing that it was the right thing to do, I forced myself to do it.

So a notice was given out, saying that I should hold a class, and any young man who liked it was invited to come. When the day arrived I went down to a room in the lower regions of the house, and found a small crowd of young men from the stables, the wood-yard, the gardens and the house waiting for me. At first I was so nervous that I hardly uttered a word, and nearly fell down from fright. I think never in the rest of my life have I felt any sensation to compare with the terror of that moment. My mouth was so dry from nervousness that I could

she imagined mistakenly that we had indecently slighted a boy who was at Eton by virtue of a scholarship, she gave us a severe dressing down. She lived on at Welbeck in a room high up, with a door nearby leading to the roof, whither she would go and sit in sunny weather. It was then said that Sister Grace was "hatching the roof." She had at one time worked strenuously among the poor, and with prostitutes, as she described in the story of her life which she wrote and had printed.

[5] Frances Ridley Havergal, 1836–79, was the authoress of hymns and devotional verse, at one time of great influence. An autobiography was published soon after her death. A musician herself, she came from a family of musicians. She was energetically engaged in religious and philanthropic work and it was in such circumstances, no doubt, that Sister Grace came into touch with her. She is said to have followed "an unusually eager, if somewhat narrow, spiritual life."

hardly speak. I remember it was about January 18th, for I took as my subject the Conversion of St. Paul. But I went on, holding the class every Sunday, and after a time had it in my own sitting-room.

I think they liked it, for more and more came, old and young, and at last the class consisted of over sixty men, so that my room was quite packed, and became terribly hot. I also lent them books, making a cupboard between two doors of my room for their library. I can still hear the tramp-tramp of the young men's feet coming down the long passage, each carrying his chair, and smell the strong smell of their flesh and hair-oil, and hear them singing hymns—the volume of sound was enough to blow the ceiling off.

My brother was Master of the Horse, and had four Royal footmen who wore scarlet livery. One or two of these used to come, and I got to know them very well. After my marriage, when Philip and I went to a garden party at Windsor Castle, I found amongst all the grand people there one of these footmen, grown large and burly. He was delighted to see me again, and I often come across middle-aged men now who come up to me with a smile and say, "I was one of your young men, m'lady."

The class became so large that I used to divide it into two— the younger ones and the older ones. They came at different hours; this was very exhausting—my head nearly burst when they were over on Sunday evening. But, oh, the relief! until the preparation for the next Sunday began. The preparation for my address was a terrible agony for me. I laboured and prayed and agonized over it, would sit up working at it, reading all sorts of books that would help me. Sometimes I would talk to them about the life of some man, Gordon perhaps, and I took any subject that I thought would help them to live their lives well.

Their confidence in me was really extremely touching. I

never had any trouble with them, they were all so simple and serious, and never so far as I could see mocked or laughed. I asked any of them who liked to come and pay me a visit separately, and most evenings one of them would come, and I would make him sit down and talk to me about his life. One of the footmen, a fat, serious fellow by name of Pottow, came one evening and seemed very upset and disturbed. He had something to tell me, he said, but had not the courage to say what it was, and after a long time of patient questioning, I found that it was that he had been brought up a Roman Catholic! (He had not dared to let anyone in the house know.)

I also started a carving class, and had a good teacher who came and taught, and tried to make them do imaginative work. Besides this I used to visit all the cottages, so that I made a busy life of my own, quite independent of the ordinary life at Welbeck. In order to secure time for reading, I woke myself up by an alarum-clock at 5 a.m., heated myself some coffee that I kept in a bottle, rolled myself in an Indian shawl, put on gloves to keep my hands warm and read in bed for hours. Indeed I hardly got any sleep, for I used often to sit up writing till two or three in the morning. I could not bear wasting any time. Blind as I was to what lay before me I never wanted to rest, and used always to be preparing for a future—not that I had any clear idea what that future would be, or exactly what I wanted it to be. Sometimes I thought I might be head of some women's training college, and then I imagined some political or philanthropic work. I knew nothing whatever of what it meant, and was very vague about it, and too shy and timid ever to discuss it with anyone, but the mania that I was to do something definite in the future, and that the time I was living in was only preparing for something beyond, obsessed me, and made me almost entirely distracted from the present, so that I was really incapable of enjoying whatever pleasure there may have been in it.

One thing I was quite clear about, clear with a sort of horror: that I could not marry any of the young men who came to Welbeck. I remember visualizing myself with dread as the mistress of one of their large houses, entertaining shooting parties, and living with a man to whom I could never talk. And yet, critical as I was of the life that was round me, I was oppressed by it, and also I felt that somehow it was all my fault that I could not enter into it. The unquestioning, unimaginative arrogance of it all had a power of impressing itself on me as "The Thing," that it was "the supreme life" and that all other existences were simply insignificant and unimportant. I was not clever enough to understand or see a way out. I felt it all so final; I never saw how I could escape from it.

There was indeed one man who was a curious contrast to the other people who came to Welbeck, Arthur Strong.[6] He was librarian at Chatsworth, and my brother made him also librarian at Welbeck. Extremely learned and biting, with a brain like white-hot steel, he was in appearance like Erasmus, and probably like him in mind. He was indeed like a being from another planet and he was very kind to me, and saw probably that I was hungry to learn, for he used to talk to me about books in a way that impressed me, although I was so

[6] It was through Arthur Strong—or strictly speaking through his wife, who was an old friend of mine—that Ottoline and I, two or three years after, renewed an acquaintance which ultimately led to our marriage. Except for the happy chance of his appointment as librarian at Welbeck we might never have met again after she left Oxford. P.M.

Fearful of how Ottoline's family would take this momentous consequence of their intervention, the Strongs, so Philip told me, sternly opposed his marriage.

terrified of him that I was quite unable to talk myself. But he gave me good counsel about reading, told me to read Locke and Meredith and Browning, and helped me with history and art.

When I was in London I went down fairly often to see my aunt, Mrs. Scott, at Ham Common, and the days there were perfectly delightful. She was very kind to me and so were my cousins. They were very religious and rather too High Church for my taste, but that did not really matter. The old house was filled with Italian furniture and pictures, and the perfume of tiger-lilies, and it was to me a haven of joy. My aunt used to take me for drives to see her old friends at Ham House and Hampton Court, and once we went to visit old Lady Russell at White Lodge. We sat and talked to her and her daughter Agatha in her stuffy Victorian drawing-room. One day I was rather astonished to find a young man paying a visit to my aunt. I was told in a whisper that it was little Bertie Russell— "He has such a wonderful mathematical brain." I sat looking at this little mathematical wonder as he sat leaning his back against the mantelpiece, his legs crossed—the same position that he stands in today. My aunt made me laugh by reminding him how, when he was a small child, someone gave him a blue Conservative rosette to wear, and he snatched it off, threw it on the ground, and stamped it under his small feet.

It was one of these cousins, Hyacinth Bentinck, who invited me to go with her to Truro on a visit to the Sisterhood there. I did not look forward to it very much; indeed, I thought it would be very dreary, but to this visit I owe my friendship with Mother Julian, one of the people I have loved most in my life. My cousin fades away, and I can only remember the little frail figure of Mother Julian, almost lost in her voluminous nun's draperies; the white band round her face, the white cuffs, the long fingers, the face extremely wrinkled and soft, with amazing eyes, rather pale and unlike any other eyes I have ever seen. They had seen the full pain and light of life, still saw the light and still felt love and reverence. Her presence seemed to radiate some lovely and loving spiritual power. She seemed to me like Saint Stephen, with heavenly lights in her face, and she gave me, above all, such a feeling of reverence that I never lost the desire, when I entered her room, to kneel to her; but it was not to her as a person one desired to kneel, but to some wonderful transcendental light in her soul. For many years, up to her death in 1912, my friendship with her remained the same. Again and again I went there to see her.

The other sisters were nice and kind to me, but not interesting. I went entirely to see Mother Julian, so different from anyone else I knew. She was intensely interested in every side of life, passionately sympathetic in every minute detail, literary, artistic and human. She was absolutely true and perfectly gentle, full of humour and quick to laugh and to sympathize in fun or in grief, reverent above all towards life and towards even the meanest individual. I remember catching sight of her sometimes as I went into the Chapel—she was of course quite unaware of being seen—and the look that was on her face, which was the combination of reverence and worship and light, still seems always in my mind to testify to a divine spirit. If all other beliefs failed, Mother Julian's attitude and face would still remain to me an unanswerable and convincing testimony to an infinite presence in life. Her intellect was extraordinarily good, very quick and just; she was well educated and expected a great deal from everyone. She would bring me a bundle of books of all sorts most mornings and expect me to read them and report to her on them in an impossibly short time. Her avidity for books never abated; she read everything, and her sisters did the same. She read all Wells's novels as they came out.

I always shrank from telling her the things I knew would distress her because her sympathy was so deep and vivid, but except for that reason there was nothing I ever hid from her. She was like quicksilver, and ran along on the subject with intensity and depth, yet always with a touch of humour. How well I remember an ilex grove in the garden of the sisterhood, where I used to walk up and down, thinking and meditating and ruminating on all the complexities of life. It was to Mother Julian that I owe the adjustment of my intellectual and aesthetic side. It was she who quelled the passion of self-denial as regarding intellectual matters. It is odd to remember that in that sisterhood was the place I found my youth and the encouragement to live with any gaiety—not in the sense most people understand youth—a sort of rush of life, impetuous recklessness, carrying all before it with energy and thoughtless courage. For I seem to have always been introspective and comparatively diffident from my earliest youth, very suspicious of flattery, and crushing the encouragement it might have given me with a fierce "common sense," as I called it to myself.

My aunt and cousins at Ham Common and Mother Julian were the only people that I was friends with except, I remember, the late Archbishop of York; he came to Welbeck for some function and took a fancy to me and talked to me a great deal. I used to go to Bishopsthorpe on a visit now and then. Mrs. Archbishop was a terror to me; but I loved the old man. He was rather flirtatious in a mild, fatherly way, but educating in other ways. I was rather jealous of Mouche Duncombe, whom I met there, and who was a brilliant creature, divinely beautiful, but chilling and freezing from her want of artistic qualities and of heart. I was too dazzled by her then to realize what she was like, but I had a suspicion that she was deep and bent on her career regardless of anyone else's feelings. She was like a Diana. I do not know how much she really cared for philosophical studies, which she was then working at in preparation for Cambridge, but afterwards I came to think that she only did them so as to make herself more remarkable. But she was dazzling and beautiful and talked well, and sometimes was remarkably frank; but her ideas never seemed to me at all original, mostly noted down in the notebooks of her mind from eminent writers. I remember a thrilling description she gave me of her sister, the Duchess of Leinster, who, she said, was like a spirit in that supremely beautiful body. I had never seen anyone who came near her in beauty; I can remember her even now as being probably the most beautiful woman I have ever seen, with the glowing sun of radiance in her whole being. I have always imagined Anna Karenina to have been as she was. Mouche told me that whenever she saw her sister she never stagnated, she was always travelling on in her mind and spirit. Somehow the description was one of those things which remain with me for ever. I suppose it answered to some unconscious idea of mine.

I do not remember what year it was that I first stepped out into the land of liberty.[7] I got so entrenched in the life at Welbeck, tired out and ill with my classes and good works, and not progressing in any direction. It was my old governess, Miss Craig, who was fond of me, and whom I saw now and then, who suddenly said, "You are being starved. You must go abroad. You must get away." I remember I looked at her with wide open eyes. Then came the summoning up of all my courage to ask for permission to go. "Why do you want to go? Are you not happy here?" After a time it was settled that a

[7] Probably in 1895.   P.M.

43

family conclave should be held about it. This was the first of these conclaves that were periodically summoned afterwards to consider my wayward desires. But you cannot go abroad alone. Miss Craig came to the rescue. She knew of a highly respectable maiden lady, Miss Rootes, who would be glad to accompany me and be my guardian.

"Well," Portland said, "if Miss Rootes goes with you I give my consent."

Of course, I regarded Miss Rootes as an angel of beauty and intelligence. The Archbishop of York smiled at the plan and recommended Cortina in the Dolomites.

Just before starting, Hilda Douglas-Pennant came to see me in London. I knew her very slightly, only having met her once or twice. We were sitting on my large sofa in my room; I told her I was just going abroad, and almost involuntarily said, "Why don't you come with me?" never thinking she would. However, the seed sprang up and became a stalwart plant. She came, and we became great and intimate friends. She, Miss Rootes and I started from Victoria and went to Brussels. We sat in the railway carriage, Miss Rootes in brown—brown hat and coat and skirt, brown gloves and button boots, white hair and long teeth, the exact idea of an English middle-class old maid. Hilda, tall, thin, very refined, shy and proud, a small head, rather nervous and stag-like. She was rather fussy about having enormous numbers of comforts: clocks, air-cushions, etc. Afterwards, on our many travels, I found that she was always packing and repacking her handbag, and when I knew her better this became a joke.

The first night at Brussels was strange, and I was kept awake most of the night by the sound of packing and the crinkling of paper next door. This was Hilda repacking her boxes.

My luggage was mostly composed of books: enormous quantities of books, large library volumes of Ruskin amongst others. I did not know how to pack them, so I got an ordinary sack, covered it with a plush cover and tumbled the books into it; it was so heavy that hardly anyone could carry it. I had also another brilliant idea, which was to put strong pockets all round the thick, full, red cape I wore, into which I packed a rampart of books. It made my cape extraordinarily heavy, and I had to walk with the utmost balance and care not to fall over. It was surprising and rather hard to anyone whom I happened to knock against.

We stopped on the way to Cortina at Brussels, Würzburg, Munich, Innsbruck and Ratisbon. I had a memory that the glass in the windows of Würzburg was most marvellously beautiful. They seemed in my mind to be like wonderful music; the colour and beauty of them quite overcame me. Years afterwards I insisted on going back there with Philip to see these windows, but nowhere could we find them; the real windows were terrible, kaleidoscopic vulgar things. At Innsbruck that statue of Theodoric the Goth struck a spark in my imagination, and I immediately set to work to read the History of the Goths. At Innsbruck it was a fête day. The air was like champagne and the peasants wore lovely costumes. It was thrilling and exciting; all these days had a feeling of strangeness in them, not quite comfortable and free, for we were very shy of each other. Hilda and I soon grew fond of one another, which of course left poor Miss Rootes out in the cold; added to which, Hilda, who was much older than I and far more critical, took a dislike to her, and was terribly bored by her. I, who was by nature kind-hearted, stood by that pathetic, dried, sapless maiden lady, and at Cortina we used to read together, and she was the first person who told me about Greek literature and advised me to read it, and I think she even suggested that I might go to college—which I had not thought of before.

Hilda was, of course, far better educated than I was, and it

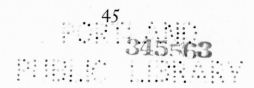

was she who gave me Keats and Shelley. I remember lovely walks with her through almost unearthly country where the mountains were like moon mountains: cold and white, not with snow, but with their own coldness and austerity. On the high ground it was very wonderful, and I love to think of the bright, vivid blue bunches of gentians that push their way through the snowy paths, and the fields of crocus and the lower grass plateaux.

In October it got very cold and stormy and we had to leave, and made our way to Venice. There the sunsets and the great barges gliding along in the evening light, laden with pomegranates and grapes, the Giorgiones and all the other rich glowing pictures there, the far-away islands rising out of the water like fair, pink water-lilies, are vivid memories to me still.

Miss Rootes simply ceased to exist. I cannot remember how she faded away, but fade away she did. We went from Venice to Padua, Bologna, Ravenna, Urbino, Gubbio, Siena, Perugia and Assisi. When I look back on these days I find that the places I went to have sunk down into my memory and have built themselves into my being like stones impregnated with beauty and romance. I drank then of the elixir of Italy—I drank so deeply of it that it has never left me. Ravenna probably above all moved me most profoundly. The dark brown buildings and houses, churches, the Bapistery all russet brown and almost unaltered since the fifth century, the dark primitive architecture with mosaics in blue and gold like peacock feathers, and black and white—mysterious and unchangeable.

Italy has ever been in my imagination the land of my freedom. It is banal to say this, for I have heard it said so often by young ladies, and there has always been a pang of jealousy in the thought, for I feel sure they never felt the same joy and rapture that I felt. The sense of being in a great rich land, rich with the profusion of nature's gifts—vines and olives, oranges and cypress and sunshine—rich with the deeds of man down from the days of the Romans to Garibaldi—deeds evil and good, but all important, all acted on the central arena of the world; and then, more eternal still even than those feats, there is another offspring of this rich land, this spoilt daughter of the gods—Art, which seems to have grown out of the soil untended and spontaneous, almost as if it had blossomed instinctively; but whether it was produced by agony or with ease and joy, it is the expression of all the finest emotions of the human heart: Botticelli and Mantegna, Michelangelo, Piero della Francesca, Leonardo—their works are not merely the dull illustrations of life, but are the intense expression of their own vision of life and beauty and religion. What wonder is it that I, poor, ignorant and starved in intellect and in the senses, should have lingered on in this rich land, in order to imbibe its spirit to the full.

As I look back on the years that followed, and trace my wanderings, I see I was more in Italy than in England, but I still peer into the past memories and piece them together. They have not vanished, for they live in me and are woven into my life, so that it is difficult to disentangle them and to isolate them.

The winter of 1895–6 I spent with Mrs. Scott in Rome, but I was not very happy, for my aunt and cousin took no interest in the things that I loved, and they cast a feeling of depression over me; but still I saw a good deal and learnt much, and I loved to walk alone in the narrow streets in the winter evenings and watch the sunsets from the Pincio and to feel the thrill of walking in the streets of Rome. I was still longing for gaiety and friendship, and when I returned to England, some chance threw into my hands a syllabus of correspondence courses in Edinburgh which prepared students for the St. Andrews University. From these advertisements I set my heart on going to St. Andrews to study.

I consulted Mrs. Dallas-York, my sister-in-law's mother, who had a good deal of sympathy with learning, and she approved the plan and spoke to my brother, and after another family conclave at Grosvenor Square I was allowed to go.

In 1897 Hilda Pennant, two dogs, my old Irish maid Ellen Dormer and a lady tutor, Miss Hurlbatt, who had been provided for me by Mrs. Dallas-York, arrived at St. Andrews. We took lodgings at No. 5 Murry Park.

It was very difficult to know what to study; my aims were so wide and vague, and I did not know the map of knowledge. I was certainly interested in Philosophy and wanted to work at that, but Miss Hurlbatt, who was a highly intellectual, managing woman, settled that, as Professor Ritchie was by far the best professor then at St. Andrews, I had better take the course of logic.

So obediently I went to these lectures and Hilda came with me. It was a curious rough class, held in one of the rooms of the old University: a few women, but mostly men, we sat at trestles with desks running along in front of us, taking notes. The men were rather uncouth and difficult to manage, very excitable and demonstrative. If the Professor said anything they could not hear, or did not like, they would shuffle on the floor with their feet, and if anyone they disliked came in they would then shuffle too; but if they liked anyone they would beat a warm applause with their feet. I am thankful to say I was never shuffled at, but was treated very kindly by all the other students. One day I lost one of my gloves. It disappeared completely, and a notice upon a

48

"Lost Glove" appeared in a little University paper, and the glove was laid on my window-sill.

Of course, Hilda took the most violent dislike to Miss Hurlbatt, which infected me. She really was disagreeable and autocratic, but on the whole, although the cold and discomfort were terrible, I loved my time there. It was interesting getting to know the students, both men and women of all classes, men who had to starve themselves six months in the year to get there at all. Hilda was a restraining hand; her outlook being formal and conventional chafed mine. I wanted to get very familiar with these young men and women, but a sort of jealous hauteur in Hilda restrained me. She could not bear to feel that we were not keeping up our dignity. The dark gabled streets, the old ruined Cathedral at the edge of the sea, the students in their red and purple gowns blown by the wind, haunt me still. But I felt very ill there most of the time and suffered acutely from the cold. The winds were the coldest I have ever felt, and blew one, enveloped in clouds of dust, along the street.

In all those years of my life I never found the secret of enjoying life, never caught the joy on the wing. The years followed each other without that essential something which gives a thrill of enjoyment. The cause was chiefly ill-health, and partly a disturbing sense of my own inadequacy; also perhaps above all, asceticism. How different my whole life would have been if anyone had shaken me and made me see that it was possible to enjoy freely, without attacking or denying the high ideals. I never found any group of people whom I could feel at home with or express myself to. I made friends with one or two of the women students, especially one who was preparing to be a Minister. She was a German. She afterwards became a Unitarian Minister in Alsace. She was a fine courageous creature. Still, logic and the cold made me resolve not to return to St. Andrews another winter.

In the Christmas vacation I first met Mr. Asquith dining with my brother Henry in Grosvenor Place. He took an interest in me and in my reading, and lent me books; amongst others, T. H. Green's[8] works. During that summer I was in London and went out a certain amount, and enjoyed it more than I had done hitherto. I imagine the time at St. Andrews had given me a certain foothold. Mr. Asquith came to see me sometimes in my sitting-room at Grosvenor Place. The room was very high up, looking over the gardens of Buckingham Palace where the peacocks screeched and old Queen Victoria used to drive in her pony-chaise escorted by John Brown. It had been my old schoolroom—Mr. Asquith called it the "tower"—and we sat on a deep soft sofa with white muslin cushions that had belonged to my mother. Bookshelves ran all round the room, packed with books and china on the top. We talked of poetry, religion and the ways of life of Wordsworth, Tennyson and Browning.

I often went down to see my aunt at Ham Common. My cousin Violet Bentinck was very delicate and suffered from terrible headaches. I had met a famous doctor in London, and my aunt begged me to induce him to come down and see Violet. I had met him lunching with my sister-in-law. He was a rather mysterious figure, very ugly, but with great charm, and he had an athletic, supple figure, very remarkable hands, was devoted to children and animals and was said to

[8] Thomas Hill Green, 1836–82, a pupil of Jowett, and brother-in-law of John Addington Symonds, was a scholarly thinker of Victorian times. As a youth he won a prize for a Latin translation of Milton's *Areopagitica*. His thought has been compared to Wordsworth's. Politically he was a follower of Cobden and Bright, and not improbably he influenced Ottoline in the formation of her radical principles.

Lieutenant-General Bentinck,
father of Lady Ottoline Morrell

Lord Charles Bentinck,
brother of Lady Ottoline

6th Duke of Portland and Lord Henry Bentinck, 1886, before going to Russia

Welbeck Abbey

have done extraordinary quixotic deeds—for instance, when
the cholera was raging in Naples, he rushed down from
Rome, where his practice was, working night and day amongst
the worst cases. He consented to go to Ham with me and see
my cousin, and it was fixed for the next Sunday. I met him at
Waterloo Station, and we went down together. At last I had
met someone to whom I could talk freely, who was not cut
on the ordinary cardboard pattern, who was subtle and free
and daring and sympathetic. He came to see me sometimes in
my room, and I remember the last party of the season when
he circled round me, and as we parted by the door he made
me promise to come and stay with him at Capri. I felt gay
and happy and free. Life was vivid and wonderful that night,
for it was the first time that I was sorry to leave a party. I
could not help a smile of triumph over my beautiful sister-in-
law, who had so much wanted to know this doctor. She was
so accustomed to sweep all before her, and I felt I had something of my own, some wonderful possession.

The next day Hilda Pennant and I went off to a place in
Savoy for my health, called Brides-Les-Bains. It was in August. We were gay and happy, and it was exceedingly hot.
Whilst I was there I had an exciting letter from Dr. Munthe,
inviting me to come to Capri, offering me a villa there of my
own. I was delighted and determined to go, but had great
difficulty in persuading Hilda to consent to it. I told her it
was perfectly *convenable*, as he was quite old. I was determined to go, and off we went, journeying through the
length of Italy. The days were baking and hot, the *gran caldo*
season, when Italy shakes off her foreign invaders and returns
to her own ways, lives her own life, dances her own passionate
Bacchic dances in the hot nights illuminated by clouds of
fireflies. On and on we went, further south, the heat becom-

51

ing greater as we went, but it was joy and life to me. The only food we needed were the masses of purple figs and ripe peaches to be bought at every station. We stopped a night or two in Rome, which, too, had returned to its pagan state. Roman women, with black crinkled hair piled high on their heads, sat outside their houses eating slices of the large green water-melon with pink lining that were piled up at every street corner. Life was lived completely in public in the streets; there were no strangers to be shocked or to criticize. But we did not linger. On we went, plunging further and further into wild Bacchanal Italy. It was vintage time when Pan again reigned supreme.

The noise of the cicala drowned the noise of the train as we went along. On the night journey to Naples a burly orange-grower got into our carriage: an Englishman who had forgotten how to speak English, but was very interested in looking at our English picture papers. The boat in which we crossed from Naples to Capri was filled with singers and musicians, who sang and played as we crossed the blue bay.

When we arrived at Capri, Dr. Munthe was waiting for us. Hilda uttered a cry of dismay at finding he was not eighty years old, but only forty, a fascinating satyr in appearance with an alert figure. However, she was obliged to acquiesce. By and by we drove to Anacapri, and then I was led through the house that was to be mine.

It was a fairy palace, perfect in everything, made of marble with blue tiles under foot and a little fountain festooned with green garlands and flowers and a hanging olive-oil lamp like magic spirits.

As I wandered through the rooms I was ravished by the magic beauty. A lovely maiden was to attend on us. Day followed day, but time had ceased to exist. I walked on

52

rarefied air in this enchanted land, and was transported by
this strange and wonderful place. The vintage was ripe, and
girls who looked like Greek nymphs were bringing in the
grapes in the great baskets that hung on their backs.

Dr. Munthe's own house was within a few yards of the
one he had lent me. We had our meals with him, and listened
to him playing the piano, which he did very well. We sat in
his garden, where there were pergolas made of Roman and
Greek pillars that had been found in the depths of the sea
near the island, and were the remains of a villa of Tiberius.
There was also, higher up the hill, looking out to sea, an old
chapel. This chapel Dr. Munthe had turned into a library,
and here he and I used to sit and talk.

Meanwhile, Hilda and my old maid, Ellen Dormer, who
had been with me for years, became more and more alarmed
about me. The more they saw that I was happy and entranced,
the more convinced they were that I was bewitched by this
archfiend, this satyr, this necromancer. Hilda felt the magic
of the place in her imagination, but with her it turned to
sinister sorcery. She heard the even beats of the men as they
plastered the roofs they were building, the cries of the decoy
quails as they cried to other quails in flight, decoying them
to come and be netted. Her attention was riveted on a
statue of Fate that was in the garden, and she unceasingly
pointed it out to me. The nights were haunted for her by men
prowling outside our little house, whispering evil things, she
was sure. As each day went by, hers and Ellen's terror and
frenzy grew greater; partly, I think, it was fanned by jealousy,
but thus my few days of bliss were soon marred and damaged
by the sense of their disapproval and terror. They soon made
me feel that I was very wicked and abandoned, and I shrank

from their critical looks. I felt that it was not possible to stop longer, and I told Dr. Munthe that I must go.

"Why must you go?"

"Oh! For many reasons."

"What reasons?"

"It is too good here. I must fly."

Then I knew that he loved me. I had been filled with a spiritual and transcendental desire to pour love into this man, had poured out everything in my heart to him, but now for the first time in my life, I realized the usual feelings of love. I was bewildered, shrinking, dazed, overcome, but sublimely happy, except for the dark fate already, in the shape of disapproving Hilda, overshadowing me. But Fate cannot strike as quickly as Love can grow, and grow it did, leaping up with all-pervading burning fire—"*Vénus toute entière à sa proie attachée.*"

In a few days we started off on a driving expedition along the coast to Sorrento and Pompeii, stopping the night at Pompeii. The heat of those summer nights on the burning side of Vesuvius was intense. I evaded Hilda in the evening, and walked with Dr. Munthe in a wood near by.

> *A turn, and we stood in the heart of things,*
> *The woods are around, heavy and dim.*
> *A moment after and hands unseen*
> *Were hanging the night around us fast,*
> *We caught for a moment the powers that blow,*
> *For it mingled us so.*

Mingled as much as one heart full of love can be poured into another, the physical side of my love was barely awake, only enough to give the abandonment of the heart with complete and passionate warmth. We slipped across the bay back to Capri in a fishing-boat; I lay covered over at the bottom

and I still can hear Dr. Munthe's voice encouraging the
rowers when the wind was against them, calling out: "Coraggio, Macaroni!"

Then after a day or two we turned homeward to England,
spending a day and night in Naples, Hilda in the last stage
of being shocked at Dr. Munthe's freedom with me. I remember that when we went to see the statues in the Museum,
he and I spent our time dodging behind statues and eluding
her, the proud, angry, tall goddess with knitted brows and
pouting mouth.

At Florence I was exhausted and numb, almost wishing
Dr. Munthe was at the bottom of the sea. That at least, I said
to myself, would stop the pain and difficulty that I felt lay
ahead of me. At Lucerne we rested in the Hotel Schweizer-
hof. I was in a dream, treading new paths in an unknown life,
sick with a happiness that was overjoyed of itself, dumb
before the difficulties that had to be faced at home, and
secretly perhaps doubtful of Dr. Munthe. I had received a
letter from him there, one quite formal, beginning, "Dear
Lady Ottoline," enclosing another tiny letter telling me that
he had been waiting for me all his life.

Yes, I was sure he loved me, but lurking underneath was
the instinct that he would not undergo the ordeal of facing
my family to win me. His vanity was afraid. He said to me in
Naples, as he held me by the arm, "I feel there is something
in you that you will never surrender to me." I was hopelessly
ignorant of the complexity of man's psychology; I could not
understand the hesitations of this man who professed to love
me.

When I got home, criticism began to hail down upon me
from my family. Religious doubts, too, assailed me. I thought
it wrong to marry an unbeliever. I wrote to him about these
doubts, wrote with intense pain, begging him to understand

and to wait. But this *enfant gâté,* who expected unhesitating surrender and submission, was outraged in his vanity by my adherence to religion in preference to him. Blinded by hurt pride to any understanding of my feelings and to all the agony it cost me to withstand him and to be faithful to what I thought was right, he turned on me and repudiated me, but before the breach had become wide I saw him once or twice in London, and went down with him to Guildford with my dear old nurse, Powell, who gallantly stood by me. But he had become irate and annoyed with me by then. I did not understand, but I still loved him beyond all reason. The happiness was gradually fading, only love and pain survived, but by this time he definitely wished to part, at least for us to remain friends. How much was my fault, how much was his fickleness, I never knew.

Then began the long and dreary journey across the desert of ordinary life; all was grey and colourless and lonely. I was burnt up by the agony of desire, by my love for this man who had wakened it all so pervadingly in me. Each day was an almost intolerable agony to me. Hilda was my only help. She poured out her devotion and love to me with a lavish hand; no friend could have surpassed her in love and tenderness. She tried to help me with complete self-forgetfulness. I did not know that one could suffer so profoundly, and yet live through it. It tortured me, bewildered me, wrung me and nearly broke me, but I was saved by a resolve to lose my own life, to cast all cares far away, and to pour it out henceforth for others, to concentrate on others. After this I arose with new courage, and with a strange force I stepped ahead singing. I never realized before how much one could laugh and sing when underneath the heart is torn with unhappiness.

The winter of this year, 1898, I spent with my aunt at her

villa in Florence. Out of kindness to me, Violet made a pretence of wishing to consult Dr. Munthe about her health, and she and I went down from Florence for two nights to Rome to see him. I was glad to have a final understanding with him, wanted to have things more clearly defined, for he would never commit himself one way or another; or perhaps it was that I would not accept the friendship that he offered me so easily. I went knowing that no good or happiness could come of this interview, but my cousin was determined to go. I went to his house, the house that Keats had died in, waited in his patients' waiting-room. There I found laid on the table for the public to read the white vellum Browning that had been my own precious possession, and that I had given to him. At last I was beckoned into his own little consulting-room. I have no clear memory of what was said, except that he wished to avoid all discussion and that he told me he considered me a religious maniac, that he had quite enough nerve cases amongst his patients, that to have one as a wife would be too much. He showed me a hole in the door where some madman had shot at him. He embraced me and I left, saddened and more hurt and torn and hopeless than ever. We returned to Florence that day. Next day I felt almost glad with that odd sense of being born again; with power to win, unshackled to start afresh, a new self replacing the old one:

"With forgetfulness comes an almost complete suppression of suffering and a possibility of well-being. This being, so unwanted, so blessed, is no other than one of those selves that destiny holds in reserve for us, and that without listening to our prayers—any more than would a clairvoyant doctor, and with even less authority—substitutes in spite of ourselves by an opportune intervention for the self that is too wounded.

This exchange indeed she accomplishes from time to time in the renewing of the tissues, but we only notice it when the old self contains a great pain (suffering or sorrow) a foreign and wounded body. That we are astonished at no more finding in ourselves in our wonder at having become another creature, for whom the suffering of the predecessor is only the suffering of someone else—of which one can speak with pity because one no longer feels it deeply." (Proust, *Albertine Disparue*.)

It is not often, I suppose, that the miracle of new birth is as swift or complete as this, for the old bruised and wounded self lies still within, and its death may be long-drawn-out and tedious, indeed for many years the old one may give many a dying groan that vibrates through the whole being, until old age comes with its numbing opiate, dimming the pains of memory.

At Florence I remember little except that I walked and walked alone in the lovely country round the villa at Arcetri; and sometimes Santa Margharita, through the *poderi* of olives and fruit trees in blossom, wandering through the old narrow streets of the town searching out hidden beauties, feeling pleasure in being alone and free, catching in myself reflections of the sometimes obscure and beautiful things around me that are hidden to the ordinary gazer in that lovely city. I was particularly fond of walking home, and by an old way called Via San Giorgio. It was steep and poor. The Porta San Giorgio has a lovely bas relief, St. George on horseback, probably by Donatello (a copy of which I had made for my brother, Henry, and which is now built into his club at Kirkby Lonsdale). How often I passed up and down this way, feeling glad to be stepping out alone and yet longing even for the love of a little puppy dog, which followed me as I went along.

I used to see Vernon Lee[9] sometimes, and she took me on several long drives in her funny ramshackle pony-carriage with a white horse. We went to some of the old Florentine villas, the Gamberia, Villa Corsini and the Rasponi Villa. I enjoyed these drives immensely, for she was extremely active in mind, and imparted her intellect and knowledge very well, and was very kind and charming to me. Through her I met Maud Cruttwell,[1] a lady of about thirty-five with a naïve boyish red face and pale yellow curly hair, a man's white shirt with stiff front and cuffs, a sailor hat, and blue serge coat and skirt, and a most charming and musical voice. We made friends and went to see pictures together. She was passionately devoted to art and was writing a book on Mantegna.

In the spring I returned to England. When I was in London I lived with my second brother, Henry, at 13 Grosvenor Place, my mother's old house. His wife was very beautiful, and I think she meant to be very kind to me, but she was ultra-conventional and completely *au fait* with the world. My rather untidy, original ways of dressing and behaving shocked her, and I now have the impression that she was always saying to me: "Ottoline, your placket-hole is open," or "Ottoline, your skirt is coming undone below your band" (my skirt and band failing to connect was a continual worry to me), or "Ottoline, your hair is tumbling down."

[9] The pen-name of Violet Paget, 1856–1935. She spent a large part of her life in Italy, and made her reputation chiefly with books concerning that country; she also wrote some fiction, which was not without merit. In her early days she was admired by Browning; Maurice Baring considered her one of the cleverest people he had known; Logan Pearsall Smith once called her the best talker of her time.

[1] Maud Cruttwell, 1859–1939, came of a scholarly Berkshire family. She is known for a number of learned works on Italian artists.

Except when I rode with him in the park, and at meals, I did not see my brother. He took no interest in my life, and was so morose that I did not dare approach him, although I was very fond of him. He was a most charming and attractive character, full of humour and pathos, but I still cannot reach him, he still eludes me, although I know the common interests we have in art and in politics must have drawn us nearer to each other than before.

CHAPTER III

Travel, Marriage and Politics

*Man is a wonderful, vain, divers
and wandering subject; it is very
hard to ground any directly constant and uniform judgement upon
him.*

MONTAIGNE, Bk. I, Ch. 1

As I STOP and breathe on this plateau of my life, I ask myself why I should burden this world with the ashes of my
past? Why disturb and distress myself by disentangling these
tangled years? The years that fate has done with, spun and
thrown aside. What use is it to anyone to remove the dust
from them, to try and make them live again? There comes
the inspiring desire of Immortality—twin voice to that ever
insistent one whose cry is for ever "What am I doing here?"
Only answered by "What have I done?"

So perhaps I live in the thoughts of those who may see
these pages. I have no events of any importance to record, no
life of any moment to describe, yet, as we all vibrate to events
in our own individual way, and each give out different music
from the chords of our being, so I will try and play a few of
the airs that life has taught me, and patch again some of the
music that life has drawn from me.

61

I was, I believe, like many other people, very late in developing anything like evenness in my character. I had been called "very old for my age." Meanwhile, my old longing to study revived in me. The more I saw of life and the more people I mixed with, the more the passion grew in me to know, to understand, to learn, to escape from my blurred world of ignorance, where I felt so timid and hungry, into that wide world which seemed to my imagination to enable those who were there to walk freely and with confidence. From past mental starvation, I perhaps exaggerated the importance of book-learning, but the idea obsessed me.

Having tried St. Andrews, I thought I might now aim at Oxford. Before doing so I turned over every other possibility, even visiting the Holloway College at Virginia Water. But Oxford seemed the best. Of course, I was not able to attempt examinations, so only went as an out-student attached to Somerville. In April 1899 I went there, having taken lodgings in the house of Miss Cooper, 22 St. John Street (a lady who taught the art of teaching to schoolmistresses). Another family conclave had to be held on this new move, but scholastic enterprise was beginning to seem quite normal and safe. I found out afterwards that what they most feared was that I should want to enter the sisterhood at Truro. There was a correspondence about this, unknown to me till by chance I found out, and rather indignantly asked why they had not asked me directly instead of trying to find out secretly. I would not allow Hilda to go with me to Oxford as I wanted to shake off all sympathy, which I felt to be weakening. I went to Professor Pelham's lectures on Roman History and also had coaching from Somerville in Roman History and Political Economy. This last was taught me by Miss Deverell, and I was very interested in it, and in all her socialistic ideas.

I used to go with her on the river, and once we went to hear Prince Kropotkin speak at a meeting. Some friends in London told Mrs. Morrell to go and see me, and I went and lunched occasionally with her at Black Hall.[1] I stayed on beyond the term during the summer, as I had nowhere else I particularly wanted to go, and began to feel a romantic feeling about Oxford as I bicycled through its deserted streets with my books in a satchel on my back; and then in the summer evenings I would bicycle out into the country. I remember now the delicious scent of the lilies in the cottage gardens on those summer nights as they were wafted to me.

Early in 1900 I stayed with Lady Bective[2] in Dean Place, for I had been obliged to leave Oxford; my health became too bad to remain. I did not care for the close exotic atmosphere of Lady Bective, although she was at that time very kind to me. It was whilst I was staying with her that I became really intimate with Mr. Asquith. He came and spent a Sunday afternoon with me, taking me to St. Paul's. Afterwards we sat and talked, and I was rather *bouleversée* by his assurance of affection, but I knew he would not and could not care for me in the way I needed to be cared for. He often came to see me after this; also when I stopped alone at my brother Henry's house in Grosvenor Place. I liked him very much indeed, but never felt really very much at ease with him intellectually, although I was naturally flattered and pleased that such a

[1] It was at this time that Ottoline first met Philip Morrell who was to become her husband, although for a time their acquaintance remained a slight one. He told me once of the first time that he ever saw her; clothed in a long, light-coloured dress, she was riding a bicycle very slowly along one of the Oxford streets. Ottoline told me that she was chiefly drawn to the house by a beautiful Flemish primitive which Mrs. Morrell possessed, but afterwards sold.

[2] The mother of Ottoline's sister-in-law, Lady Henry Bentinck.

well-known man should be interested in me and come to see me. His intellect was forcible and logical, but I never felt that it was very exciting talking to him. He was never spontaneous or intuitive, nor did he ever soar into the wild unknown regions of life, or of the mind. He would make me feel shy of expressing my real thoughts as I felt they might not stand his unimaginative logic. As I look back on this intimacy, I regret many things, above all that my hypersensitive conscience made me nervous about it, so that I was prevented from drinking its full pleasure and riches.

Soon after that I had to go for a rest cure to a nursing-home kept by Miss Nelson Smith. Whilst I was there I read a great deal and enjoyed it immensely. During that time I remember hearing the roars and wild shoutings that went on all one night at the relief of Mafeking. My youngest brother Charles had been in Mafeking all during the siege.

In April 1900 Hilda Pennant and I went to Monte Generoso in the vain endeavour that I should become well and strong. I read most of the day. Sometimes old Mr. Llewellyn Davies came up the mountain to see us and to read Wordsworth to us. Very soon after this, my health being still exceedingly bad, I was advised to go and consult a famous specialist, Professor Beigel, in Germany, and as I could not speak German Miss Nelson Smith was sent out by my London doctor to explain matters to Professor Beigel. We arrived at the dreary little town, strange and lonely, feeling that infinite boredom that always accompanies the search for health. The old Professor came to see me, and instead of the usual gross and stupid red-faced German a very tall, aristocratic man appeared, about sixty, like an old Jewish Rabbi with long, sensitive, artistic hands. I was stripped and examined, which caused me a great deal of shyness, and he

ordered me to be sent to Wiesbaden where I should be under
his supervision. I was rather taken aback when as he left me
one day he bent down and kissed me. Hilda was still with me
and we went to Wiesbaden, spending three dreary months
from October to December, occasionally going over to Giessen
to see the old professor. Before Christmas he made us go and
stay there. The only possible place where we could lodge
was at the Protestant sisterhood, and we spent Christmas
there, listening to German carols, and my old Professor became passionately devoted to me. I do not think anyone has
ever been so devoted to me as this man. I was very fond of
him, but as of someone who was much older, like a father.
He had married when he was young, a nice amiable fat
woman, and he was quite fond of her and of his two daughters, but all the hidden, pent-up, idealistic side had obviously
never found a home. Once wakened, it poured itself out un-
swervingly upon me. As I could not talk any German, and he
could not talk English, our conversation was limited, but he
could understand French, and he could write it fairly fluently.
He wrote to me every day henceforth. I was determined not
to go back to England and settle down with my family. I
easily induced my Professor to say I needed long months
abroad in the sun to complete my cure. We hurried back to
England to arrange for a further escape to Sicily and spent a
few weeks in London.

In January 1901 I saw Mr. Asquith several times; he gave
me Thucydides to take with me and read at Syracuse. We
went to a hotel just outside Taormina, high up on a cliff hanging over the sea. We wandered and sat amongst rocks and
prickly pears, lemon trees and orange groves, looking down
on Scylla and Charybdis, or away to Mount Etna, always
changing and terrifying. Perhaps I was romantic, but I used

to feel a certain limitation when I saw any marvellous places like Taormina, a sense of not being completely free or not in tune with such perfect and wonderful surroundings. I still felt too ignorant to enjoy them to the full and as I look back I feel it was true. I was also still too pent-up, too conscientious and not liberated enough from tight inward discipline. I seemed to be under the spell of some tyranny which forbade me to enjoy freely, or to drink deeply of the cup of life in my hand. This perhaps was partly ill-health; partly it was the remains of my old life, partly also hunger for something I had never found.

One day, walking inland up the steep rocky hillside along a little rough old path between wild lavender and marble, there came dashing down upon me a flock of goats with their goatherd—Pan himself, alive and wild, dancing down in wild career singing a queer song as he went. His face was thin and pale and almost green, his cruel yellow eyes slanting upward, and ears pointed like horns. High up as I went, I caught the tender lovely thrill of the Sicilian's pipe, and its answering notes came across the valley. I stood entranced, searching to see where they came from, whether from man or god. There on a rock high up I saw a little brown figure sitting with his pipes to his mouth, and then following with my eyes across the valley found his fellow, who was answering him back.

Another day we went on a picnic with Professor Butcher[3] and his wife, who were also at Taormina. We found a lovely place beside a stream, perfect in beauty, smelling of the

[3] Samuel Newby Butcher, 1850–1910, was professor of Greek at Edinburgh from 1822 to 1903, and Member of Parliament for Cambridge from 1906 to 1910. His name is known to the public chiefly for his collaboration with Andrew Lang in their prose translation of the *Odyssey*. He was a singularly handsome man.

crushed herbs which we sat on. We read Theocritus, and drank of the wine that had been brought with us, wine freshly made and unfermented, tasting of crushed flowers and peaches and strawberries. It was the only wine that has ever seemed to me worth drinking.

We saw a good deal of Professor Butcher and his wife, and made expeditions with them, going to Palermo or to Monreale.[4] I remember looking down on the great orange groves spread out below, stretching down to the sea, dark green leaves foiling the oranges that hung beneath them. The little chapel lined with mosaics was most exciting and beautiful. Mass was being celebrated and I remember the ray of sunlight falling on the priest in his white vestments as he was celebrating in this jewelled shrine.

From Palermo we went on expeditions out into the wilder parts of Sicily: to Segesta, the huge temple that stands lonely and high up on a hill in wild and desolate country: to Selinunte—the temple that once stood there lies shaken down as by a giant. The pillars are enormous, like great limbs lying on the golden sand by the seashore surrounded by vermilion poppies and white asphodel, and the blue sea washing in upon the sandy, golden plain. It is a moving sight to see those helpless, useless columns lying there, as level with the sea.

We spent the night in a little inn at Catalafiumi; the *padrone*, like all Italians, was very inquisitive about us. He asked Mrs. Butcher what we did. At some vague answer he exclaimed: "A! you live the *'vita leggiera.'*" Yes, we lived the *"vita leggiera."* On we went, driving under hot sun to Gir-

---

[4] Here, as perhaps in other places, Ottoline's topographical memory is not reliable. The cathedral of Monreale, which she seems to be alluding to, could never be called a little chapel. She probably had in mind the Cappella Palatina, in the royal palace of Palermo.

67

genti,[5] which seemed to me bare and arid. Temples were scattered about, the earth was red and it ought to have been perfect. But I still recall discomfort when I think of it; people were extraordinarily savage. We then went on to Syracuse, that low-lying antique harbour, the Roman theatre recalling the pastorals of Theocritus. It is very moving to be in places where rushing life has been lived, life terrible and tragic, and mad and gay, but now all past and gone, leaving only dry shells behind, overgrown with vegetation, and with the vague thoughts of the gazers. How few really feel or are moved by the life that was lived so passionately in these ruins some two thousand years ago?

Soon after, Hilda and I left Sicily for Rome, where we had arranged to meet Mrs. Strong to see Roman antiquities together. The journey from the south on a May morning was a dream. How much I imagined what I saw, or saw what I imagined, I cannot tell. Castles and mountains and rocks and valleys, mists and colours divine flew by; and then on a flat, glowing, sunny plain with the sea washing and lapping up to its feet, stood the temples of Paestum, standing low, with their amazing colour of burnt cream and rosy pink in the early morning sunlight, standing lonely and supreme, as if built by the gods, asphodels growing all round them.

We arrived in Rome and found it lovely—full of flowers, roses tumbling everywhere over the walls in glorious cascades. Mrs. Strong was an accomplished teacher and guide; she took us to many places unknown to me before: to the Villa Albani, which I enjoyed almost more than anything else, the little Pallas Athene by Phidias, the ilex grove and the quiet formal garden statues by Scopas with the rose garlands. After Mrs. Strong left us, Hilda and I remained on at Rome, going out

[5] Now called Agrigento.

into the country in a delightful little victoria which we hired. The Via Appia, the Campagna, the Corso, great palaces built by Bramante and Michelangelo, the Villa Madama built by Raphael, with its ruined cascades and terraces, and the glowing russet earth beyond; and then, to end our time, on a wonderful day in June we went to Hadrian's Villa and to Tivoli and the Villa d'Este, creeping along over the Campagna in a little black tram.

We alighted at Hadrian's Villa, the ruins of which are so vast that it might have been a town spreading out on that wonderful spot: the halls, the courts, the private rooms, the fountain and gardens of what had been the treasure house of that one supremely civilized Caesar, now indistinguishable ruins on every side. Here had stood a villa, not built by vulgar, ignorant riches but by one whose poetic and sensitive taste had culled from Greece and Egypt and Asia Minor the most perfect and exotic flowers of beauty and of art—all gone, all demolished, the lilacs and the nightingales alone left to speak of its beauty. As we wandered over it, we found a ruined tower perched high up looking down on the terraces and the Campagna. Here we sat for hours, musing and talking. Nightingales were singing, the scent of the lilacs and wild roses on all sides. I remember that talk very vividly: What were we going to do with our lives? We had decided to live together in a house in London. Yes, then that was all right. But that was only outside. What was to be the inner life? That fruit of all my passionate desire? Hilda said, "I suppose the great thing in marriage is that it solves that question and naturally gives interest and occupation." I inwardly resented and denied this, but no one could solve the eternal problem except oneself, and one's inner energy. It can only be a shifting of the décor, leaving one still learning to dance one's own part in the ball of life. I got up dazed with doubt and wonder as to what the future would involve. The curtain was not raised. I could not even to Hilda unfold the almost unconscious hopes and expectations that I felt, but the beauty of that day will never fade.

We crept across the Campagna to Tivoli, wandering in the gardens of the Villa d'Este, another empty shell of another grandeur. Much as I loved Hilda, and much as I loved seeing these wonderful things with her, I never lost a feeling of void, a desire for someone with whom I could be more satisfied, who would take the larger views. I felt that her interest was too detailed, too personal, too minute, and that she could not sweep along with large rich views which were the outcome of knowledge and experience. I hungered for other thoughts and other subjects to feed upon and to discuss. She imprisoned me intellectually, and I secretly dreaded being with her in London, knowing that I should find it difficult to get out beyond her into larger and more interesting fields of thought and life. I had always tried to persuade her to undertake work of her own, and had stipulated that she should find something to do if she lived with me, so as to leave me free for my own life. But I felt sure that her fastidiousness, and what I used to call her pernickety ideas would not allow her to find anything that would suit her. We left Rome very regretfully. We went to Florence and met Miss Cruttwell there, starting off with her on a tour.

We went to wonderful places: Mantua, that poetical city with its gargantuan castle, with tower rooms painted by Mantegna with frescoes, its immortal ghosts of the Gonzagas, who still hold their static court, as if suddenly spellbound: the windows looking out over the bridge of boats which crosses the river on to the marshes beyond. I stood entranced seeming to hear the song of Swans being sung. It was this window that Mantegna painted in the Death of the Virgin with St. John, now at Madrid. The town with its arches and dim remains of frescoes, the museum where Mantegna's one precious antique possession still stands, the beautiful classical church where Mantegna was buried, and which contains his head in bronze, done by an unknown hand, fierce, savage, haunting—only he himself could have done it, and done it when he was old with his last fierce passion, looking as if he had cut his own head off and poured bronze over it. As I was wandering along the wide, grassy-green streets I met an old man with an exquisite ornamented hand-organ, playing a Mozart air.

From there we roamed on to Ferrara, to Monte Oliveto, to Ravenna to Lucca and Pisa. I remember wonderful long drives in the hot summer nights surrounded with clouds of fireflies and fragrant odours. Another long drive from Pisa to the sea, passing through the pine forests and along the river where stands one of the King's palaces. I saw his camels coming down to water at the river, looking mysterious and tall and strange amongst the dark pine trees. It was almost unbearably hot on our drives across the rocky, sandy country to Monte Oliveto and San Gimignano. Miss Cruttwell would insist on sitting on the box by the driver in the full blaze of the sun, smoking a huge cigar, with her pink innocent face beaming with enjoyment.

I determined to go to Carrara; the heat of the journey through the white mountains was almost unbearable, but extraordinarily beautiful and strange—the long, narrow, white roads and the rough carts drawn by ten or more white oxen carrying blocks of marble, the men covered with marble dust and the pink sunset light over it all.

Siena, too, we went to, driving miles around the country,

searching for the fields of lavender that Maud Cruttwell assured us existed. She said they smelt for miles, and so on and on we went, sniffing the air to catch the scent of lavender on the wind, but which we never found.

Then back to Florence, hot and gay, delicious with the smell of gardenias, under our windows, feet passing swiftly and with the sound of song and guitars, carrying my heart away with them, and waking the haunting hunger that I never lost, for someone, someone or something—with whom I could be perfectly free, to do wild things—someone who would sail with me on the clouds, run with me on the earth, whose hand I could clasp, and escape from the narrow world in which I lived.

Mrs. Morrell asked me down to stay with them at Black Hall for a week-end. She was busy making a strong mixture of wax and perfume for pomanders; it was so strong that it made us all feel very sick. Although nothing had been said, it was here that I had first the impression that Philip wanted to marry me. I sat up all night in my bedroom by my fire trying to push away the feeling of pressure that was closing upon me. I felt his personality almost physically elbowing in on me, a pressure of Fate. I wished to withstand it.

I didn't really think of marrying then, and clung to my solitary liberty. I believe in many women there is a strong intuitive feeling of pride in their solitary life that when marriage really comes it is, to a certain extent, a humiliation.

"I have succumbed" is, as it were, a lining to the words, "I have humiliated myself." I also felt too burnt-out by the old love affair that had lasted many years.

The crisis came when I went to Welbeck for Christmas, and Philip went to join his father at Pau. I would give no definite answer; I said, "Impossible." It just was no special reason. I know I was very pleased with a lovely bunch of lilies of the valley that he brought to the station, and treasured it all the days that I was at Welbeck. My old friend Mildred de Lotbinière[6] travelled down with me in the train, and we discussed the situation. I have a vivid impression of our talk, she and I sitting side by side in the railway carriage and the bunch of lilies between us, larger in importance than in size. She was on the whole favourably impressed, and at this I felt disturbed and distracted and undecided, but yet with a happy feeling underneath of close companionship and love.

I have no vivid recollection of my time at Welbeck, except that I felt undecided and yet happy.

When I returned to London I had to go to bed with a feverish attack. Philip was away at Pau writing to me, pressing his suit.[7] I lay tossing in bed undecided what to answer. At last I made the plunge and wired to him to "Come back." The answer came that he was returning at once. My old Nurse Powell was with me—indeed she was always there at any crisis of my life. I realize now how very reserved I must have been. I certainly never spoke of my indecisions or worries to anyone except Powell. I remember her bending over me in bed with the telegram from abroad. He arrived; I see him as he came into my sitting-room, and I remember where I stood by the piano waiting for him; but I remember nothing more except that he smelt of violets. The pressure of fate that had laid its hand on us had been responded to and had pressed our two lives together.

[6] Sister of Ottoline's sister-in-law, Lady Charles Bentinck.

[7] This is merely a conventional phrase and not very accurate. For, in fact, I was filled with doubt as to whether I could ever make her happy in consequence of the great differences between us in respect of upbringing and way of life. So I was determined not to be too persuasive or pressing and must have often seemed, as my letters clearly show, a hesitating and backward lover.   P.M.

73

Our wedding took place on February 8th, 1902, at St. Peter's, Eaton Square. My family made no objection to it, indeed I think they were relieved that I had not chosen a wild and lawless man of the woods for my husband. One of my sisters-in-law said she had had "a horrible dream," that Philip was a Radical. Poor dear, little she knew then that it was a fact as well as a dream. Indeed, part of our mutual interest was that both Philip and I were what is called radicals.

No one could have been kinder or more generous than my family were to me then, except that my youngest brother said to Philip at the wedding, "Well, I am glad I am not in your shoes. I wouldn't undertake her for anything."

These mysterious warnings and doubts that fly past one brushed me with their wings and woke me out of the romantic illusion that married life would be without any hitch or trouble. In a flash I saw, as if I were looking through a window into the future spread out before me, that the road would be rough and steep, that I should have to walk side by side with my companion, and that I should have to be my own guide. A voice told me that if I started on this new life, it would mean difficulties that I must bear alone. I saw and I heard, but gladly determined to go ahead and have never had any regret. It is not often that one is taken to these windows that look into the future, led there by some mysterious hand, but the visions that are seen are always true. Sometimes indeed one isn't taken as far as the window. A sharp arrow is darted into one and that is all. It is well not to disregard these flashes of light—for they only happen once.

I stepped out on February 8th, 1902, into the outer courts of my real life. The years that had gone before were curiously unformed compared with those that I was to live in the future. I didn't leave a home or a mother. Those would have been a continuous influence with me. I left two rooms, a sitting-room and a bedroom, and a much-loved friend, Hilda Douglas Pennant, and my old nurse.

Is a honeymoon ever an ideally blissful time, as the name seems to denote? I doubt if it is for anyone over twenty-five. Old habits that have been formed by living alone have to be broken, adaptation begins, and to anyone serious and nervous these first days of joint life assume an exaggerated importance, mutual likes and dislikes are watched with microscopic eyes, and if in all things they do not correspond, the whole of the future seems at stake. The small fact even of new clothes and shoes tends to make these days uncomfortable and odd.

However, we found nothing to despair of, and our days were very interesting and happy, sightseeing in Florence, Naples and Rome, reading aloud Carlyle, *Past and Present*, poetry, Gibbon, Milton, and meeting on our way old friends of Philip's and mine, Logan Pearsall Smith[8] and the Berensons. Here indeed was one of the microscopic troubles. Logan had been a very intimate friend of Philip's and was, of course, critical and suspicious of me. Of this I became exaggeratedly conscious. Another complication arose from having taken with me my old and devoted Irish servant, Ellen Dormer. She had been with my mother as housemaid, and had clung to me at her death with a loyalty and fidelity that are only perhaps possible in an Irish woman. She had followed my wild and rash footsteps over the world, protesting often, but always ready to slave, to sew,

[8] Logan Pearsall Smith had so much disliked the marriage that he went abroad to avoid being present at it, and declared that the friendship was at an end. Meeting them later, he brutally told Philip that he could come to the house after all, not as his friend, but because he found Ottoline very interesting. He was evidently fascinated by her for a time, but he never forgave her for marrying his young friend.

75

to cook and to pack and to nurse when necessary. She now found that the sight of her loved charge and mistress married was too much for her to bear. She became quite unbearable, rude and unruly. She had to be left to spend a week at Naples by herself, and eventually sent on to London alone. Knowing what this dear and naughty creature suffered, I felt very disturbed.

One of our longest stays was at Ravello, that wild and pagan village near Amalfi. Staying in the *pension* with us was R. C. Trevelyan and his wife.[9] He also had not been long married, but marriage and its obligations and ties did not trouble this Pan-like creature. He would spend whole days out on the crags and cliffs alone, writing poetry, and then, when he returned to his meals would, when the macaroni was offered to him, put the whole contents of the dish on his plate, quite unconscious of the sad and horrified hungry eyes of the other pensionnaires. At night we would call him and he would come on to the terrace probably half undressed, and walk up and down, declaiming about Shelley's poetry, on and on, in a loud and half-controlled voice, hesitating yet explicit, very interesting and very full of charm. He was so full of the desire to be a poet—and indeed he had great promise—that he had adopted it as his profession, and luckily was well enough off to be able to do so without difficulty. But that Muse is a flighty, fastidious and proud mistress, and will hardly and rarely come to those who woo her even with much learning and rhetoric. But few

[9] Many years later, when she was old, Mrs. Trevelyan described to me Ottoline's entrance into the hotel at Ravello—all a vision of long, pale, fluttering draperies. "I was amazed; I had never seen anyone like that before"—an observation true of all Ottoline's acquaintances. Yet, as the narrative shows, they very soon recognized one another as creatures from the same world.

people had at the time of his life so much whimsical charm and oddity as Bob Trevelyan. It has since solidified; but perhaps a next generation or two may discover that he was one of the remarkable poets of our time.

Rome followed Ravello and we both, I think, remember that as the happiest time. We had lovely rooms and a large sitting-room in Hotel Molaro,[1] where we lived in peace and Philip read Gibbon aloud and we spent long days alone. I took him to see all the places I most cared for in Rome, and it was wonderful sharing these things with someone so educated, artistic and appreciative. I think the old convention that a honeymoon is to be spent *"à deux"* is with many other of the old-established conventions regarding manners and personal life, very wise. There is so much to learn about one's new companion, and indeed about oneself in these new circumstances, for one sees oneself with his eyes, and this is accomplished more happily alone and when not interrupted by casual friends.

On re-reading some daily jottings of these days, I find how intensely religious I was then; indeed, the writing that I did was almost entirely religious, spiritual meditations. It was the centre and ground of my life. From it radiated all my other activities. I speak of it as if it is in the past, for though now in 1925 spiritual life is still strongly alive in me, yet it is more transfused, more sublimated into other ideas. It is the core of my life, but other ideas and interests have grown strong and waxed full.

The first months of our return home were spent in settling into our house, 32 Grosvenor Road. We went before that to No. 36, a furnished house belonging to Percy Feilding. Questions of servants, housekeeping, have faded from my memory.

[1] Then a hotel in the centre of the city, quite near the Piazza di Spagna. The house still exists, but is no longer a hotel.   P.M.

I only remember the maids and their names. How they came to me I don't know.

Philip had to go every day to his office (a branch of the Oxford solicitor's business), and I generally went to meet him at luncheon at the Vienna Café in New Oxford Street, when we would see in the distance Laurence Binyon and his friends. In the evening he would read aloud to me, sometimes poetry, sometimes Gibbon, sometimes Macaulay's *History*. Then there was always endless work in arranging our house, which really became very lovely. The drawing-room was panelled pale grey, and the curtains a vivid rose-pink Chinese silk, and I had a sitting-room on one of the top floors overlooking the river. It was so high up that it seemed suspended over the river. I loved to watch the blue evening lights and the yellow gas lamps, and to see the great barges being pulled up the river, the men's figures outlined against the lights. Philip had great energy and taste, and devoted himself to making our little house perfect. His taste was so architectural and accurate, at first it was quite bewildering to me, who was not accustomed to so much care in details of furnishing and house decoration, but I soon learnt my lesson and was stimulated to many developments of my own, more romantic and wilder inventions, he curbing and pruning.

The next few months passed in a sort of novitiate for the life that was to develop. All too soon was the peace and happiness of it to give way. Visits to Philip's father and mother at Black Hall, Oxford, were fairly frequent, and in the summer to their little house at Clifton Hampden. They were at this time very kind and uncritical of me, and we were happy all together. Philip was devoted to his mother, who was a most gifted and an unusually charming person, lively, witty, critical, with immense artistic ability, especially in decoration and embroidery. Her nature was that of a very enchanting child, loving all things beautiful and gay. She had been an important figure in Oxford, very much more remarkable in taste and in entertaining than any other woman there. She had gathered round her in their beautiful house many interesting people, who found her a delightful and witty friend and hostess. Indeed, Henry James, it is said, took from her the inspiration for *The Spoils of Poynton*.

Philip was the only surviving son. He had become a solicitor much against his will and taste to please his parents, more especially his mother, who was curiously devoid of ambition for him, but liked to have him near her. It was not at all a happy career for him. He was far too creative, too fastidious in temperament, to feel satisfied with a business career, and his life would have been very much more complete if he had been allowed, when young, to devote it to some form of artistic or literary work; but parents are blind and autocratic, and sons of those days were dutiful and submissive, or rather perhaps in this case, tender and hopeful of finding a way out after serving an apprenticeship in "the office."

I felt with him the unsatisfactoriness of his career, and together we discussed all ways of escape. We were both interested in politics and social reform which seemed a possible outlet, as it could be combined with law. In 1902 and 1903 politics were a very living and inspiring career. There were groups of young men on the Liberal side enthusiastic for reform; land reform, housing reform, old age pensions, international friendship. These and others were all castles that could be built on earth. "Building Jerusalem in England's pleasant land" was no high soaring song, but a real possibility.

Our smouldering project was fanned into a flame by a visit to Logan Pearsall Smith at Haslemere, where we met the Sidney

Webbs. This meeting and the discussions we had there were as a finger-post for us pointing along a road that led us away from all our old friends, across a gulf that separated me from my family, and for some time, though less widely, from Philip's also.

Having taken the turn, we trod on bravely, and toiled many weary years in the political vineyard certainly gaining knowledge and experience of human nature, and also we took part in many interesting and exciting events. But the task was hard and baffling, the workmanship difficult to learn. Others pushed and jostled, possibly less idealistic in thought and action. In 1914 all that was promising, all that was already accomplished, was overturned by the declaration of war.

On looking back I am astonished at the light-hearted, quixotic way we started forth on this career, which meant much weariness, much self-denial, so much that was hoped for ending in such bitter disappointment. But fate has a deceitful way of veiling the eyes of her puppets. Should we have still stuck to our post if we had known all it entailed?

If I had been asked this in July 1914 I should have said yes, willingly. In August the answer would have been beyond doubt, no. The Liberal leaders revealed themselves as having been undecided, underhanded.

But to return to 1902. Philip, by my advice, went to see Mr. Asquith, who advised him to join the Liberal League, and to see Mr. Freeman Thomas.[2] This advice coincided with that of

[2] Then a recently elected Member of Parliament. He afterwards became Junior Lord of the Treasury; and later, having been created a Peer, was Governor of Bombay and Madras successively; and later still, having risen to be Marquis of Willingdon, held the post of Viceroy of India. In all these offices he was extremely successful, not from any remarkable intellectual talent, but from his extraordinary tact and charm which, though often no doubt exaggerated and artificial, seemed

Mr. Sidney Webb, who had sung the praises of this off-shoot of the young Liberal Party, who were, they said, the most enlightened branch of the Party.

Appointments, conversations took place between Philip and the Chief Whip; we were welcomed into the Party, election expenses were promised, and after much discussion it was settled that he should stand for South Oxfordshire against Sir R. Herman Hodge.

In October 1902, eight months after our marriage, our political work began. The constituency stretched from Oxford to Henley and Caversham.

The first dark cloud arose on the horizon. His family, and all his old friends in the country, were outraged that he, coming from an old Conservative family, should have the audacity to fight an Oxfordshire seat as a Liberal. What they thought he was gaining by standing as a Liberal I do not know, but every evil motive was imputed to him.

His father and mother were also grieved and indignant, and in fact never quite forgave him, and after two or three years he was forced by his father to retire from the business as it was thought that a Liberal partner would damage it and alienate Oxford clients.

Now began our new life. All Philip's free time and holidays were spent in going to meetings, large and small. We generally drove to them in a high dog-cart. How vivid are those endlessly long night drives. A hurried tea and dinner at six, and then out into the night, driving on and on, long miles through lanes, over commons, climbing the Chilterns, and through mysteri-

---

based on genuine kindness of heart. Ottoline and I stayed with him in the Viceroy's house in Delhi, and found him just as simple, as amiable, and as charming as when we first made his acquaintance thirty years before in London.   P.M.

ous woods. Arriving at a Town Hall such as Thame, where large enthusiastic audiences were waiting, or Watlington, where there were large and adverse crowds ready to hoot, yell and boo and even throw eggs and stones, and overturn our dogcart.

And then the small meetings in village schoolrooms, where a few agricultural labourers sat on small children's forms, their corduroy trousers tied round with string, and their huge great bodies and rough faces stolidly facing us, and occasionally nodding their heads and groaning approval. And the knots of "doubtfuls" clustered round the door, whispering in hoarse voices, or, if unfriendly, calling out crude and silly insults.

Who could help not being moved to desire better conditions for these men, more enlightenment, education and better housing, more freedom to obtain the land. It seemed to one to be simple and obviously right that such glaring inequality should be abolished, and we pushed and pushed with vigor at the heavy weight that lay upon their lives.

How blind then we were to the avalanche that was to come from another direction and that was to overwhelm us all.

The notes that I find of these next years are almost entirely about political meetings. Names of places jotted down: Checkendon, Caversham, Chinnor, Goring, Wheatly, Ipsden, Nettlebed, Peppard and Garsington, Ewelme, Tetsworth. How little I realized then that we should live many years at Peppard, and still more years at Garsington.

As I go through the villages now, the old dead struggle like ghosts. The names of supporters come to my mind, seem remembered often with affection and admiration for their service in the cause. Long drives at night, as I have said, and very often visits to rich supporters living in large and pompous houses, combining the most elaborate decoration with great

Ottoline, aged about 8

Lady Ottoline, 1902

Philip Morrell
by Henry Lamb, R.A., 1911

Henry Lamb at Peppard Cottage,
Henley-on-Thames, 1911

IV

discomfort. There was Friar Park, Henley, belonging to the rich solicitor, Sir Frank Crisp. He worked hard, and earned and ate much, and diverted his mind from company promoting by erecting sham Swiss mountains and passes, decorated by china chamois, which had to be spied through Zeiss glasses, and elaborate caves and underground lakes, lit up with electricity, and festooned with artificial grapes, spiders and other monsters. He took his visitors round the caves and the garden (which was also filled with china hobgoblins and other surprises), dressed in a long frock-coat and top hat and with a large umbrella in his hands, as if he was walking to his Throgmorton Street office, his manner perfectly serious when warning one against the danger of a monstrous spider alighting on one's hat. We were then floating in small boats on the underground lake, lit up by electric light.

How much this serious, comic, overgrown child mocked at himself or at his visitors, I don't know, or whether, with all his commercial clear-sightedness, he was colossally simple and really thought these vulgar and monstrous jokes amusing and beautiful. At least, I imagine they were a refuge from his work and his family.

We also stayed with the Pears of the soap, who were living at Watlington Park. Mr. Pears met us in a brougham lined with bright blue satin. Poor Mrs. Pears was lonely and uncomfortable in the large Georgian house, and was hoping soon to retire to her villa at Isleworth.

Mr. Pears smoked large cigars all day, beginning in his bath at 7.30 a.m.; naturally he looked yellow and depressed and his eyes bloodshot. I well remember the uphill talk with Mrs. Pears, on the morning after our meeting.

But there were other houses where our visits were a pleasure. One was Shiplake Court, belonging to Mr. and Mrs. Harrison. He was the President of the Association. She was an intelligent woman, caring for books and art, and their house was filled with beautiful things, Whistlers and Sargents. I was fairly happy there, but perhaps not really so, for one had to be on one's best behaviour, and he was always, I think, conscious of being our patron.

Another political resting-place was Newington House, where Ethel Sands lived, but this had quite a different atmosphere and we made real friends with her, and have always remained so. This exquisite, very fine figure came of American parentage. Her mother was, I believe, an extremely beautiful and fascinating lady—a friend among others of Gladstone, Sir W. Harcourt, Sargent and Henry James: her father a very passionate Free Trader and Liberal. She had inherited his political ideas and her mother's intelligence and friends. Her adoration and admiration of her mother was unbounded. When a young girl, she realized that she had no place or part to play on the stage of her life, and gracefully removed herself to Paris, where she lived with a friend, Miss Hudson, and worked seriously at painting.

At her mother's death she had to interest herself in bringing up her two brothers. Partly for the sake of being within reach of Oxford, she bought that most lovely and melancholy house at Newington. A square grey stone house, built by Inigo Jones,[3] with a forecourt and great stone gates, ornamented on the other side by a formal garden, looking away over a great stretch of meadow land, a line of old elm trees like old men ambling across. The beauty of this place ravished me. I loved the old grey stone house and the exquisite decorated rooms. The garden, a small flight of grey stone steps with pink roses

[3] Beautiful as Newington is, I do not think that this attribution to Inigo Jones would now be accepted.

climbing over them, gave me a thrill of joy every time I passed them. When I first knew her, she and Miss Hudson had only recently migrated from Paris, so that with the exception of a few of her mother's old friends, she did not know many people in England, and it was through us that she afterwards became friends with a younger generation of artists and of literary men.

The days that we spent at Newington were certainly the happiest among our political visits, indeed the monotony of practical politics here merged into discussions on political ideas —and gradually mutual interests in art, literature and life grew up between us.

In the winter, unfortunately, Miss Sands had to leave Newington for London as the green meadows turned into silver-grey floods.

And many a time as we passed at nights on our way to and fro to meetings from Oxford, I have seen in the moonlight that lovely grey house, arising out of a grey mirror of flood, desolate and spellbound.

The last time I went over to say good-bye to the house— Ethel Sands had already left—I wandered round the garden one early summer evening, with its lovely terraces, listening to thrushes and nightingales and smelling the purple lilac, the white syringa, the sweet-scented pinks. I sat on a seat overcome with melancholy that life for us here was past, that the lovely décor was put aside, that other actors would perform here. I called to the spirits of my old companions to come and say farewell. I thought of tall Sir Walter Raleigh, sitting at a tiny tea-table with my little daughter Julian, aged six, Herbert Fisher, Logan Pearsall Smith. But more vivid than others are William James and his brother Henry.

I walk again in memory with William James across meadows

and down the long Elm Avenue. He was so appreciative and "ravished by the greenness and luxuriance of the English country. The villages and lawns: the streams," as he said, "are endlessly perfect in their way and interesting. A country in equilibrium with itself and to Yankee eyes fabulously antique and finished."

But perhaps more vivid to me was his talk about his brother Henry. He was distressed that Henry should have written *The American Scene* about his own country; especially painful to him was the chapter about the Commercial Traveller's breakfast. "How could he have written that about a fellow human being—one for whom Christ died?"

He confessed that he found it difficult to appreciate his beloved brother's novels. They were too involved and elaborate for his taste. He had once asked Henry to write before he died a book for little brother; to which Henry had replied, laughing: "Dear brother, I will do so, but I know if it pleases you I shall go down with sorrow to my grave." Both of them had such great capacity for affection. I felt that William's nature was intensely lovable, simple and human, with immense sensitive kindness and understanding of life and of other human beings —he had above all people the intellect of the heart. His brother Henry had perhaps very much the same temperament, but added to it there was the inexorable artist who, when it takes command of a personality, is an autocrat over all the instincts, and a jealous taskmaster.

I always felt that this great artist had unbounded sympathy and a good heart, but from his devotion to the lady he worshipped—his art—he dared not give it free play. So little meant so much to him—a grain of real life expanded so rapidly in his mind to a large and complicated and tangled tree that he was obliged to protect his windows, to curb his outgoings or outpourings of interest and affection. Who can tell what those unique, rather bulging pale eyes saw? They were entirely unlike any other eyes I have ever seen—they were not fierce and piercing as Tolstoy's must have been—or tragic and worn and suffering as Conrad's were. They were of the kind that sees the intangible. The eyes themselves were of a fluid quality that absorbs and distills what they apprehend. They seemed to see the complex, spiritual tangle that is hidden to most of us—who are content to dwell in the outer hall of the majority of mankind, and indeed often of life itself. Henry James asked only to sit in the hall, but the far rooms of the house were open to him. He had no need to trample and tread and intrude, knocking against the ancestral furniture—for he saw too much— walls and doors did not hinder it—his vision wandered at will. Perhaps this clairvoyant exhausting vision was an inheritance from his Irish parentage, for I always traced a very strong Irish strain in him.

Of these memories that come to me, above all were those of our friend, Ethel Sands—who delicately had made all her surroundings so lovely—perhaps almost too exquisite, but nothing could mar her gentle sympathy and understanding.

I wandered away, bidding it all good-bye—as I left, my eye caught a black iris, like a snake rearing its head, wicked and evil, among the lilies growing under the house. Perhaps in beauty detached from life there is a sort of corruption? For the house and its garden had grown more and more spellbound by the exquisite—and seemed as if it was the castle of the Sleeping Beauty.

CHAPTER IV

Life in London

WHEN NOT BUSY ON POLITICAL WORK, our life in London was quiet. Philip going to his office every day and spending the evenings reading aloud: Saturdays and Sundays going to concerts at the Queen's Hall. Indeed, I remember on a dull London Sunday afternoon Philip crying out: "We must make some friends. We haven't any friends. The only person that I can go and talk to is Mrs. Sidney Webb." This *cri de cœur* was an arrow that aroused me, and I saw that it was true. Both he and I were indeed two stranded wayfarers, both having left our native land and arrived in a new strange country. As yet we had not found Liberal politicians very sympathetic or particularly friendly. Ardent with the enthusiasm of youth, we never spared either time or energy. I am, indeed, astonished as I look back on those early years to think how hard we toiled. Up and down the country we went—the way always illumined by the light ahead, of hope that if only we could bring into power a strong Liberal government, some of the worst wrongs would be righted and a new era begin. The work in the country—those uncomfortable hours—I never regret. It was human and enlightening and has helped me to a greater understanding of life; but the attempts which I made to know

88

and to be friends with our fellow Liberals in London and Liberal society, I only look back on with a complete sense of weariness. These were people, I felt, like ourselves, enthusiastic for the same cause as we were—of course we should find them sympathetic and interesting—and for several years at least both Philip and I tried to think they were. We went to functions and dinners given by Liberal hostesses—Liberal leaders' wives—struggling and pushing candidates' wives. But it was all time and energy wasted, and I look now back to the ghosts of these entertainments, as I do to all formal Society parties, as dead and vanished hours.

A few of the younger and sincerer fellow Liberals, who have now joined the Labour Party, we worked with very happily, above all at the beginning of the war in 1914, when for a short time we joined together and hoped to arrest that catastrophe, or at all events to shorten its horrors.

One figure who fought the battle of Liberalism bravely week by week, H. W. Massingham, Editor of *The Nation*, stands apart from the crowd of other politicians. It is always tragic that a journalist's work, however brilliant and constructive, should be written on the wings of weekly print—cast forth into space and rarely remembered. Massingham certainly deserves to be remembered with affection and respect, for he carried on his work with rare courage and adventure.

Each week he and his faithful and devoted staff (H. M. Tomlinson, Brailsford, Nevinson and others) sent forth his paper with as much care as if it was the only issue. His quick, nervous abilities commanding, directing, inspiring those remarkable articles on politics at home and abroad, literature and art—his own writings had indeed in them the glint of the rapier.

He loved talk and fun and human life with all its wickedness and failings—though he himself was not a brilliant talker. His brilliancy all went into his writing, but he was so young, so alive and interested in life, that I find it difficult to remember that he is dead.

Another man whom I knew less well but admired was Edwin Montagu, who died in 1924. He was of the ruminating, brooding type of man—gloomy, but with a touch of genius somewhere hidden in his ugly, awkward body. When quite young he was rather repellent from the effect he produced of ambition gnawing at his vitals—but later this became sublimated into his work, especially for India. He had a really good and rather ponderous mind and was, I believe, a poetical and tragic character, with a heart which had fire in it for good. He threw himself into the work for India with great intensity and with a noble self-sacrifice.

But the friends that came to us mostly came from other sources than politics. I had met Augustine Birrell before my marriage, and he had been, I think, interested in me—because of my love of literature and religion—and I believe it was through him that I met Herbert Paul,[1] who would often and often come to tea and dinner and sit puckering up his odd, soft, rather gutta-percha face into odd expressions. He had grim, dyspeptic moods alternating with brilliant talk about history and politics, and a continual barrage of anecdotes. If anyone was present that he found unsympathetic, his manners would be atrocious; he would sway himself backward and forward, and mutter under his breath, "Good God." I remember taking him out to dine once when he was staying with us in the country, and his protest to boredom that evening was to

[1] Politician and historian. He wrote much on the liberal side of politics, besides producing a very able *History of Modern England*; also a *Life of Froude*, which was published in 1906.

sink down in his chair at dinner and fall asleep when not eating. Melancholy and bad health so overcame him in after-life that he withdrew himself entirely from public life—and indeed from the society even of those he was fond of.

His wife asked me to have him on a visit at Bedford Square when he first became actually melancholy, as she thought a change of scene would help him. Naturally I was only too glad, but the experiment was a dismal failure. He lay on my sofa all day with the blinds drawn down, groaning, groaning, quite oblivious to the fact that he was causing inconvenience to anyone else. On the third day I went to him with a message from his wife, saying, "Oh, Mr. Paul, I have just heard from your wife that she is coming to see you this afternoon." He groaned a deep groan, jumped up from the sofa and said, "I must go to the House" (he was then in the House of Commons), and fled, I after him; I caught him and took him to the House in a taxi. He was greatly attached to his wife, but couldn't face anyone that he knew well.

But the real stream of friends, the river of whose lives still is united to ours, came from two other sources.

When I was staying with my brother Henry and his wife at Underly, I often walked across the park to see Mr. Llewellyn Davies who was Rector of Kirkby Lonsdale. He had been a friend of F. D. Maurice and Robert Browning and even Thomas Carlyle. He was a shy, sensitive, reserved man, and had rather a stiff, dry, unsympathetic manner, but after a time I had broken the outer ice. I found this old man, sitting in his little study, a great solace and very interesting. He had a large family of sons, all remarkably clever; one married the daughter of Du Maurier, and their children were, at their father's death, adopted by J. M. Barrie. (One of these, Michael, many years later we were to know and love, alas for too short a time, for he was drowned bathing at Oxford). Another son, Theodore, was drowned bathing in a river in Westmorland, not very far from home. It was a hot day and he was walking to the station—took off his clothes to have a bathe on the way, and was found drowned. He was one of the very rare people whom one seldom meets with in life, combining brilliant intellectual powers, a warm and tender heart and great charm. He could never be forgotten by anyone who knew him. Another son, Crompton, had his brother's intellect but was more reserved and more intensely passionate. What he did say was almost always something so sincere and so witty and true that it impressed one.

For many years he threw himself into the cause of Taxation of Land Values. It was always said that he thought it would cure all evils, even measles. He married a very charming Irish lady and he became an ardent Sinn Feiner. Since I have lived in the country I have seen but little of him, except indeed when we joined our energies in the attempt to save the life of that fine and remarkable man, Casement, who was condemned, to the disgrace of England, to be hanged. I had once met Casement at the house of Mrs. J. R. Green, and had always admired his magnificent work in the Congo.

Crompton always stands out as one of those little known but very remarkable Englishmen. It was indeed through him that we met most of our intellectual friends in London. When we were living in Grosvenor Road, he was in Barton Street, Westminster, and would often come and dine with us. I heard some years later that when others who knew us were slightly critical or suspicious, it was he who would always stand up for us and say that we were worth knowing. His sister Margaret I also first met at Kirkby Lonsdale. How well I remember asking her about a photograph of Tolstoy that hung in her room there, and saying shyly that I had never read any of his books. She told me about him and mentioned *Anna Karenin* as one I should read; I don't think I had ever heard it correctly pronounced before, but I went away determined to read *Anna Karenin* as soon as possible.

I continued to see a great deal of my very dear old friend, her father, up to his death, for they moved to Hampstead. His mind remained vigorous and alert, and interested in modern things until the last.

I think it was at this time that I first knew the Sangers, who were then living in the Strand. It was, I believe, Crompton Llewellyn Davies who introduced them to us. High up above the hustle-bustle and roar of traffic of the Strand lived this couple, not long married—and one day of the week they were at home. He was an intensely passionate, intellectual Cambridge man, with a most delightful character, and she an equally passionate philanthropist—untidy and emotional and self-sacrificing.

I felt shy, going off to see these strangers, climbing up the endless stairs and at last finding myself in their little plain room with matting on the floors and a gas stove. I think they were alone when I arrived, and we sat round the flames of gas. The only person that I remember coming that first evening was Lytton Strachey. I had already met him—soon after we married when we were at Haslemere. He had come over with his mother to see the Berensons. His tall, bending figure and a rather long, cadaverous face, with long nose and a drooping moustache, made him then a not very attractive figure, but I found him most sympathetic and everything he said was of interest.

I see him now sitting in a long basket-chair by the Sangers's gas fire leaning forward, as he would still do, holding out his long, thin hands to warm. I think that he had just come from one of Bernard Shaw's plays. Altogether I enjoyed my first evening at the Sangers's immensely and came home quite excited. Amongst others whom I met at the Sangers's parties was Desmond MacCarthy, who became for a time one of our closest friends.

How elusive are the first impressions of these people that one knows well! Years of intercourse and experience of their characters have laid a patina upon them, difficult to move. The first impression, that vivid and generally truthful *coup,* has an elusive quality, that one has to chase as a will-o'-the-wisp— always fleeing from one until one catches it and holds it, and then for an instant it stands before one's eyes. The first impression has probably struck the tuning note to the air that this character has since played in the fugue of mutual life. Occasionally, of course, quite a wrong note has been struck which may lead to many subsequent discords—or in the hurry and excitements of life that first impression may be so entirely erased and forgotten that it has gone dumb—and experience alone has supplied the theme.

It is only standing far off and calling back; the first sights that one can catch once more, the first impression of that well-known face and figure. Desmond MacCarthy has hardly altered at all in my mind—yes, slightly—but very little; very few discoveries have I made in him that contradicted the first, most delightful, impression I received, talking to him at the Sangers's on one of those Friday evenings, now moved to their new house in Oakley Street, Chelsea. His photograph needs very little retouching. I was very shy and timid, but he was as kind then as he would be today to anyone who needed encouragement. I don't remember the subject of our talk. I feel I could if I knocked long enough at my buried past, but it probably was unimportant, except that it was sympathetic, ruminating, suggestive and original. He reminded me slightly that evening of Belloc, but that impression was a superficial one and has since been worn away by experience. It was, I believe, the same evening that I met George Moore, the Cambridge philosopher, who had such a great influence on the men of his time. I had a long talk with him about Tolstoy—but I have never seen him again.

Would it be worth while to have the gift of looking down and through the years that are to come and of foreseeing in the little theatre of one's life those characters that are to play any part there?—of that one is never conscious at the first meeting. A character that enters and one anticipates will play quite an important part, makes a few gestures—remarks—and disappears—and the Exit is for ever.

CHAPTER V

Days with Conder,
Days in Spain

THE OTHER CURRENT that enlarged our life was the artistic one. Philip's friend, Percy Feilding, who lived near us in Grosvenor Road, brought in one day to show us a most charming little picture of a lady sitting on a sofa, thinking we might like to see it—it belonged, I believe, to his sister. I asked who it was by and was told James Pryde. I called out to Philip, "Here is the artist to do a portrait of me!"—he had been anxious to have one done. I found out his address, which was at High Wycombe, and when next we were at Oxford I induced my mother-in-law to come there by train with me. It was an exciting adventure. After wandering about and looking at the lovely Town Hall, we found the very dreary little house. I cannot remember whether he showed us any pictures, but I invited him to come and do some sketches of me when in London. Poor man! when he arrived his spirits failed him. I sat in my loveliest lace dress on a delicate eighteenth-century sofa, but all in vain. He fled out of the house, probably to gain inspiration by drinking whisky at the nearest pub—but chance threw in his way a photographer called Cavendish Morton—this treasure was brought back and he set to work with enthusiasm. His photographs are lovely still, far more beautiful than any other photographs I have ever seen—which generally enchant one for a week and then are only of value to be put away out of sight and looked at occasionally as mementoes. Pryde withdrew for a time to think over the portrait, then reappeared to stay with us at Oxford. I wandered about the town with him, and took him to see the Botanical Gardens, which has always been a favourite place. I think it was the tall, dark gates here that suggested the portrait that eventually arrived—or perhaps some odd prophetic vision of the yew hedges at Garsington.

When he brought the picture finished and opened it from its wrappings I could not suppress a gasp—"Oh, Mr. Pryde, do you think that is like me?" "That is how I see you to the depths of your soul," he replied in a deep, solemn voice.

Perhaps he was right.

It was to Pryde that I owe one of those occasions of chance that fate throws to one to take hold of. He was interested in dress, for the sake of his work, and spoke to me about a remarkable dress that had been made for one of his sitters by a dressmaker called Mrs. Neville (Max Beerbohm's sister). Of course I found out where Mrs. Neville lived and went to see her. "Why don't you let me make you a dress painted by Conder?" she said. I hardly believed my ears. I had heard of Charles Conder and his work from Philip and from Logan Pearsall Smith who had known him slightly, through their beautiful mutual friend, Louise Kinsella.[1] That lovely and radiant woman always gave one the impression of being an

[1] Conder's picture, now in the Tate Gallery, entitled "The Green Apple," is, in fact, a portrait of her.   P.M.

Logan Pearsall Smith, in *Unforgotten Years,* tells of Conder's first meeting with her and how "falling in love with her at once (he) never really painted any other human being."

emanation from Conder's imagination, for she seemed always to carry with her the atmosphere of beauty and romance, and to walk through life on green lawns, through groves of dark trees and statues attended by nymphs and peacocks, dressed in lovely full taffeta dresses and flowing veils—"A green thought in a green shade."

In later years in Rome I spent many happy days with her, and found her a most witty and enchanting companion, generous and kind, above all to the young. In a monotonous modern age she stood out rather a lonely figure as if left behind by a wittier, more exquisite age. Now she has gone to join her companions, and all who loved her are sadly left looking at the portraits by Conder and by Whistler and wishing they could hear her deep, amusing voice, and see the gaiety in her eyes and the light on her lovely fair hair. She could never have been old; she left us when she was still beautiful and gay and courageous.

To return to Conder. Mrs. Neville promised to take me to see him at Cheyne Walk to discuss the painted dress. The dress never was painted. It seemed desecration to put those lovely paintings on to a dress that would get crushed and soiled, but from the first visit to 91 Cheyne Walk, with its delicious transparent taffeta curtains and painted satinwood chairs with blue silk seats, Conder became our delight and joy. I "sat," I stood. We dined, we talked. He and his wife came to our house. We enjoyed their happy evenings when all their friends would come. We went on expeditions together to Hampton Court. He was always painting. Even at night he would sit at table under a lamp, painting, on and on, the most lovely visions, inventing, extemporizing as he drew, with his magic hand of chance. Conder also came from another age, but really from no one age. He had much of Villon—and as much of his painting ancestors, Watteau and Pater, from whom he was in fact descended. Then at times a flavour of Giorgione. He was all artist—a child. He loved singing and songs—and he loved wine too well; but this he resolutely abjured when I knew him. He loved beauty and romance, and his talk meandered in a soft, slightly incoherent, charming voice, and he had the habit of running his hand through his hair with rather a helpless movement.

How entranced I was when he recited some of Villon's poems to me.

Où sont les neiges d'antan?

If he could have been anything besides a painter, he would have been a troubadour. When he looked out on the world, he saw his own lovely, fantastic vision. If he went to an hotel at Brighton, he would sit at the window all day and paint and paint, but what he saw and painted no other eyes at Brighton saw—a frieze of lovely ladies in pinks and blues and greens, walking before the sea with parasols—waves playing round them and possibly a mermaid arising from the sea to greet her sisters on the land.

One of the happiest days we spent with Conder was at Hampton Court. He and I went down early one summer's day, and his wife and Philip and some others followed later. He and I arrived at Waterloo laden with easels, paints, canvases, baskets of delicious food, books, etnas, parasols, Spanish shawls. Arriving at Hampton Court we found we had forgotten two necessities—ginger-beer and fruit—so after loading our chaos of goods into a cab, so many that they seemed to fall over the sides—we drove to the town and bought still more: gooseberries, grapes and ginger-beer. How we got out into the Palace gardens I don't know—but we did, and found a lovely spot near the long pond. Conder, forgetting hunger and thirst, put up his easel and at once started on a portrait of me, in a long white muslin dress that I was wearing, and long hours flew by in that green avenue. The picture we have adds to my memory, but to us alone it speaks of the enchanting child with all his confiding fun and his happiness and delight in that summer's day, the statues on the grass, the avenues of lime trees.

It was a great surprise to me to find him so good, so innocent, and entirely guileless, for I had often heard him spoken of as sunk into degradation and debauchery. If this had been so, it had slid off him, leaving him untouched. "Stella, dear, do sing me *L'Heure Exquise*," he would call out to his wife. —"Stella, may I have some money for paints?"—"How much do you want, Conder boy?"—"Oh, can I have £1?"—"No, Conder, I have only ten shillings." And off he would go with it, quite satisfied, in his hand. Stella was devoted to him and understood him, and helped him to be cured of drink. One day when he was taken ill and fainted, the doctor said, "Give him some brandy." He opened his eyes and said, "No, I am a teetotaller." He was proud of it as a child would be of some great distinction. He often spoke with admiration of Augustus John's work, and one day he came back laden with drawings that he had bought from him. He had been to see him and found him in bed, as he was then so poor that he had to remain in bed while his wife mended his clothes. Conder, who had the tenderest of hearts, was so moved by this that he carried off a bundle of drawings, which he bought from him. I was then less accustomed than I am now to nude drawings, and I felt slightly shocked by the redundancy of the flesh, but they must have made an impression, for I can see them now, as Conder arranged them round the room, praising and admiring them as he did so.

One day that I was at Conder's studio, I found a tall, rather mysterious-looking man there. He seemed intensely silent and rather *méfiant*. His hair cut like a Renaissance picture, gold ear-rings and a black sweater high to his neck, and he looked at

everyone very intensely with eyes that absorbed what he gazed
on. They were remarkably beautifully-shaped eyes, and were
of that mysterious pale grey-green colour, expanding like a sea-
anemone, and more liquid, more aesthetically and poetically
perceptive, than any of the darker and more definite shades.
His voice, when he did speak, was not very unlike Conder's,
only rather deeper and more melodious, but like Conder's
hesitating—and he also had the same trick of pushing his hair
back with one of his hands—hands that were more beautiful
almost than any man's hands I have ever seen. Conder murmured "Augustus John." Three years after this I met him again
and began to know him.

I have wandered on, tempted by the lure of Conder, to 1905,
which was the year we met him. We had just returned from
Spain, going by P. & O. to Gibraltar and Algeria and wending
our way northward.

Each day of this time in Spain was filled with delight, even
the long, meandering, slow railway journeys across that great
wide country, seeing at the stations horses tied to a tree, waiting
for their owners to arrive by our train, and then watching them
ride off, sitting like grandees of old—legs almost straight in the
stirrups—some carrying their ladies behind them, and then
the train going so slowly that one could follow them across the
great endless plains. From Ronda we plunged down to Malaga
—perhaps principally for the sake of the journey through
orange and lemon groves—great tracks of green and gold and
yellow. We were driven from Malaga when we got there by the
attentions of a tactless guide who would not leave us in peace.

Shall I ever again walk through the Sierpes at Seville smelling the lavender that is scattered on the Braziao and finding a
pyramid of golden oranges piled up to ripen outside the
Cathedral, that Cathedral which seemed to me so perfect,
mounting up and up in purest, pure Gothic, so lofty inside

that it reduced the slim, delicate ladies fervently kneeling in prayer, or standing by the pillars dressed in black, with lace mantillas on their heads, to little swallows skimming low upon the ground.

Each morning we would return there to hear Mass sung in the old Gregorian music, to watch the naughty urchins who were "serving"—running up and down the altar steps playing games together until the end came, when one would have to stand alone, dressed in his red cassock and white tunic, and sing aloud, his childish, uncertain voice echoing up and up and then dying away in the grey arches. No service ever was as sweet as that which was sung in that Cathedral. Then wandering one day into a side chapel we heard a Requiem being sung. The coffin in the middle of the floor, draped in black velvet, trimmed with silver and pink—silver candlesticks all around and dark-faced priests attending. Thinking it over now I cannot believe that I was not looking upon one of Velasquez's great pictures come to life.

In the evenings we went to a charming café, where there was Spanish dancing. The first night that we appeared at the door the whole of the people already seated inside rose *en masse*, and rushed to the door to see the wild strangers arriving. They surged round us. I had an orange feather in my hat, which was a thing unknown as yet in Spain. The patron of the café hurried up to us, and tactfully said, "The café is full now, would you return a little later." We had the happy thought of returning to the hotel, taking off the hat and putting on instead a black lace mantilla. We then went straight back to the café, entered without any excitement, and went there every night, sitting at little round tables, drinking tea or Malaga wine, and surrounded by charming, dignified peasants and girls with carnations tucked into their beautiful polished hair. The sad antique

Moorish singing, the castanets, and the long-drawn-out move-ments of the Spanish dance: women in long trains and frilled cotton dresses, and shawls crossed over and pinned behind, tell-ing in slow movements, with sudden sharp quickness, the story of desire, love, in all its thousand forms. It is a language which can only be thus spoken by a Spanish woman. She speaks to those who for nearly a thousand years have understood it. It has come down in her unconscious instincts from the East; once initiated, almost all dancing becomes slightly vulgar in comparison. One evening a small boy about twelve years old sang one of the old minor Moorish songs. It came out from the little boy as if his ears were catching an antique plaint that had been sung by the Moors hundreds of years ago, still floating on the air, haunting the hearts for generation upon generation. The full, but childish, voice soared up, and then with the subtlest tones suddenly twisting and turning as a thought might turn and rouse itself into a new melancholy, heart-rending cry. The audience applauded and applauded, and made him sing over and over again. At last the fat man who ac-companied him on the guitar grew weary and refused to play any more, but nothing would check the insistence of the listeners. If the guitar could not be played, he must sing with-out. The child had to obey. Their desire compelled him, and I see the little fellow now, detaching himself from everyone, standing behind a chair, and clutching the back of it with both hands, looking out into space, beginning again his lonely cry of the human heart—the lamentation of those who desire and do not attain on this earth. I think of "Pan, to whose music the nymphs danced, who has a cry in him that can drive all men distracted," that he must have sung rather like this, and yet it was not the cry of Pan; it was the cry of human desire.

The Spaniard, who seems too antique and finely modelled

and formed and complete, has, after all, shut away within the fine casket of his being the eternal cry.

Granada's gardens and pools and the Palace shining and gold —Cordova, Madrid, Toledo—its dark citadel towering up high. I could trace the shape now as I saw it across the great bridge. Towns like Toledo have been so built together, chance has so shaped them that the far-away effect is perfect in balance and composition. Time, the invisible Architect, has so crowned the efforts of the individual, one can but cry out, when you see the town from afar, "What a perfect building."

Someone—I think it was Sargent—had commended us to go to Aranjuez outside Madrid. We left one morning and had lunch in the large Railway Restaurant, which is panelled with tall, grey looking-glasses, and then went forth to see the original of the lovely painting by Velásquez which hangs in the Prado: the gardens and Palace, long alleys of trees: stone statues and fountains so tall and grandiose that they make human beings look like children playing round them.

More wanderings in Madrid at night seeking for dancing, and when found being asked, after the girl had finished her dance on the table, also to perform. "But you and your brother are artists, aren't you?"

Somehow Wilhelm Meister is threaded in and out of Spain, for it was here on the long, slow railway journey that I first read that enchanting *Life and Wanderings*. No book was so suited to the environment as that was.

We arrived home on a dark, cold Saturday night in January —Victoria Station and Vauxhall Bridge Road—gloomy, damp and dripping—men and women brawling out songs as they staggered home drunk and dishevelled. We had come from a land of old civilization into the capital of the new.

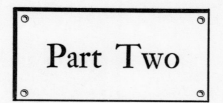

Part Two

Bedford Square: The Advancing Years

CHAPTER I

A Lost and a Living Child

AS I STOP AND BREATHE on this resting-place of my life, I try and draw breath.

The years 1904 to 1906 I will pass on one side—save that they are disagreeable and painful, at this time they do not appear to me very significant. Perhaps I shall return to them if days and health are given to me. Now, as I write, the wings of the dark bird that comes to carry us across the gulf into the unknown are still brushing my cheek.[1] I still hear the soft and gentle fanning in the air of these great muffled wings. They hover over me, and if I am still I can almost hear the strange song of the unknown—calm and august—but with the heart-rending melody that is always in the air when, even for an hour, or a day, one parts with those one loves—which is a knell.

It is not hard to forego life on this earth, with all its interests and seeming pleasures, pains and endeavours. My will is pliant and submissive when I am asked to do that; to set out on the distant journey. But can I not turn back when I am asked to leave the one with whom my love is entangled, my interest

---

[1] Written in 1929 when she was recovering after the terrible and agonizing necrosis of the jaw from which she had very nearly died; she had been left with pitted scars along the angle of her lower jaw.

plaited, my laughter threaded? How could I see him alone at night walking up a dark, hushed and empty staircase? My call of welcome home would be too faint to reach him from another world. The small companion who so adores him will not live very long. He too must depart on his four little legs, and then my cry goes up, "Leave me, leave me—broken, disfigured, chastened. Take my will, I will obey in everything but in that. Take him first. Let me be there to hold his hand as he sets forth, to say, 'It is all right. I am coming with you.'"

We have had only each other to cheer and to encourage in all the disappointments and mistakes that we have made. We cannot part now. It is he who has always given me courage when timidity and diffidence have made me shrink and despair, and it was I, perhaps, who kept alive his desire.

What is the attraction that has beckoned together two souls, as kindred as brother and sister, in the vast crowds that people even our own little island? What is the strange chance that acts as a magnet to draw two personalities to each other? I see that in some among my intimates I have sought out—attracted by their thoughts and writing; but in others they have not come to me thus, but by an unseen pressure: a magnet that works its attraction through the vast crowds that run on the earth.

In the great torrent of humanity that flows from the unknown into the unknown, tumbling, falling, jostling each other as they are carried along, two atoms are tossed together, two kindred souls meet, and are held together: husband and wife, companions, brother and sister—no matter by what name they are called—they are to each other comrades, and they do not part.

The river flows on and on and we are carried forward ever nearer to the great sea. Often standing on some old stone bridge catching the great swirl of a rushing river underneath, have I seen in its life, chaotic and yet with a wild compelling order on and on—no turn back—no retreat—lives tossed together, perhaps for ever, or maybe only for a brief companionship to be diverted and carried so far apart that no meeting again is to be within their fate.

In 1905 we sold our little house in Grosvenor Road and turned to my old favourite quarter of London, Bloomsbury, and took 44 Bedford Square. I was expecting the arrival of a child, and this was not very welcome to me. It seemed an invasion, a burden, an unknown existence breaking into ours and upsetting the wonderful intimacy and companionship of our life together.

To most mothers I hope it is a lovely and warm invasion, fulfilling their destiny and enlarging their lives; to me it came otherwise—indeed, I felt classed with those unfortunates who have to bear the burden of a child alone, without a husband to share the responsibility. Never did I feel that I was bringing a new and beautiful creation into the world. I felt helpless to form or to mould the life that lay dormant within me.

I confess it even now with unhappy shame. Could I have altered it? Could anyone have turned the current of my thoughts into a normal direction? Perhaps so, but I was too ashamed to confess them. I looked forward with apprehension to the years ahead, feeling myself incapable of bringing up a child. The warm and happy maternal instinct towards an unknown child was omitted from my temperament. But when the first cry was heard, the voice of the little stranger was answered by a new and strange echo in me. That cry was not in vain— as the child awoke, so did the instinct within me.

The cry was from two lives, for I had given birth to twins at 10:30 on May 18th 1906. The little girl was so fragile and small that her life was despaired of; the little boy was apparently strong and well. But he who was our joy was taken suddenly ill on May 21st.

I copy what I then wrote in my journal:

"Little Hugh suddenly taken ill at 9 o'clock; sent for doctor; haemorrhage in the brain. Doctor came to operate; slowly sank, and died at 1:30. Agonizing, cannot write of it."

Wildly, pushing, pushing fate back, I lay in bed, all my being passionately concentrated on holding and keeping the little life next door. He cannot be taken, he who already is so fair and beautiful, and who is the delight of our life, the centre of our hope, living, breathing, with apparent perfection these three days. It is not true—it is a mistake.

Intent on every sound, I wait. I cry to God, "Leave him, leave him." I see Philip's face of pale misery.

But no human desire can hold him back. He is gone. I cry out, I call, in vain. That personality that bid fair to be unique is gone. He has not tarried here, to pass through this life.

Wildly I plan to have another child, but truth answers, no other would be he, on this earth you cannot see him again. He was brought in to me to gaze at, to stamp upon my visual memory the vision of mortal beauty, the face modelled as in white marble, bearing upon it an impression of experience and wisdom, lovely and serene. Where had he dwelt to know all that was reflected in that little face? What had he known to show such wisdom and beauty? Where had he gone?

Perfect little body, without fault or stain on thee
  With promise of strength and manhood full and fair!
    Though cold and stark and bare,
  The bloom and the charm of life doth awhile remain on
    thee. . . .

Bedford Square: The Advancing Years

So I lay thee there, thy sunken eyelids closing—
  Go lie thou there in thy coffin, thy last little bed!—
    Propping thy wise sad head,
Thy firm pale hands across thy chest disposing.

So quiet! doth the change content thee? Death, whither hath
    he taken thee?
    To a world, do I think, that rights the diasters of this?
      The vision of which I miss,
Who weep for the body, and wish but to warm thee and
    awaken thee?

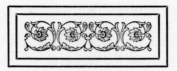

CHAPTER II

Painters, Politicians and Others

LIFE HAS TO BEGIN AGAIN. The door that opened for us into mystery and suffering must be closed quietly. Life, a lonely visitant, came and is gone, to be inwardly remembered always and mourned and wondered at. But the little fragile sister remains, and upon her care has to be lavished to keep the flickering flame of life alight. Small hope at first, but I have an inward confidence that she will come through. Philip bends over her with that peculiar tenderness which only a man can show, and which always is so moving. Her little personality, already independent asserts itself. When she is strong enough to bear the drive through London, we take her to St. Paul's Cathedral to be christened by Canon Scott Holland on July 5th 1906. She, one of the smallest of babies, dressed in an old lace robe, is held in the arms of that very tall man in the vast Cathedral, and is christened Julian after my old friend Mother Julian. It is the first public act of this tiny body, carried out in this huge church—a few friends and relations kneeling round her, offering her to God to fulfil His will in the turmoil and seeming chaos of life.

When I was well enough to get about, I had to devote myself to arranging our house, 44 Bedford Square.

Furnishing and decorating houses is a thing my friends like to think that I have a special talent for. Perhaps it is true, but if so it bears out my conviction that no talent can be exercised with any measure of success without great effort and trouble. When people say to me, "How you must enjoy decorating houses. It must be such fun," I turn away, and in my thoughts answer, "How little you understand or know all the anxiety and travail that this task is. It is no more pleasant or amusing than to paint a picture or to write a book."

The rooms in Bedford Square were beautiful in their proportions. Philip, who has far more critical and constructive taste in architecture than I have, rearranged doorways and chimney-pieces. My own interest was always more for balance, rhythm and colouring. The expression of form is to me so necessary in life, from beginning to end. Necessity is not perhaps the right word—it ought rather to be desire for form and balance and rhythm.

However great the chaos of storm and violence may seem, yet if there is a return to balance after the rocking and upheaval, then life is not shipwrecked or broken. No symphony could stand repetition without fundamental rhythm and harmony, however wildly chaotic it may appear to the uncultivated ear.

I have felt at times that the most one can do for one's own well-being and development is to safeguard this inward poise; to attain and to keep it in perfection always has never been possible to me, but to realize it for moments or even perhaps for days has been possible. Some turn of all the diverse chords of one's nature has come about, and lo! one is conscious of a feeling of well-being that one can alone name rhythm. Winds and storms of daily life break through and upset it again, but there it has been, and if it has been attained for a time, it surely could be held together for ever, if the absurd irrelevancies that invade us were reduced to their proper value.

I have wandered far from the task of house-decoration, but all creative activities, however seemingly transient, have fundamentally this need, whether it is one's own life or the thing one has to create. Is there anything new? The creative instinct pushes, but new leaves, new flowers on each tree—is there really anything unique or completely new? Is not everything entangled and interlaced? Shakespeare is unique, but he added his own imagination to many an old, forgotten, musty play. Cézanne is called unique, but how many painters before him helped to make him so? Who can say that they stand alone without having derived some ideas, some suggestion from someone or something—perhaps trivial and valueless in themselves—that scattered the seed into their imagination, and which has grown into something infinitely beautiful? And so it goes on—Dickens gave birth to Dostoevsky, Ruskin to Proust, Velásquez to Manet, Manet to Degas.

But to descend from the sublime to my own small efforts—a description in a book of Marcelle Tinayre of a French Pavilion, and a picture of a grey dance studio by Degas were, I believe, the source of my image in decorating in Bedford Square! Pale grey walls and yellow taffeta curtains—this was the setting of our life for the next nine years (1906–15).

Friendships, gaiety and politics jumbled themselves together in this period. We also had a small cottage on Peppard Common where we spent some months every year, and where Julian's youngest days were spent.

There were so many threads, difficult enough to keep disentangled while they are being unreeled, even more difficult after they have been woven together. Julian gradually learnt to run about in the garden of the little house there—a little fairy-like child, fragile and yet wayward and independent. As she ran along the grass paths of the garden with the sunlight behind her, and her little transparent muslin dress blowing in the wind, she seemed more like a vision of Blake's age of innocence than a mortal child. She was always impatient of being led or taken care of. Her father often took her out on the Common, carrying her on his shoulder. One day, when they had gone a little way, she said, "Now, Daddy, put me down, and don't follow me. I want to walk back alone."

The hopes I had cherished of having another child were to be entirely put an end to. About a year after Julian's birth, I was obliged to have a very serious operation—the first of many of these journeys—for journeys they are into a land unknown and mysterious and only vaguely remembered.

When the doctor told me what was before me—with that kindly, tender, bending manner, revealing nothing definite that they always use—I felt stimulated, as I generally am by definite peril. It was a relief to know that what I had been suffering could no longer be called hysteria.

I put my house in order, and was taken off to the nursing-home of my old friend, Miss Nelson Smith. I catch glimpses from her of the rough crossing that lies ahead of me, but I push ahead.

Next day Philip comes—nervous but cheerful. I comforted and encouraged him, hiding my secret terrors. I asked him to read me something familiar and gay—Keats's *Letters*. The call comes from upstairs, and up I walk to the operating-room where my body is to lie. I throw off some inane joke to the three white-masked sterilized figures standing round. I jump on to the table; one more smile, as if to wave a farewell, and an inward silent commendation. I felt for a hand to hold, and breathed, breathed, breathed into the black mask . . .

That little dark trap-door through which my spirit escapes up, up into regions of colour and golden haze, until it reaches the Mystic Rose, the ultimate source of all—and for a millionth of a second—or is it for an hour?—I know that the eternal exists and I am at rest, for I had reached truth.

My eyes opened. Great stillness reigns. I see not God but a nurse's cap and a kind face looking down on me. I sigh to find myself in this dull, still, bare world, sick and bruised from my fall from Heaven.

Now I remember that while my spirit was away on that aerial flight they had done strange things to my body, had given it back to me racked with pain. They had set wolves upon me to devour my inside. I was on Ixion's wheel, turning round and round.

Time and reality became confused.

In one hour of darkness there are ten thousand hours of pain. It ebbs and flows with ever greater force—until what happens? I don't know, but called for him I love most to hold my hand and stop me slipping off the earth. I was half over—a gulf below me. I hung over. Everything seemed far off—words failed, but they are pulling me back.

A prick in my arm, then came a lull in the storm and the pain faded gently away, and everything became muted and muffled. I seemed to be falling, falling through the bed down to the centre of earth, but it is all so gentle. Was I escaping that way—but I have heard that the "Everlasting arms are beneath you."

Light shines in; the room seems fresher. It seemed a long time since I had looked on daylight. I asked what day it was— Tuesday. What day did I come here? Saturday. But I thought I had been here three weeks? The nurse's head is shaken. I asked for my book. Am I holding it upside down? For I cannot understand what it means.

After a few days my little bark becomes steadier, and then came a period of bodily rest and mental activity, when the mind is delivered from material worries. They may clamour and tap at the door, but wise, deceitful nurses shut them out, and I lived in blissful ignorance of the outer turmoil, which only floated up from the street in a comforting companionship of murmured noise mixed with the music of a barrel-organ. In these spells one plays with one's thoughts, and moves the marionettes about at will. Or when tired of playing with one's own small theatre one lets one's mind fly off like a kite caught up by the winds of fancy into a world of vague dreams and desires—perhaps stimulated by a line of poetry, and one imagines that life's problems are solved, and with one moment of vision one has arrived at perfect peace. The two halves of life are equally balanced; material so blended with the spiritual that never again can they become out of gear, disordered and unmanageable. But this luxurious Thebaid does not last for ever. There is no withdrawing here into a life of contemplation for those who were human in the nineteenth century. The poise once seen must be worked out, the vision matured by life. Real life has to be faced and dealt with; so easy in theory, so waving and complicated in practice.

Our life at 44 Bedford Square gradually became more settled and more spacious than before. Politics were the dominant theme. Philip was Member for South Oxfordshire from 1906 to 1910, which necessarily entailed many visits to the constituency and eager and interesting meetings in London with his political friends, the younger Members of Parliament: A. Ponsonby, Charles Masterman and C. Trevelyan. Indeed, as I read my old diaries and notebooks, I am amazed at the great activity of our lives during those years (mostly scribblings—no time or temper to write fully, I having constantly to stay in bed

from acute headaches—but next day or even that very afternoon flying off to see someone at the other end of London by
bus or cab). And then in the days that followed I read with as-
tonishment of giddy activity in seeing people. It seems now to
me feverish energy, and I threw myself into the pleasure of
knowing people that were intelligent and sympathetic after the
years of friendliness that I had traversed.

Conversation, talk, interchange of ideas—how good it was! I
felt greedy for friendship and launched recklessly on the sea
of London. So many people were interesting, attractive, and in
many ways sympathetic. I was easily tempted, and caught many
a cord thrown to me, often getting these threads very entangled
—many a time friends of very diverse personalities sat staring
at each other, but with such zeal, such enterprise as I then had,
nothing daunted me!

Comings and goings—tea parties and "At Homes" on Thursday evenings—all were accomplished. I gave myself in reckless
energy and sympathy to these people. Seen now, as I read in
my diary, writers jostled politicians, serious ladies had to meet
young and unkempt artists, such as Epstein the sculptor. My
brothers dined, and were taken off to see Isadora Duncan
dance. Henry James faced Max Beerbohm—whom of all others
he was afraid to meet, fearing that terrible power of caricature.

Dinners with Miss Edith Sichel,[1] who was protecting and
encouraging to me. She asked me to meet her friends—the
memory of one of whom lives with me as a lovely, almost
Blake-like figure, Mary Coleridge. Her tall, short-waisted
figure, with rather small head and lovely violet eyes, was very
much in accord with her writing and her elusive, delicate and
mystical poetry. We liked each other, and bitter was my annoy-

[1] Edith Sichel, 1862–1914, was a minor writer, who published works
on history and literature. She edited some posthumous prose works of
Mary Coleridge.

ance and disappointment that, when she came to tea with me and our mutual sympathies were beginning to spring up into a delicious fountain—we were laughing together about our powers of magnetic attraction for egoists—when a smart young man was announced, whose presence brought us both back to London life. Before she left she asked me to come and see her, and she was to read me Robert Trevelyan's poem, *The Rat*. This never took place, as she was taken ill a few days after and died.

Ethel Sands, who had a house in Lowndes Place, came and went, dining with us and we with her. Our friends interchanged. Soon after my operation we went to dine with her. Walter Sickert, Prince Antoine Bibesco and Augustus John were amongst those that I remember that evening; but as I didn't feel very robust I crept into a corner. Prince Bibesco seemed very elaborate and exotic. John came late; he was dressed, to our surprise, in evening dress and looked slim and handsome, but rather odd to me in such conventional clothes— as I had last seen him in a black sweater. He still wore his gold ear-rings! I was again impressed by the movements of his hands, long, fine and sensitive, and the way he passed them over his hair so reminded me of Conder; and he had the same hesitating way of speaking, although his voice was even more beautiful, having a deeper, more resonant quality.

I saw him standing in the middle of the room before dinner, looking self-conscious, shy and slightly aggressive, until his glances caught sight of me whom he had already met—his brows lowered and his gaze was focused—he forgot himself.

I sat next to him at dinner. Gypsies, Romany gypsies, was the theme of our talk. Conder, too. That troubadour. Painters. "Will you sit to me?" he said abruptly. "Come and see me tomorrow at my studio."

In the afternoon of the next day Philip and I walked round

to his studio, 8 Fitzroy Street (Whistler's studio).[2] How ram-shackle and dark and dirty the hall of this house of studios was. An elegant gold console table in the hall, letters scattered about on it. Up and up and along rickety passages, down steps and up others—at last, after groping and peering, we find a piece of paper pinned to a door, "Augustus John."

We knock, and John himself appeared—in his usual clothes: a greyish suit, the coat long and full in the skirts, and with a bright green velvet collar, a large silk handkerchief round his neck. He waved us in.

A large studio, very clean and tidy: on an easel stood the first oil painting I had ever seen by him. It was called "Sera-phita"—a girl dressed in a tight black dress, standing on a mountain top with strange ice-flowers growing at her feet. But crude and almost childish as this picture seemed then to my uninitiated and uneducated eyes, it made an impression of such strange unearthly poetry and imagination that attraction was greater than repulsion. I often wish that I could see it again. Another large canvas was of a boat and fisherman on a grey lake, more lovely and finished, but almost reminiscent of Puvis de Chavannes.

Before we left, Clive Bell and his wife Vanessa arrived. I looked at them with a certain amount of awe. I had already heard of her and her sister, Virginia. They were both daughters of Leslie Stephen; Vanessa was herself an artist, Virginia lived with her brother Adrian in Fitzroy Square and was the centre of the younger Cambridge intellectuals. "Do you know the Stephens?" I had been asked. "Who are they?" "They sit

---

[2] I had already been to this studio many years before at Louise Kinsella's invitation, to see Whistler painting his portrait of her, and had stayed to luncheon and listened to his talk, and he had shown me some of his pictures—one of the great occasions of my early life. P.M.

round the fire in a dark room and say nothing, except occasionally, after a long silence, one of them makes a very clever remark. Virginia and Vanessa are both beautiful, and like their father, very intellectual."

I was thus very interested to see with my own eyes one of these wonderful remote beings, who lived in a world of intellect and art. Vanessa had the beauty of an early Watts portrait, melancholy and dreamy. They stood in front of the picture of the lake, Clive Bell gesticulating in an excited way, showering speechless admiration, Vanessa, head bent, approving.

When I asked him shyly to come and see me, John returned with us to tea. I wish I could give an impression of John's appearance in those days. His dark auburn hair was long and cut across the front like a fringe, and with a square beard, his curious pale face and sea-anemone eyes, he might have been a Macedonian king or a Renaissance poet. He had a power of drawing out all one's sympathy. But I have no clear remembrance of the remainder of that day—except that he asked me to sit for him for a portrait.

We went to our cottage at Peppard for some weeks, where we were snowed up. Sitting in our little house with ramparts of snow I read Balzac's *Séraphita*. I absorbed that strange book, soaring and gliding over mountain and glacier and snow, only half understanding the Swedenborgian philosophy, but feeling elated and as if I too were living in this high and rarefied atmosphere.

On our return to London I asked an old friend of John's to come and see me, feeling curious to hear from someone who knew him well what he was really like.

"I cannot touch his melancholy," I said. "What I can give is not what he wants. He calls for something strong, reckless and rampant, which will carry him off his feet, and he knows too well that it is not mine to give."

"You are right," she answered. "I was afraid he might have carried you off your feet, and that perhaps you felt you could lead him into your paths. That would be hopeless, my dear, you could never divert him. He spoke of you when I saw him lately, spoke of you with admiration and, for him, a good deal of reverence. 'She is an angel,' but," she laughed, "I know an angel and he could never walk long together. Still, there is ample room in the world for an angel to hover over John. He will need a host of them to keep him good."

The portrait that he began of me was not finished, but many a drawing was done—torn off the block, thrown on the floor and afterwards sold. I did not like then to ask for them, or ask to buy them, thinking he might want them for his portrait; and now they are scattered over the world.[3]

These days, when I first knew him, led me into a new world, where there were no barriers. Conder's life, when I knew him, was comparatively well ordered. He lived in a charming and exquisitely furnished house, had a devoted wife and entertained his guests with parties. John's sole foothold was his studio, where he slept and lived, and at the prompting of his spirit he would go forth, take to the road on his feet or live in a caravan. He would loiter in pubs, he would stare at a woman he saw in the street, and compel her to sit for him. He was indeed a vagabond, free to wander untrammelled.

[3] Four or five of these sketches were afterwards offered to us at a high price by various dealers, and are now in my possession. One of them, a full length washed in water-colour, though face and head are quite unfinished, is perhaps the best portrait ever done of her.   P.M.

This drawing is reproduced as the frontispiece. The oil portrait, long lost sight of, was recently recovered from among the artist's possessions. Although unfinished, it is a beautiful work and an excellent likeness.

Engagements were intolerable to him. Luxuries, possessions, responsibilities were alien to him. When I mixed in an ordinary London life, the figure of this man, so unquestionably remarkable, living a life so completely different from anything I saw around me, haunted and disturbed me. He would appear to me in my imagination as if he passed through the room, suddenly making the conventional scene appear absurd. It might seem less strange to me now, but John then lived his life with greater simplicity and freedom than other English artists. I received a letter from him asking us to help his friend, the sculptor Epstein, whom he counted as one of the greatest artists that England has produced since Blake. Epstein had done eighteen figures for the Medical Council in the Strand, for which he was paid £1,000 and he had to supply the stone, which had cost him nearly all that sum. Some neighbours in the Strand had objected to them on the ground of their supposed indecency, and were threatening to have them removed. Poor Epstein was in despair; he was meanwhile on the verge of starvation. We went to see him at his studio in Cheyne Walk. Could anyone live nearer starvation than he and his wife did then? The room was indeed bare. Life lived at the very edge of subsistence. The cupboard seemed bare. He had no orders, and work as a sculptor was impossible without stone. Stone was very expensive. We gave him an order for a garden statue and I took likely clients to see him—amongst others W. B. Yeats and Lady Gregory, who asked him to do a bust of herself.

Memory, that controller of one's past, has blurred the scenes that I find sketched in my diaries at this time, where names, names fly round like bees. Names of those that have mostly flown away out of our life—some indeed out of this life altogether.

Luncheons, dinners, teas—each day filled up recklessly with engagements, and on every Thursday dinners, parties or people afterwards. How did I survive? Why did I do all this? I was intensely interested in these people—most of whom were remarkable in some way and I who found them so exciting, so thrilling, was anxious that they should know each other. If I liked a personality my instinct was that I wanted that one to meet others in whom I was interested. It gave me immense pleasure to effect these meetings, and to bring them about I would take infinite and exhausting trouble—for this reason my Thursday evenings were an agonizing anxiety to me. Had I introduced such a person to the other person they were suited for? Why, oh why, had I done this, or that? Had I neglected someone else? Such thoughts hurled themselves at me after the evening was over, assailed me and made me groan with remorse . . . Is it too late? Could not I run out on to the pavement and catch them now? No, the last cab has gone, leaving me whipped with regrets and piling up new resolutions, new efforts for the following week.

I was encouraged and egged on to entertain interesting and intellectual people, who were not of the smart world, by Philip's old friend, Logan Pearsall Smith. He was extremely encouraging and fanned my endeavours with praise. I was one of the few people, he said, who could do this kind of entertaining and keep it from being worldly and smart, and yet not dull and dowdy. He indulged his love of power by urging me on, sometimes bringing people to see me who he thought would interest me, or who ought to be included in the circle—the young and unknown who would like to meet brother writers or painters.

These Thursday evening parties were continued intermittently until we left Bedford Square in 1915, the colour of the stream of people varying slightly, but varying more from the incoming of the younger generation than from any difference in quality. The only people I cared to ask were artists and writers, and generally those who had not yet arrived. An evening dress suit was not seen, except on such strong adherents of the conventions as Henry James or Max Beerbohm—but Henry James usually came when he had not the pain of seeing the undressed crowd of "irreverent young people." His very great sensibility to external behaviour was indeed pained to see me what he called "descending amongst them." I recollect that in distress he laid his hand on me one day: "Look at them. Look at them, dear lady, over the banisters. But don't go down amongst them."

His words I disobeyed; I was already too far down the stairs to turn back. I have often felt myself standing on some old musicians' gallery, side by side with Henry James, both of us looking down at the hall below, my other self being knocked and jostled by the "young irreverents."

I find at this time in my journal a few chance sentences that reflect what was passing through my mind.

"How I strive to *do* something here (Peppard) and have worn myself out and failed. The District Nurse. The Women's Liberal Associations and libraries for them.

"How difficult it is to find the work that is right for oneself.

"I don't get on with these people who are 'all work.' I hate them. No dreams, no thoughts or ideas. And then those others who are like stupid super-animals. I see them from my window, playing golf morning to night. Red faces . . . stamping across the Common. How hard it is to live a balanced life and work. I fail utterly. I feel my best and happiest life is when I read and think and meditate, and have space around me, and write these foolish things in my book. When I am at work here or in

London a senseless pressure carries me away. I feel harassed
and overdone, tired in brain and spirit. Is it better to live like
that, or fresh and clear and well, doing but little outward work,
but *living* inside, growing, developing."

¶ *October 1908*

"I cannot forget the impression arriving into Italy, Verona,
from Austria, in August. The wonderful great green-rind mel-
ons, with pink flesh inside at every corner, and the scent of lake
roses, and the women in black shawls and little fans.

"Again the old question which never has ceased to haunt me
—work—work and contemplation. I wish I were ordered and
practical, and could help Philip more with his work. I should
feel happy then, but I am not clever or capable. What is it
urges one to help 'good causes,' and works, when one is not
suited to it? The wretched inherited instinct of responsibility
for the country's good, I suppose.

"But I always fly too high, and accomplish nothing.

"Why, I wonder, when one is at work or talking do scenes
pass across one's mental vision? Scenes in a street abroad, just
moments flit across. They were of no importance at the moment
one had them, and yet they hang about one, cling to one, and
waft themselves across one's mind unwanted.

"The dreariness, the depression of the human side of country
life had become too great an agony to me, and yet the country
people are freer, cleaner, happier than the neurotic towns-
people. So cheer up and open yourself to see and enjoy the
world around. It has music as lovely as Mozart. It has colour
like the Venetians. It has sadness as Giorgione. It is the background of Keats and Shelley and Blake—or rather it gave them
birth.

"New thoughts, new fullness and material gather within me

here in the quiet of the country. In town all this inner spiritual growth is checked. It is too rushing, exciting, wearing, except for that other side, the understanding of men and women that one learns in London—too much sometimes!

"After all, it is not my barrenness of fruit, but the outcome of laziness in building up something within myself. What can I give if I am not rich?

"I feel intense boredom and effort of doing 'works.' Is it laziness or is the thing not meant for me?

"Gilbert Murray says:

" 'Such lines, "Wind, wind of the deep sea," they carry in time that inexplicable beauty, that quick shiver of joy and longing, which, as it was fresh then in a world whose very bone and flesh have long since passed into dust, is still fresh and alive, but still like most other things of the spirit it will die if it is not loved.' "

¶ *February 9th 1909*

"Heard of poor Conder's death. Sensitive to the end of every light that could inspire his vision, even the most banal things served and were transmuted into visions of beauty by him. His imagination responded to the slightest prick and in spite of all his wild life he kept his spirit as a child. Adieu."

¶ *March 30th 1909*

"We are both so depressed at the military frenzy that has overtaken the country. It is all commotion, and a craze, an emotional craze that has seized on the man in the street as a music-hall singer's latest song might do.

"It is a smart set convention—as false as any other Public School convention. Why should there be attacking? Why should there be resistance even? I believe even if one did not resist an attacking nation one would not be worse off. The hatred, fury and madness of war is a thing to be ashamed of. If we see two dogs fighting or two rough men, we say how horrid. What is the difference? Why settle national or commercial quarrels in that primitive manner?"

¶ *March 1909*

"I sat to John in my dull violet velvet dress with green sleeves. Dorelia was there and came in and out with the children."

Was that the first time I had seen his wife Dorelia? I believe so. She had the dignity and repose of a peasant from a foreign land (her family really came from the Hebrides), extreme cleanliness, nonchalance and domination towards the children, a slightly mocking attitude to John, and shyness, *méfiance*, towards me, which melted by degrees. Between my sittings we sat round the large table for tea, the children eating slices of bread and jam, John looking a magnificent patriarch of a Nomad tribe, watching but talking very little. I saw that in every movement Dorelia made there was such grace and rhythm that she was indeed a stimulating model for any painter. He came back to dinner with us, and Roger Fry, the Clive Bells and Virginia Stephen.

At Easter I invited two of John's little boys to Peppard to stay with us. I was rather nervous of having these two little fellows, but I hoped they would be companions for Julian. Fearing that they would arrive with only a cotton overall each I went and brought them an outfit of clothes. We found it difficult to get them to eat, and when we asked them what they were accustomed to eat at home, they only answered in a deep voice, "Bones." After a few days they grew happy, and both John and Dorelia wrote them charming letters when they were with us.

I took to flying kites on the Common and the two little boys used to come with me. On April 14th I find noted:

"This has been such a heavenly spring day. We went on the Common and flew a new kite. It was most exciting feeling this thing twitching at one's hand 'frantic to be free'—dipping down and then up again, fainting and soaring by turns. I loved seeing it high up, carried along by violent breezes and in an air so rarefied.

"John writes very depressed at getting back to London streets after his caravan. He wants to know when I can sit."

¶ *April 21st 1909*

"I have been so tired the last few days that everything has seemed dead within me. Nothing but an aching pain in every nerve in my head. It is horrid to know anything is happy and lovely around, and yet to feel utterly wretched oneself, and always haunted by the thought of the uselessness of my life. It is like an angry fury, driving and lashing me, and yet I feel too utterly tired to do any practical good to anyone. I often wonder if other people feel this to the same painful degree I do. My life is haunted with it every hour.

"Carlyle's letters to his wife are good. Never was he serene. He was for ever groaning and travailing in pain, and her self-centred nervous temperament could not stand the strain. He needed a big, great-hearted, understanding woman. Jane was a quick, little, prickly female. He urges her to 'make the choice' between the world of amusement and the world of ideas and work. She made it by his pressure, but not from her own choice.

"Her own letters are sparkling, racy, critical, complaining and rather catty. Carlyle's full of splendour and grandeur of soul, pathetic in his struggle and poverty.

"Devastated by ill-health and depression, in a fog of gloom his love for Jane was the one bright happiness of his days, and how little that self-centred little glittering lady gave him—warmth she never gave him.

"I remember hearing that Whistler would tremble and shake with passion and resentments against people, but would be calmed in a moment by his great peaceful wife putting her white arm round him. One feels that this was what Carlyle needed, instead of the little stinging female he lost his heart to. But, after all, she has great charm. I hate her in one letter, and in the next she bewitches me. She is a most scoffing, disbelieving little creature, with no heart to speak of and very little faith, except in Carlyle, and yet she has the charming directness that he loves. I expect he was self-absorbed and intolerant, but what man is not, and, above all, a genius?"

¶ *April 24th*

"The thing I should really like to help on would be education. It is almost deplorable in the country. Young people always mock at what they don't understand, and as their understanding is so low it means they are for ever mocking. It is their form of poetry and happiness. When they meet one they enjoy a good coarse jeer.

"I believe the only thing that touches their imagination is the Army and anything to do with soldiers.

"The Church which ought to direct them and inspire their imagination never does.

"After all, their stupidity and coarseness is only the outcome of what they are given to learn. How utterly wrong was one's own standard until one evolved."

¶ *April 25th*

"I have never felt the spring to be so entrancing and fair as it is this year. The pale loveliness of it makes everything seem unearthly. The air is cold and clean, creating a vivid grey-blue background for the vaporous dream of pale blossoms—they seem as if they are feathers shaken down from angels' wings, each one with a hidden pink and perfumed centre which, when the moon is on them, shines through the white lantern of the blossoms.

"I stood amongst them enthralled at the vision, which like a lovely ecstasy dwells with us but for a brief moment."

¶ *April 28th*

"And now I am back in the great whirlpool of London, chaotic, noisy, clanging. Motor-cabs and buses all charging each other in a most unamiable way.

"I sit to John most days in a long white dress.

"The spring, the spring even in London, it floats on the wind over the roofs of the houses, and flows under the pavements. I can breathe it in the air. I feel melancholy at being here in this cage, but I can live with it in my imagination.

"In absence I seem almost to know scenes and people better than in their presence. They seem to unfold themselves as if in a vision. I feel at moments stripped of all my immediate surroundings, and as if I were in contact with that far-off scene or far-away person—feeling, seeing, hearing in a more real and vivid manner than if I passed them by and stood in their presence. And it is in these moments that I *understand*. Understand even the horrid sides of these personalities that in "real" life so puzzle and disgust me. For instance, I understand better the complications that exist in John's personality. His direct, ruthless, animal gypsy side, loving primitive men and women, and things ugly and crude, and his simple, nervous, sensitive, gentle side—the imaginative, idealist poet."

¶ *May 2nd*

"We went to Hampton Court with Miss Chadbourne and Mrs. Kochlin (two American friends of the Johns and of ours —two ladies who entertain and live on taste—exquisite, refined taste, and who faded away, having no roots in England and very little vitality). We picked up John and Dorelia.

"What a comical party we must have looked! The two American ladies dressed in immaculate tailor-mades—coats and skirts, tight little pork-pie hats. Philip would make me dress very smartly in a pale silk taffeta coat and large hat with a floating veil; Dorelia looked very beautiful in a long velveteen dress with buttons down the front, a long cape and a fur cap; John looked magnificent, with his big high black hat. We wandered through the rooms of the Palace, John apparently very bored, admiring quite bad things that took his fancy. The Giorgione and the good painters do not move him at all, except the Mantegnas, and these he gazed at for a long time. I find few painters really have got the instinct for cultivation. They feel antagonistic to old art, and don't want to absorb it. Traditional beauty such as we enjoy is alien and dead to them. We call such people uneducated, but it is possibly a protective instinct that shelters their own creativeness from being crushed and discouraged by the past.

"Time after time I find they will admire some apparently crude or ugly scene and turn with boredom from something that one would expect them to admire, some masterpiece of painting or architecture or even a group in nature that one thinks would move them to raptures. The French painter,

Derain, whom I met in Rome, found nothing that he could paint there. 'It is all too beautiful'—and it is. 'There is nothing for me to do. I must go on to where I can find something unformed and crude.' "

I think the only moment that John really "saw" something that interested him on that day was as we were driving back through Bushey Park—a herd of white and pale dun deer fled through the dark trees.

¶ *April 1909*

"Roger Fry brought MacColl of the Tate Gallery to lunch. He is a sympathetic critic and appreciative of Conder and John. We went afterwards to the Tate Gallery to see the Alfred Stevens's drawings that he has collected. Stevens seems to have been one of the few Englishmen with real direct genius—he and Blake and Turner.

"How hard it is for any genius to get on or to live!

"I feel strongly now that every penny one can save ought to be given to young artists. At least, we who really feel the beauty and wonder of Art ought to help them. There are heaps of people who understand philanthropy and who can help it, but so few can hear the cry of pure Art, or see the beauty of it. And young creators have such a terrible struggle."

Roger Fry and MacColl and C. J. Holmes lunched with us to talk over our scheme for starting a fund to buy the work of young English artists. At luncheon we began proceedings by quarrelling wildly about the different merits of Watts and Rothenstein—Roger Fry holding Rothenstein up as brilliantly clever and Watts as comparatively stupid. But what is cleverness? Is it imagination or intellectual ability?

After luncheon we set to work to hammer out the Fund Scheme, whether it should be connected with the National

Arts Collection Fund or a separate thing. It was decided that it was to be separate. Robbie Ross and Holmes are to come on to the committee.

This scheme definitely materialized and floated. I asked Lord Howard de Walden to be patron of it, and it has grown and flourished under the name of the Contemporary Art Society.

Visits, tea parties, evening parties, week-ends in the country —how hard it is to recapture the feelings that one felt, the acute shyness, the veil of self-protective criticism that is spread across one's inward retina, and that keeps the unknown from entering too readily into one's inner life. The consciousness or the imagination of what one suspects one's hosts are thinking of us; the extreme discomfort, in fact, that one suffers seeing oneself through their eyes, for the thoughts that lurk there are so rapidly felt by their poor, self-conscious, silent guest!

Why does one go through this exhausting experience and delude oneself into calling it pleasure? Curiosity, desire for friendship, fear of losing some unique experience that would be illuminating to life. But would not a play which could be watched from the stalls be as useful and as enlightening? No. That demands no effort from oneself. It does not break up anything inside oneself, or rub off mould and moss from hidden corners, or open up fresh vistas into new countries. Such excursions may not lead one to an abiding resting-place, but they build up those little distant castles that one sees in the background of a primitive picture, which if viewed through a magnifying glass show minute phantom figures going in and out under gateways and walking in formal gardens.

In June 1909 my little mirror shows that we went to Crabbet Park in Sussex to stay with Neville Lytton. He had asked to paint a portrait of me, and I sat to him in the mornings.[4]

[4] Strictly speaking she stood; for the picture, which represents her in a highly elaborate red dress against a dark background, is a standing

The large untidy house built in the grand style by Wilfrid Blunt (Mrs. Lytton's father) had all the charm of a really old eighteenth-century house—the beautiful empty architectural rooms, the woods near by, were fascinating and romantic.

It seemed at first almost to be the Palace of the Sleeping Beauty and Neville Lytton the Prince Charming, standing in front of the house in fancy clothes, tall high-boots, and playing a flute, his brown hair in curls over his dark poetic face. Judith, dressed in gorgeous Arabian dresses, hardly appeared. She did not sleep, but was as one under a spell—*sans pitié*. The breeding of toy dogs and Arab horses, arduous games at tennis in their newly built tennis courts, were done by her without a smile, as if impelled by some cruel fate, known only to herself and about which she is silent. She is beautiful—as beautiful as an Eastern princess, or a highly coloured archaic statue. Her three children run about the garden, their long white bare legs glinting out of the laurels, the two girls with long dark hair falling down over rather sad pale faces. They would peep and peer through bushes and trees to catch a glimpse of their remote, mysterious, cold, spellbound mother. The only time that I ever saw them together was at early Mass on Sunday, which the priest would come to celebrate in an upper room.

The atmosphere of the house was so devoid of pomp or conventionality that we might have been in Poland or Russia. The bare rooms, the good simple vegetarian meals, the one eccentric manservant, the beautiful rather formal garden, and the smell of the lime trees in flower that was wafted through the windows, the waves of brilliant bluebells surging round

---

full-length figure. After her death I gave it to Portland, and it is now (1942) at Welbeck.   P.M.

the trees in the woods around—made an entrancing scene. Neville Lytton himself, so fresh and with so much enthusiasm for painting, socialism and Bernard Shaw, for folk-dancing and music. Indeed, he seemed as if he could dance through life accompanied by all that was beautiful and good and advanced. Here, too, were the Aranyis, who had just arrived in England, and were beginning to make an appearance in public as violinists. The youngest was about fifteen years old, with black hair falling straight down over her dark cream face, making her look like a figure in a Puvis de Chavannes fresco. She played the violin with precocious knowledge and fierce young passion, hardly realizing difficulties which she had met and conquered. While I stood for Neville to paint me, she played duets with Donald Tovey, who accompanied her on the clavichord. He, too, gave me the impression of a genius who had immense knowledge of the theory, history and philosophy of music, about which he discoursed in an involved and entangled way.

Neville Lytton took me for drives through the forest, driving one of the Arab horses in a light cart. We flew along over heather and grass, winding in and out of trees as if we had been riding, passing several of the sequestered little homes in the woods that Wilfrid Blunt would, when the mood took him, retire to, accompanied by a young lady. This remarkable old man, then nearly seventy, was preparing to get a divorce from his wife, Lady Anne (Byron's grand-daughter). I tried my best to have some contact with Judith, but failed entirely. She seemed without desire to know human beings and turned her back on her guests as much as on her children. The only human being that interested her was the professional tennis player whom she kept to play with her.

Some years later the dark mysterious princess awoke, and like a fury she quarrelled with her father and refused to see him; she quarrelled with her husband and turned him out, and now she reigns supreme. I do not know if she still retains the tennis professional. Certainly Byron's great-grand-daughter had very strange blood in her veins.

Neville Lytton lives now in Paris with a French wife. He is poor and disapproves of modern art.

Earlier in June we stayed with Ethel Sands at Newington— Whitsuntide party arranged to surround Henry James with sympathetic atmosphere. Our fellow-guests were Howard Sturgess, Miss Una Birch, Lionel Holland and an American, Schuyler Warren. Henry James didn't arrive until Sunday morning, with his foot in a gout-boot, looking ill and in pain, but he talked incessantly. "Golden stuff," I called it in my diary. "His words came out like little hammers and hit every nail they aimed at. He has a kind and penetrating spirit."

Should I now call it kind? I hesitate to say yes—but yet it was, for he had penetration without humbug.

His sensibilities were perhaps too easily shocked by what would appear natural to a later generation, and being American he held on with tenacity to the polish and conventions of English society. But his perception was far too penetrating and clairvoyant to be deluded by falseness however thickly veneered. His conversation enthralled me. Although I could not always agree with him, yet the sharp turns and thrusts of perception when he appeared to be lengthily fumbling or rummaging round a subject, and when with a sudden quick thrust of phrase would hold up his victim pinned on the point of his sword—made me thrill with pleasure.

He called on me once in London and as I was not in left a visiting card on which he wrote:

"Life is a hard struggle and full of complications."

One laughs, and yet it is true.

Life certainly to Henry James was not an easy thing. He was absorbed by thoughts, ruminations, glimpses, vibrations— there was no time in his later years for any action beyond writing. The swarm of images, possibilities, that filled that capacious brain would make anyone cry out "Life is indeed very complicated." And who can deny the truth of this?

The mystic who sets his heart on God alone and who forgoes and prunes from his life all worldly and human contacts, or the restless man of affairs who forges ahead, trampling on anything that impedes his success, may find life simple, but one who, like Henry James, was aware with a wizard's instinct of the teeming currents and cross-currents of thoughts and feelings in each human being, and who out of the vast tangle of these wireless vibrations was creating his own individuals and putting them in motion, beseeching them to live, to think, to speak and consider each other, can not but turn away at times from too much stimulus.

I see him—as indeed one can see all real literary creators— writing in a study and invoking out of his imagination phantoms into which he breathed his own complicated, subtle and mystical spirit.

I was shy and self-conscious in his company, being aware of how little might mean to him too much! And yet, after all, I might have had more confidence, for although he was ruffled by tactlessness and bad manners and outraged by vulgarity, what he fundamentally appreciated was goodness and absence of pose.

One day we drove over to lunch with Miss Alice Rothschild, who had been a friend of Ethel Sands's mother. We were shown over the house, and all its priceless works of art. It seemed more oppressive even than an ordinary museum, which is after all open to the public. This, on the contrary, was guarded from human view. We were marshalled round the rooms by Miss Rothschild, and I was told by her "not to touch" when my hand rested for a moment on a table.

I felt as if I was moving in the interior of a Louis XIV clock that would cease ticking if I stepped off the drugget that was laid across each room. A breath of criticism was indeed cried into my ear by Henry James; his basilisk gaze had absorbed the company of seven-foot-high footmen that waited on us, the hothouse flowers and the dish of enormous white strawberries that were in front of the plates. He looked up at the footmen, he looked down on the strawberries. "Murder and rapine," he said, "would be preferable to this."

So inhuman was the atmosphere of this private museum that none of us were directed to the place which is after all so necessary a provision even in a museum. When Howard Sturgess suggested asking one of the young giants where it was to be found, Henry James threw up his arms and said to him, "Howard dear, what I thought was an Elysian dream you have made into a physiological fact."

I remember nothing of our drive home except that my hat was so blown about by the wind that I took it off and tied my head up with a lace scarf, conscious of looking dishevelled and plain, which was indeed my constant obsession. Henry James told Ethel Sands afterwards that he admired the shape of my head.

I have an instinctive shrinking from compliments, but this is one of the few that I have kept and put into my little cabinet of treasures. One other stands on the shelf as its pendant.

The evening before he left, Henry James told me of two dreams that he had in his youth, and which had obviously made a lasting impression on him. He awoke trembling in a great state of nerves. He had become aware that a terrible beast had entered into the house where he was. He realized that the room in which he was had four doors. He rushed to the first, the second and the third, turning the key; when he arrived at the fourth he was aware that there was something awful behind it, and he began to hold the door to with all his strength. But as he was doing this, he felt a sudden *volte-face* within himself, and he called out, "What a vile, cowardly creature you are to be afraid." He dashed open the door and determined to pursue the monster; as he opened it he found he was on the threshold of a long beautiful gallery, flooded with sunlight. He rushed out, waving his arms, and at the far end of the gallery he saw a monster rushing away, and as he fled after it he woke.

The other dream was that he found himself in a house or shop full of furniture, huge rooms of beautiful cabinets and chairs and tables. He wandered all over the house feeling a vague mysterious presence. At last, arriving upstairs, he found himself in a room in which was an old man sitting in a chair, and like the other dream he had a sudden change from fear to strength. He called out to the man, "You're afraid of me, you coward." The man said, "No." Henry James answered, "But you are, I know it. I see the sweat on your brow."

As I am gazing down into the pool of memory I catch sight of a few more opalescent, faint, intangible anemones, waving to and fro in the waters of time, I will bend down and try to hold them by the magnetic hand of memory.

I realize, now that I have had more experience of remarkable men, what a wonderfully sympathetic listener Henry James was; critical, I am sure, of expression or jargon, and of foolishness and conceit, but not really intolerant or impatient—indeed, the great head and the pale eyes were turned full on to the speaker and absorbed and absorbed, valued and ruminated. His own talk was akin to his writing, unlike any other talk, but not unlike Bach's fugues. It might seem to halt, dwell and ponder, and wander, but then suddenly, unexpectedly, there was a swoop and swift twirl, and with often a happy and humorous thrust. Never did I hear Henry James repeat his talk or repeat phrases, which is a rare thing among talkers. Even the best seem to have innumerable gramophone records in their minds which, if one knows them well, seem scratchy, monotonous and mechanical. To the tight-rope-dancing society talkers, who delight in the pirouettes and acrobatic feats of talk, Henry James probably appeared cumbrous, slow and boring. Indeed, Margot Asquith called him "an elephant that had picked up a pea." But she did not see what a magic pea he had found.[5] They little knew what a merciless observer and critic he was; he would take them into his camera obscura, and then the little flashing pirouettes would seem very tawdry and vulgar. I was told that when he was sitting with an old lady in her boudoir, Mrs. Kemble was shown into the drawing-room next door. The lady turned to Henry James and said, "You will come in and see Mrs. Kemble, won't you, Mr. James." His reply was, "A tight-rope—banisters—backstairs, anything to save me from meeting that battered mountebank, dear lady." When a party of actresses came down in char-à-bancs to see him at Rye, he entertained them most courteously and generously, but afterwards with a

[5] The philistine H. G. Wells, in *Boon* (1915), had written of Henry James as "a magnificent but painful hippopotamus resolved at any cost, even at the cost of its dignity, upon picking up a pea which had got into a corner of its den. Most things, it insists, are beyond it, but it can, at any rate, modestly, and with an artistic singleness of mind, pick up that pea." Which conceived this image must, and perhaps for ever, remain uncertain; certain it is, however, that one of the two had borrowed from the other.

sigh said, "A char-à-banc full of mimes; but there was one poor wanton, not without a certain cadaverous beauty."

On his way to tea with us one day he had chanced to meet Princess Bariatinsky who lived near by. She had been a famous Russian actress, who though now married to a man of high position in Czarist Russia still could not free herself from the glamour of sawdust and orange peel. He gave a vivid description of her talking in her loud, raucous Russian voice, insisting that he should come and see her act "some terrible play." Alas, I cannot remember all he said, except the end: "This remarkable woman—intense, insistent, passionate, in her stage vanity so over-dressed in furs and mock diamonds, in the street was dressed in old rags, pinned round her with a pin that . . . that she had picked up in the Tottenham Court Road."

There were certain things that angered him—above all, irreverence and disrespect. I remember him speaking to me about some young people who had invited him down to Cambridge, and had rather freely and disrespectfully tried to make use of him. Somehow this hurt him and aroused his indignation, for he said: "I feel now that I don't wish to be trodden under foot."

Alas, I fear that I was the cause of much distress to him, for when he came to my Thursday evenings he found many young men dressed in rather rough day-clothes. This appeared to him almost as if they were sitting in my presence with their hats on. His niece, who lived with him, told me afterwards how distressed her uncle was at what he felt to be their want of courtesy and respect towards me. I am sure he felt that I had done wrong to disobey his advice not to descend the steps into the arena, but to look over the banisters at "those below"; "those" being such people as Augustus John of whom he said that "he paints human beings as if they were animals, and dogs as if they were human beings."

I have always thought that he owed much of his ultra-sensitive imagination about life and personalities to his two Irish grandparents, and perhaps to his Swedenborgian father. I have heard people discuss whether he was or was not religious. Desmond MacCarthy wrote of him that as regards religion he was purely eighteenth century, which strikes me as strangely inaccurate. I believe all religions interested him intensely. He dwelt in thought on them, and voyaged out at times into very strange fields, but could not imprison himself in any definite dogma. When I told him that my mother-in-law had become a Roman Catholic, he thought for a few minutes, and then in a ruminating tone of voice his answer came: "How happy for her that she is able to." I know that he was certainly not anti-religious as Lytton Strachey or Bertrand Russell were—my impression was that he was by nature very spiritual and reverential, and that his mind had a strong mystical quality is obvious to anyone who reads his books, for does he not always endeavour to express the power and influence that character—soul, thoughts—have on one another? It is not deeds, acts, that he values as important, but thoughts, personality, goodness, the "invisible man," and the conflicts of the spirits of good and evil. The head upon which he lays his hand in blessing is always that of the good and pure in heart. I believe, as I look back and remember certain things he let fall, that he had himself travelled into obscure regions, seeking the battleground of spirits dark and light. But of this he did not wish to speak; he only said that he was exhausted by experiences that he had been through. I do not know how anyone who has read Chapter VI in his book *Notes of a Son and a Brother*, where he actually describes his father's Swedenborgian spirit-

ual life, could think that he was without God. He here laments
that the religious life of his home, though so real and so deep,
took no outward form. "Religion was a matter to be worked
off more than to be worked in."

When I hear people discuss Henry James, or any of my old
friends, I often wonder at the blindness of human beings towards each other. When we observe each other do we only see
what is within ourselves? The limitation of our own natures
perhaps limits our understanding of others. When we condemn
and criticize other people, it may be that we are really criticizing ourselves. The sensitive inner eye that can see into the
depths of our fellows and feel their tangles and complexities
under layer upon layer of habit is, I suppose, rare; for it demands a self purified from envy and malice, and lit by the
penetrating lamp of love and understanding, and a sincere
wholehearted compassion for tangled, shot-silk human nature.

Newington, lovely as it is, seems a great weight on Ethel
Sands. The tables are spread, the candles lit, the flowers arranged, best cushions put out and all is made lovely and exquisite—for an occasional week-end party, where friends talk,
croquet is played, French dinners are eaten. But what happens
after the cabs have driven away on Monday morning—after
the last waving of hands from the lovely old grey stone porch?

I remembered as I drove away what W. B. Yeats had said
to me once: "We who create have to cultivate our wild beasts;
most people have to subdue them."

Were there any wild beasts at Newington to subdue? Do
they hide themselves discreetly behind the rose bushes in the
garden? Or take refuge in the bodies of the French bulldogs
that are so petted?

It was a strange contrast to go to a large luncheon party that

144

Philip had organized at the Holborn Restaurant in support of the Land Taxes. Asquith and Lloyd George were the principal speakers. There were about five hundred people present.

I sat next to Lloyd George, who was attractive and witty. During part of the luncheon he wrote his speech. I glanced down at his notes and found that he was writing them in Welsh.

Asquith spoke well; as Lloyd George said: "He is a lawyer and speaks to his jury. This is a packed jury."

The only contretemps was the interruption of a suffragette who had to be led out, kicking and biting and fighting.

I say in my diary:

"It really has strengthened the cause of Land Taxation, I think. Asquith is so squashable, and the rich Whigs are so against it that they might easily carry him with them."

How far away, unimportant, phantom-like, this all seems now, the war having washed away, for good or for bad, such questions as these. In 1909 they seemed of real importance, and in working for them, we hoped we were toiling for something important.

A few days later a party of Liberal women from South Oxfordshire came up, and I took them round London in large brakes, and provided tea for them at Whitfield Tabernacle, and they ended their day by coming to Bedford Square to inspect baby Julian.

It was during this summer that we went to stay for our first week-end with Lady Horner at Mells. A visit here was more alarming than one to Ethel Sands, the atmosphere less familiar, more assured, and more of the past, and the thought of it filled us with dread and nervous misgivings.

We were aware that in comparison with these established people we were but wayfarers in life, outsiders, and I felt rebellious against their cynical political views, and their opinions about such elusive and uncertain subjects as art and literature, and their half-mocking attitude to anyone who had not as yet public approval; they had the power of making those who were not of their intimate circle feel the pain of sheepish inferiority.

However, when the invitation came curiosity triumphed and we accepted. I packed my best dresses, which somehow, when shaken out and worn, seemed absurdly fantastic and unfitting for the company and the surroundings. These that at home I was so proud of and thought so lovely would suddenly be transformed into tawdry "picturesque" rags, making me feel foolish and self-conscious in wearing them. I see ourselves sitting in the loggia talking to Lady Horner, Mr. Haldane and Raymond Asquith; I making a brave, but only half-successful, effort to transpose myself to their key, to talk in a way that would be harmonious to them. All my own feelings and enthusiasms, like my dresses, I felt sure, would seem absurd and fantastic if I allowed them to be seen. I entirely failed in courage to express what I really thought, indeed I felt absolutely immature and unable to talk with the easy, nonchalant certainty that would have been successful, and I was therefore obliged to relapse on to the easy couch of sympathetic questionings and listening.

From time to time I would escape up to my own room, fling my arms out and cry aloud: "Oh to be free, free!" Then sedately returned and paced the lovely medieval garden with its grass paths and flower-beds within its frame of grey walls. To walk up and down listening to Mr. Haldane, who like a modern Buddha would suavely pour out words of worldly philosophical wisdom. "Sly old thing," I called him at the time, feeling annoyed at his half-veiled contempt for Radicals and his worldly attitude in politics. Across our path would come

Lady Horner's son, Edward, who at that moment had the dazzling beauty of a Greek athlete. His beauty was indeed too perfect to be more than transient. It was fated never to fade, for early in the war he was one of its thousands of victims, he and Raymond Asquith, whom I can still see sitting in the loggia, in a long basket-chair, reading D. H. Lawrence's novel, *The White Peacock,* which he admired, but which puzzled him he said, as he could not believe peasants could talk as Lawrence made them talk, nor could they have any knowledge of art or music. It must be artificial—he forgot that Lawrence was himself the son of a Nottinghamshire miner.

Underneath Raymond's cynical exterior there lay a streak of charming gentleness and tenderness, but it was not easy to find the way to it through the armour of sceptical cleverness that had been hardened and polished by Oxford and by the smart set in London who flattered and admired him. He had been leader at Oxford of all that was clever and reckless and contemptuous. Whatever Raymond thought and did was followed by the other young Olympians (the Grenfell brothers, Patrick Shaw Stewart, Edward Horner and others). He drove the foremost chariot and woe betide any poor individual that found himself in the way. The intellects of these young men happened to be excellent and they carried off prizes and fellowships with as much ease as they could win a steeplechase. Health, beauty, intellect, all had been showered upon them by indulgent Fortune, and they were intoxicated by their possessions. Life was "too gloriously happy" to feel any discontent or doubt. Those amongst them who were not rich were going to the Bar or into High Finance, destined, as they gaily said, to be millionaires, so as to be able to indulge to the full their love of comfort, good food, good drink, bath salts and other luxuries. How Dizzie would have loved them, and how they would have admired him! But while we were basking in the sunshine and peace and beauty of this lovely English garden and smoking cigarettes, and scheming, planning, doubting, criticizing, there was a dark figure coming nearer and nearer, which laughed to see these simple children of earth so at ease, so confident and so unseeing. Did none of us have ears sensitive enough to hear that whisper: "Your dreams and efforts are but as the smoke of your cigarettes"? Even when that hideous creature came into our very presence it appeared to those young men as one clad in bright armour, radiant and beautiful, beckoning them to come to new adventure—"to a glorious picnic," as one of them described it.

One evening Lady Horner brought out a collection of letters from Burne-Jones and read them to us. He was obviously devoted to her. His language was very whimsical and fanciful and rich. She has books full of his stories and conversations. Perhaps she was once an inspiration to his art.

Lady Horner is one of those remarkable and capable English-women who, with a certain amount of artistic and literary culture, can manage society, friends, a family, garden and household with ease and success. She has few doubts; perhaps at times she has wondered what life comes to, but whatever the results of her questioning she has faced it bravely, and although she has had great losses—her two sons, and her son-in-law, Raymond Asquith, she remains unsubdued and undaunted.

But how disturbing those excursions into the smart set were! Its members are so sure, so certain, that they are on the right road in life, so untroubled by complications and struggles, either of their own or of others less fortunate. They possess so much that dazzles and attracts: cleverness, beauty, ease in relationships one with another, and life generally. They hardly need to knock at the gates that lead to success, or to push, for they are so welcome.

It was a relief to return to our own house and own queer and imaginative friends, our scallywags, as Virginia once called them.

I was now beginning to see more of Virginia Stephen and her friends, and to go to her Thursday evenings in Fitzroy Square, where long-legged young men would sit in long basket-chairs smoking pipes and talking almost inaudibly in breathless voices of subjects that seemed to me thrilling and exciting. When the pool that lay between us grew calm and overcast, Virginia's bell-like voice would be heard, swinging, swinging and resonant, awaking and scattering dull thought, and giving warning that a light would be thrown into the darkness, the rays of which would light up her own lovely face and our stagnant prosy minds. She would lead us swiftly along into the streets or the lives of any she may meet, and the world of poetry, showing her light into dull corners, and making them appear full of fantasy and beauty. This strange, lovely, furtive creature never has seemed to me to be made of common flesh and blood. She was rather like some Diana of the realm of the mind who, though she had forsaken forest and the chase of deer, now treads the ways of man still carrying hidden under her veil her crescent of light. She comes and goes, she folds her cloak around her and vanishes, having shot into her victim's heart a quiverful of teasing arrows.

She walks in London streets, she travels in an omnibus, and with her penetrating light searches the hearts of those she meets. She sees their thoughts and feels the tenderest and frailest vibrations of emotions traversing their beings. She hears the distant song of beauty or the sigh of despair.

To this visitant from another sphere our lives appear more

149

strange, more vivid and fantastically exciting than they do to oneself.

As years have gone by, and her sojourning here has inured her to our ordinary life, she seems now to sit with almost familiar ease in my room, and I no longer feel the fear that this enchanting and bewildering goddess will sail away before I have recovered from her entry and before I had caught a glimpse of her crescent light. I feel I have made her see into my heart.

Since the days of Fitzroy Square, when she led her followers on to the *Dreadnought*[6] dressed up as an Eastern princess, and out to Covent Garden at dawn to buy armfuls of flowers, she has known the love of many, she has married, she has written, and she is now recognized and admired. But I like to remember her in the old days with her little circle of companions: her brother Adrian, her sister Vanessa, Vanessa's husband, Clive Bell, that happy, flattering, good-tempered Autolycus holding out gay leaves for us to admire. Roger Fry, who had not yet set sail on the sea of modern French art; Lytton Strachey and Duncan Grant—what a delightful company they seemed!

Of Lytton Strachey I used to feel most shy, for he said so little and he seemed to live far away in an atmosphere of rarefied thought. His voice so small and faint, but with definite accentuations and stresses of tone, giving a sense of certainty and distinction, appeared to come from very far away, for his delicate body was raised on legs so immensely long that they seemed endless, and his fingers equally long, like antennae. It was not till I knew him better that I found how agile those long legs could be, and what passion and feeling lay in that

[6] The full story of the famous hoax alluded to here was eventually told and published in *The Dreadnought Hoax* by Adrian Stephen. Virginia Woolf, though a willing and conspicuous participant, was not the leader.

delicate body, and how rapidly those long and beautiful antennae could find passages in Racine or Dryden, and the strength
and vigour of his voice when he read these passages aloud
to me. But at this time he seemed so melancholy and aloof
that I hardly dared approach him, though he would come to
see me now and then. Duncan Grant, too, was shy and vague
and elusive, but always bewitching.

It was in this year that the first Russian dancers appeared in
London, not the Diaghilev Ballet, which did not arrive here
until a year or so later, but some forerunners who seemed to our
unspoilt sight as winged fairies. How lovely, how gay, how
enchanting they were, as if Conder's pictures had come to life.
I was so enthusiastic about them that night after night I took
friends to see them: John and Dorelia, and Desmond Mac-
Carthy and Roger Fry, Virginia and Duncan Grant, were all
led there. How anxiously I watched their faces to see if they
were as thrilled as I was. I often lost whole precious moments
of this all too short joy by scanning the faces of those I had
taken to see the effects on them. Their appreciation never really
satisfied me.

Then one day the Clive Bells asked us to go with them to
Artists Revels at the Botanical Gardens. What a picture of
gaiety the two words evoked, "Artists Revels." Philip and I
dressed up, he in his black velvet court suit, I in a very full
black taffeta dress, with black lace mantilla.

It was my first and only experience of a fancy dress ball and
I visualized a Mozartian scene of lovely gaily-dressed youths and
maidens flitting in and out of dark trees lit up by coloured lights
—a ballet in real life. But even at the dinner in Gordon Square
with the Bells a certain disillusionment began. I felt that our
companions had not chosen very appropriate costumes. Vanessa's Madonna-like beauty surely could have found a happier
alias than that of a Pierrot, and Virginia was hardly suited to

pose as Cleopatra, whose qualities, as I had imagined them, were just those that Virginia did not possess. Adrian, her brother, too, was not very convincing as a young Cardinal, but I excused these little lapses as high-handed carelessness on the part of intellectuals.

On arriving at the Botanical Gardens, however, the scene that I had anticipated was nowhere to be found. I searched indoors and out. I recoiled from the jumble-tumble of awkward young men waving long, raw, red arms and legs, and young women equally crude and ungainly, pretentiously and unsuitably decked out in badly adjusted garments of all ages and periods. What a different scene to the one I had expected of ordered and exquisite beauty! Has the past indeed so literally vanished that no trace of its minor arts and finery remains in our instincts? Are our ancestors so completely buried under their monuments that no spark of their delicate taste and courtly grace remains in our blood? We still live in their homes and recite their poems, but to wear their clothes clearly is a vanished art. The bouyant, athletic bodies of these young people have grown sadly unsuited to the buckram of the past. Their minds have developed their bodies into a different mould.

From behind the dark trees I caught the sound of mocking laughter. Was it from these lords and ladies whose earthly garments were being so travestied by the ungainly young revellers? I seemed to hear them say, "You think we looked like that, do you? Silly children, how blind you are not to see and understand us better than that. Go and put on your cricket flannels and tennis skirts, your football shorts and motor goggles, and play your hoydenish games which you understand. Leave ruffs and farthingales, embroidered stomachers and waistcoats, powdered wigs and minuets to us."

I put my arm through Philip's and drew my black lace veil close round me hoping that no one would search my face that night to read the melancholy disappointment that I felt at the sight of English artists revelling!

Perhaps, after all, I belonged to the time of hoops and loops and billowing skirts—a rare survival—one of those who were laughing from behind the trees.

John had asked me to go down to see him and his family at Grantchester. He was living in a caravan there, while he painted a portrait of Jane Harrison at Cambridge. Philip was averse to this expedition, but gave way to my pressure and I went gaily off, dressed in my best muslins. John met me at Cambridge station with a horse and high gig. Directly I climbed up into the cart the horse, which was a huge ungainly half-trained animal, began to back, slipped and fell down. John rapidly descended from our high perch; he stood calmly smoking a cigarette, looking at the great brute kicking and struggling, but made no attempt to help. However, station loafers came to the rescue, and we adjusted the horse and harness. Up we got again, and slowly trotted through Cambridge to a meadow where he was camping with Dorelia, her sister and the children, who were running about like little gypsies.

How damp and cold and cheerless and dull it seemed. John was morose, with a black eye, the result of a fight the night before with one of the men who looked after the caravan horses. Dorelia and her sister, absorbed in cooking and washing, treated me with indifference and taciturnity, and made no friendly effort to make me feel at home. But after all it would have perhaps been a difficult task to be at home in a melancholy, sodden meadow outside a caravan.

I was given a crust of bread and some fruit for my dinner

and I returned to London, chilled and damp and appreciative of my own home and Philip. I brought back some beautiful drawings, slightly coloured, that John had done of Dorelia in Turkish trousers, which I sold for him to my brother Henry. They were some of his most delicate and beautiful work. How much I regret that I did not buy them myself! I suppose they were more than I could afford at the moment, or perhaps I was anxious to interest my brother in John's painting. When I first spoke of it to him he used to scoff at it and deride me for thinking it good.[7]

The habit of my family of criticizing me was not broken down even by my marriage. The only difference was that I was removed from hearing it. Philip was by my side to support me.

"No cords bind us together except to Henry. They are unaware of it, they have not spun or woven the web of friendship and so there is nothing to break, except the old fear and nervousness that I feel with them."

If they only knew how they crushed and terrified me. How well I remember the wild relief and delight when I reached my own room and shut the door—to be alone, with a door between me and their criticisms.

I loved beauty and colour and loveliness and poetry, but they said it was "degenerate." That word was said in a contemptuous, superior, righteous tone, meant to knock me on the head. I looked up amazed, but no look could penetrate the armour of complete self-satisfaction and of assurance, for if they held in one hand a cudgel, the other held a complete moral code.

How well I remember travelling by train with my brother Henry. He asked what I was reading. I showed him a volume

[7] As I have said in the preface, Lord Henry made in the end a fine collection of contemporary art. For this he bought some of Ottoline's pictures when she was forced to sell them.

of Spenser. "How can you waste your time on that rot?" was
his comment. Inside me the cry went up, "What does it all
mean? What's your rot is my reality."

In September 1909 in my journal I find the following entries:

"Philip went to a large meeting at Birmingham arranged by
Sir Charles Maclaren. Asquith's speech very disappointing and
lacking in courage and inspiration. It fell rather flat. The
11,000 people who came full of expectation and enthusiasm
went away damped, but a man cannot give what he has not
got."

"Suffragettes threw small bombs, and a large piece of iron
was thrown at Asquith into the railway carriage."

In September of this year (1909) we went to Black Hall
for the week-end and from there we went by motor-car which
Logan Pearsall Smith took us in to see the Bertrand Russells
at Bagley Wood. Desmond MacCarthy was there.

"Bertrand Russell," I wrote, "is most fascinating. I don't
think I have ever met anyone more attractive, but very alarming, so quick and clear-sighted, and supremely intellectual—
cutting false and real asunder. Somebody called him 'The
Day of Judgement.'"

His notice flattered me very much, and though I trembled
at the feeling that in half an hour he would see how silly I
was and despise me, his great wit and humour gave me courage
to talk.

Vernon Lee came to see the Russells while we were there;
she entered with her head on one side, pince-nez on her nose
and dressed in a white cloth dress, looking younger and happier
than when I had seen her years ago. She at once sat down
and said:

"You are all politicians and Liberals. Tell me why you don't cultivate more the friendship of Germany?"

In vain we all protested and professed our love of Germany, and boasted of all that had been done by politicians. She did not attend or listen; her voice went persistently on, with its rather charming intonation and lips; whenever she saw one of us attempting to answer she would hurry on, fearing an interruption.

Bertie Russell grew very restive, and had visibly to control his longing to burst out and say something harsh. We all sat round watching.

But she really said many good things about Germany and France. The Germans, she said, are much more subtle and full of doubts than the French, who labelled everything with stock phrases—"Le Vrai," "Le Beau," "Le Bien." It was like a sky-sign over a music-hall, which sometimes showed one name and then another. The French had the name of being unconventional because they treated of subjects that we English don't generally mention, but as a nation they are very definite, very cut and dried.

Next day, Mrs. Morrell drove me over to Court Place at Iffley, to see old Mrs. Pearsall Smith. She is keen and interested in everything. Alys Russell was there. She said that Bertie had enjoyed our visit and would like to come and see us in London. It would be very delightful, but I really have not the courage for it. In ten minutes he would be disappointed and bored. He makes me feel as if I was as empty as an old drum.

¶ *September 22nd*

"We went to lunch with the Arthur Ponsonbys at the House of Commons, with Prince and Princess Bariatinsky (whom we had introduced to Arthur Ponsonby), Prince Kropotkin and his daughter, and Massingham. Kropotkin was delightful; he gave one an idea of Tolstoy in appearance, so genial and merry, and clever and full of knowledge. He was delighted to meet Princess Bariatinsky as he had heard so much of her fame as an actress. His pleasure was so fresh and keen and expressive —how unlike an Englishman! Massingham talked to me about Mark Rutherford's works, praising them highly and comparing them to Rousseau.

"We went outside on the terrace. John Burns stood at the end, evidently longing for us to come his way. He waited about in his coxcombly way."

Soon after this we went to our cottage at Peppard, and Logan Pearsall Smith came to stay with us. He pounced on the volumes of the new edition of Henry James that I had there, and sat reading them. He read me an article by Max Beerbohm in imitation of Henry James, about two children on Christmas Eve, full of intricate sentences, only half of which had any meaning. I find it difficult to talk to Logan. He makes me nervous and shy. He pries into one's life; I lose my head and talk nonsense.

"He took us over to the Kellys at Marlow. The Bob Trevelyans were staying there. Bob was very argumentative and positive and contemptuous of other people's views.

"After luncheon he began to scold me about Augustus John's clothes. He said they were worn for effect and vanity. He was such a remarkable looking man that he need not do it, and that it only put people off him. I replied that he did not care a rap for that! Bob answered, 'But he ought to—'

"We had another argument about Henry James. He maddened me by quoting people's 'opinions' about his work—men like George Moore the philosopher, whose judgement about literature and psychology is obviously worthless. I should listen to it if it was given about metaphysics or some abstract subject, but about life and art—no, no. Bob Trevelyan does not like or understand intricate or entangled thought.

"We stayed late, listening to Mozart and Brahms, and Debussy's *L'Après-midi d'un Faune.*

"While Logan was with us his niece, Ray Costello[8] (now Mrs. Oliver Strachey) came over in her motor-car which she drives herself. I was amazed by such wonderful self-reliance and independence in managing your own life like this. She devoted her life to the Suffrage Cause, and motors about speaking from her car. We had a great discussion on riches. Logan said it was unbecoming and did not produce happiness. Ray frankly said she wanted plenty of money to spend on political work. Like all these questions it is so intricate. I think very often we might be happier if we gave up Bedford Square. It gives an impression of grandeur and wealth, too gorgeous for what we are or wish to be.

"What a foolish, childish dreamer I have been, always thinking of beauty and piling up colour. Shall I do it again and again, I wonder? I heap up beautiful things, oriental cloths, old embroideries, Italian damasks, painted silks. The same ungoverned love of beauty. My austere intellectual friends censure it, perhaps rightly, but they don't feel the passion of it— except Philip, and he is too lenient to me. I wish I could feel it wrong. On the contrary, I really feel the dreary, ugly rooms I see in other people's houses to be all wrong. If it were more permanent, I might be allowed to do it as artists paint their pictures, but they say it is ephemeral and soon passes away, and that houses and rooms ought only to be *convenantes.* I murmur to myself—'Birds' feathers are beautiful as well as *convenantes,* flowers are beautiful.' "

[8] Daughter of Mrs. Bernard Berenson by her first husband, Benjamin Costello.

¶ *September 29th*

"Why, oh why, does the question always and for ever haunt me like a menace of the utter uselessness of my life? Why don't I feel that Philip and Julian are enough *raison d'être*—a tie to earth? Every moment of the day I am haunted by my utter uselessness—a body lumbering the earth, fit to be cast into the fire. Is it true or is it an obsession? I feel so tired always. I cannot face any work. To get through the necessary letters exhausts me utterly and my head aches all the time. There is hardly a moment that I am free from pain . . .

"I wonder if it will ever pass? or whether I shall be able to feel again the thrill and joy of living, the pleasure of reading and working, instead of having to force myself with a will of iron to do the most trivial things, but I must be gay and cheerful for Philip's sake; it is so depressing for him. Luckily he is absorbed in his work, and I hope he doesn't realize how bad I feel. I am dead—dead—and yet I can laugh at myself."

John and Dorelia still came and went in our lives. She and I used to go out on shopping expeditions to buy him a large black hat at Heath's—a copy of the one they made for Thomas Carlyle. Which he puts on his head with a smile and marches off looking triumphantly splendid. Another expedition to buy her a large Leghorn hat which she also puts on her head with her own smile and looks mysteriously, secretively beautiful.

We also went to inspect a school for the boys. She wished to leave a message for Henry Lamb at his studio in Fitzroy Street. I waited for her outside in the taxi. It is the same house in which John had his studio. I sit and ponder, recalling the world of emotions that I traversed coming here day after day. Each visit a turmoil. What tension, fear, pain I felt with every step I took walking here. Thank God it is over, I murmured half aloud. "Won't you come in for a moment? Dorelia sent

159

me," I heard a voice say. I awoke from the past and saw standing by the door of the taxi a figure that seemed to come from
a vision of Blake, a pale, slim man, dressed in an old-fashioned
mustard-coloured coat, a green and yellow silk scarf round his
neck, an almost transparent face and pale golden hair starting
back from his forehead in pale flames.

I followed him into the familiar hall, up and around the intricate dirty stairs, to a small studio at the top of the house.
Here was Dorelia, and another young woman dressed in the
then unusual John-like dress—light bodice, long-waisted and
full skirt, tall black hat with a feather dropping down. She had
arched eyebrows and a drooping, plaintive voice, small and slim
figure. A bed was in the corner and a large easel and canvas,
paints, clothes all in disorder. I looked again at Henry Lamb.
His smile is angelic, but the mouth has long, curving, rather
thin lips—what do they express? But the slim visionary figure
must not be looked at too much. The three came back to tea
with me in Bedford Square.

A few days after this in early October I started off to Paris to
stay with Miss Chadbourne at the Hôtel Crillon. Philip was
to follow in a few days. I had jokingly suggested to Dorelia to
come with me. I said Miss Chadbourne would "love to have
her." I did not expect her to come, but she accepted without
hesitation. John came to the station to see her off, both arriving at the last moment, John looking grey and draggled.

Off we went together, I feeling very worried as to how I
should explain Dorelia's arrival to Miss Chadbourne. Would
she welcome her, or would she feel annoyed with me for bringing this uninvited guest? She is rich and fond of Dorelia, but
one never knows. Dorelia herself did not give it a thought, I am
sure.

At the station Miss Chadbourne met us attended by Mr.

Pritchard.[9] I hurriedly tried to explain about Dorelia, and suggested that she should come "for the night," knowing that if she was housed even for a night she would remain. Miss Chadbourne took it all for granted, and we glided off to the Hôtel Crillon in her motor. Pritchard at once began a disquisition on aesthetic philosophy, and preached his theory of existence without food. As I had not eaten anything all day, I was nearly fainting, and had to interrupt his theories by asking for some soup and toast. Dorelia, I believe, even suggested a lobster. I felt very strange and lonely without Philip in this suite of luxurious, over-heated rooms. It was uncomfortable to me to be the guest of anyone (and at such expense) that showed so little warmth or cordiality in welcoming me. Why had she pressed me to come? Did anyone's presence make a difference to her? She appeared so completely detached, as if she was absorbed in contemplation—but of what?

Sometimes I felt that she had drifted into our passionate and exiciting modern world from a novitiate in a Buddhist temple. Money was her only tangible means of contact with this European life, but even this brought the East to her door, for she gathered round her dark and dusky dealers from whom she would buy rare Persian carpets, priceless Persian plates that

[9] Pritchard, Ottoline once told me, was unkindly referred to by some people as "the little brother of the rich." Logan Pearsall Smith had a story of a fashionable lady saying about him, "It's wonderful! He lies on the floor, and bites the hearth-rug, and says 'There is no God!' " From the same authority I had it that during the 1914–18 war he claimed to have kept raiding Zeppelins away from London by his own will-power. When I was at Oxford, he read a paper to an undergraduate society concerned with the visual arts. His thesis was that art is ceremony, and that nothing of aesthetic value had been produced in Europe between the decay of Byzantine art and the early paintings of Matisse.

would be stored in the mysterious, dimly lit and asphyxiating rooms of her flat in Park Lane.

The rooms that she now occupied were on the top floor of the hotel. Outside was a wide terrace with a stone balustrade round. Even here I had the impression of standing on the edge of a remote Eastern temple looking down in imagination rather than in reality on a vision of Paris, so far below and distant did it seem. The rushing, tearing life of motor-cars with their lights darting across the open Place, the dark Bois de Boulogne with its blue and yellow lights stationary, speculating on its secret life. Far away, faintly outlined above it all, the dome of the Invalides.

Standing there by the side of this little, quiet, pale, composed, remote woman, with her toneless American voice, I felt that it was she who had come, not from a new country but from some old, old worn-out land where all enthusiasm, all power of feeling had been burnt out, and who watched and watched—occasionally smiling a very charming, sad, disillusioned smile at the antics of these silly people.

How separate and remote we all were from each other: Dorelia, nonchalant; I myself so torn with feelings, interested and aware of the tragedy and frenzy and recklessness of life below and so unwilling to be ignorant of any corner of life, following in my imagination the threads that shot through the darkness.

Next morning we all walked over to the Salon d'Automne. It was my first sight of the very modern French pictures which were soon to be called Post-Impressionist. There was Matisse with his dazzling and beautiful colours and spreading and sprawling figures, Fergusson's large violent portraits, Valadon's leaden-coloured nude male and female boxers, outrageous portraits by Van Dongen of nude women with black eyes and black silk stockings, and Van Gogh paintings of flowers and landscapes of Provence, passionate and flame-like, pure and beautiful, in their midst. I felt excited and bewildered by the newness.

After luncheon we went to see the famous collection of Manets and Cézannes belonging to Monsieur Pellerin at Neuilly—a gentleman who had made his fortune in margarine. The Cézannes were new to me. At first I found them a little cold after the heated, excitable pictures I had seen in the morning, but as I looked and looked they unfolded their great beauty and nobility. Groups of nude figures against the grey-blue background, with perhaps a touch of red. Rocks and villages of Provence, rough and rugged Nature remodelled, re-created into something in which rhythm and pattern were condensed—a vision that to most mortals would have been seen and forgotten in an hour was by him absorbed and held and re-expressed as by magic and made permanent. The Creator certainly allows some of his children to take a brush and to gaze at a particle of this old earth, and transform it by absorption in their imagination into something so new, so illumined, that it surpasses the original.

We went from here to Rumpelmeyer's for tea. Horrible place, full of money-grabbing repulsive women—I hated it so much that it made me feel ill. Then Dorelia and I went off to the Quartier Latin to look for Gwen John, and found some charming red slippers for the John boys and Julian. Dorelia spends with the care that women who have no banking account do, whose all is in the strong dark purse they carry.

Next day we went to Versailles, and wandered about the gardens and alleys, and found some fountains that I had never seen. It is inexhaustibly beautiful, but I missed Philip dreadfully. None of my companions really enjoyed it or had any thrill of pleasure in its beauty and romance. They seemed dead, and as if they saw nothing. Pritchard is only interested in his own thoughts. He will only eat salads and his only sign of being human is his extreme irritability.

On Friday we went to Matisse's studio, through a most delightful part of Paris, deserted and overgrown, round the ramparts and out beyond on the great straight cobbled roads. Matisse gave me the impression of a commercial businessman. I could not trace any connection between him and his art. He seems exceedingly competent, but it is difficult to imagine that he has an inward vision of beauty. Obviously he has great sense of design and form and ability of hand. He looks more Flemish than French with his fair beard and square face. Miss Chadbourne and I sat before a chair on which a portfolio of his drawings were propped. He stood turning them over for us to see and choose one to buy. She appeared to take no interest, indeed hardly looked at the drawings, but from time to time picked off little bits of dust and fluff from her black skirt. She gave no heed to his remarks and explanations. When he had gone through the drawings she silently got up, without any comment, wandered round the room, took up a small bronze figure in her white-gloved hand and said she would like to buy it and walked out to her motor, Matisse bowing to her very graciously on seeing his bronze figure depart with her. I wondered if he thought her as strange a figure as I did, or whether he simply held up his hands and said, *"Encore une Américaine!"*

Leaving him, we motored on out of Paris to the place where the aeroplanes are tried. The country was very beautiful in the October evening light, flat, with hayricks, and we flew along the long paved avenues, double rows of poplars on either side. We passed a man who had been knocked down by a motor-car. The poor hunched figure and high shoulders being lifted into the car made an awful picture by the side of the lonely long road.

The flying machines seemed very ugly and made a deafening noise. We stopped and watched them from an old bridge.

That night Philip was to arrive from London. At the barrier of the dark station I waited for him, one of the ever-changing group that waits, waits for the great roaring, panting engine to arrive and vomit forth its load of tired travellers. Around me they stood, anxiously straining their eyes, having come through dark streets to show that there is one ardent heart the lonely traveller can rely on in this great chaotic rushing town where, if one enters alone, one feels one must disappear for ever. I look at some standing by me and caught the vibrations and doubts that I see passing over their faces, half afraid to be "sure," half afraid to be "glad." "Will he come?"

It has arrived and figures hurry along the platform. Valises in hand, one passes through; he waits; he searches, no face is found that gives him a smile of recognition, and out into the dark night he walks alone. Was I too to be disappointed? I search, but at last in the distance I think I see Philip's tall figure, and then I see him waving, and a great rush of relief flows over me—he has really come!

We went back to the hotel and found Dorelia sitting in an armchair just as I had left her, passive and imperturbable.

Next day Philip was caught up into the motor and whirled off with us to see more modern pictures. Monsieur Vollard took us from his shop to his private house, where on a top floor, like a great gruff bear, he hoards his treasures. Gauguins, Manets, Picassos and, above all, Cézannes—amongst them his own portrait. He puts on a pair of old gloves and brings them out one by one from piles that are stacked against the walls. He is a

165

large, bearded, taciturn man—a character that might have been known to Balzac.

After dinner we went to see more pictures at Mr. and Miss Stein's. They are American Jews and have their great bare rooms lined with pictures by Matisse. An astonishing sight, glaring and gay, crude but great beauty of line. There was one lovely one of a woman sitting in a wood. It was one of those interminable evenings where we continually wandered round the room, and no one dared to talk, silenced perhaps by the clamour that seemed to shout from the walls. Miss Chadbourne stood vaguely about with a bunch of flowers in her hand.

The remaining two or three days are rather a bewildered kaleidoscope. Visits to Montmartre searching for Picasso, where the old houses and studios and a little open *place* are scenes that have sunk into my memory to illustrate Paris life. *Cafés Chantants* and *Bals Tabarins* at nights, excitements about the execution of Ferrer, a Spanish educationalist. *Feuilletons* were wildly sold in the streets, inviting people to come and protest. How far off and past it seems now!

After a couple of days Philip and I started off on our journey to Provence. It was good to find ourselves sitting in the railway carriage, free to live as we planned and glad to escape from so much unconnected, luxurious excitement. That lovely October morning, after gazing out of the window and enjoying the wide fields and long alleys, I turned my attention to our fellow-passengers. Opposite to me was a square-built, middle-aged man, obviously French, of the lawyer middle-classes. I was surprised to see that the newspaper he was reading was our English *Times*. After an hour or two, I said to him in English, "I see you are reading an English paper." To my surprise I found that he could read but not talk English, or even understand it easily. However, Philip and he started a long and interesting talk about French and English politics, and he was interested to find that Philip was a Member of Parliament. He said, "I also am a Député." They discussed the important men in both countries and it was on the tip of my tongue to say, "I suppose one of the most remarkable men in France is Jaurès—"

Philip asked him if he would show him the Chamber. "Certainly, if you don't mind being seen with a Socialist." We laughed and explained that we were Radicals. After more friendly and very interesting talk, he wrote his name on a card and passed it to us and begged us to let him know when we were next in Paris. I looked at the name he had written, "Jaurès, Député de Carmaux."

We soon arrived at Lyons where he was to address a large meeting that night. He was met by a small crowd of men and we watched them from the carriage window gathering round him in excitement and deference, escorting him out.

He was the first man shot in the war in August 1914. He not only gave his life for France but died for humanity and peace. It was at a large meeting in Paris in August 1914 to protest against the war that he was assassinated.

On our return to England we had to devote ourselves to preparing for the election that took place in January 1910.

For nearly two months we toiled night and day. "The horrors of the election swallowed me up," I noted at the time. Two or three meetings a night, with the tide against us.

Very few of these days stand out in my memory. At some places we were stoned and booed at.[1] Watlington was particularly violent. Bertie Russell had come with us to speak at a large

[1] Ottoline writes with concern of these occasions but, in fact, she found something exhilarating in them. I remember her talking about scenes of the kind and saying, "I loved it. I wanted to cry out to them, 'Go on! Shout at us! Throw things at us! I don't care.'" And she threw out her arms as if in an ecstasy of martyrdom.

meeting there. There seemed no chance of anyone being listened to, much less anyone so quiet and remote as Bertie Russell, but undaunted he stood up and began to speak. Catcalls, whistles and yells redoubled, but something in his passionate sincerity and intellectual force arrested them, and in a few moments, much to our surprise, he was being listened to with attention. Very seldom have I seen intellectual integrity triumph over democratic disorder.

After the election, when we were beaten, we returned to London, depressed and weary. A telegram was waiting for Philip asking him to help in the organization of the Gladstone League,[2] which was being started by the *Daily News*.

Philip was made secretary, and he devoted himself with great energy to the work. It was a difficult task, as his fellow-workers were inefficient and unpractical. I also worked there every day, going down to the office at St. Stephen's House, Westminster, early every morning and remaining until six in the evening.

It was my first experience of office work, and I found it intolerably wearisome, sitting all day at a table opening and sort-

[2] It was a huge unwieldly collection of people who had no relation to each other beyond being readers of the *Daily News,* and being ready to contribute, in response to appeals of the paper, the sum of a shilling a year to the League's funds. But the notion of a political league has always been attractive and highly successful. The most famous of the political leagues has been the Anti-Corn Law League, founded by Cobden and Bright to effect the repeal of the Corn Laws, which it did. Besides that there was the Primrose League, founded by Lord Randolph Churchill in memory of Disraeli, and run by fashionable ladies and their friends to promote the interests of the Conservative Party— which also had considerable success. After that came the Liberal League, founded by Lord Rosebery and his friends to promote the interests of Lord Rosebery; and now there was to be the Gladstone League, founded by the *Daily News,* to promote the interests of the Liberal Party and the *Daily News.*   P.M.

ing letters. It was only with the greatest determination that I compelled myself to continue. After a week or so I grew more interested in the work, and gradually found the routine of office life a rest from the management of private existence; but from entries in my journal the other life still seemed to go on in the background.

I still had my Thursday evenings, preceded often by dinner-parties; Augustine Birrell, Lytton Strachey, Virginia Stephen, the Clive Bells, Arthur Ponsonby, Duncan Grant, Roger Fry, Henry Lamb, Bertie Russell were those that I saw most frequently. Bertie Russell attracted, frightened me; but everything he said had an intense, piercing, convincing quality. The first time that it dawned on me that he was not happy in his own life was one evening at dinner. Sitting next to me, he said with intensity: "There is always a tragedy in everyone's life, if one knows them well enough to find it out."

It was probably the same evening that Mr. Birrell was dining with us. I was describing with enthusiasm my delight in music-halls. "Come one evening and pick me up in a cab, and take me with you."

I picked him up a few days later, and I took him to the Tivoli to hear Harry Lauder, who was to have sung. Unfortunately he was ill that night and didn't appear. However, Victoria Monks was there, so I felt I had not brought him in vain; he was not untouched by that woman who expressed the essence of Cockney London—its vulgarity, its vitality, its human kindness, its tragedy, humour and recklessness. What charm that woman had! Her vulgar body in a tight red satin dress, short skirt with flounces and spangles, brown hair done up "on high" with a huge fringe. Her rather hoarse, thrilling voice, which had such a power of stirring and rending one when she sang "Pay Day," "Don't turn me out for it's raining tonight," or

"Give my regards to Leicester Square and remember me to the boys round there," or "I throw my affection in your direction; for you are my size and style."

Her charming little hands with black ribbons tied round the wrists would give a beckoning gesture to the audience and the whole Tivoli would join in her chorus. I often felt impelled to ring up Victoria Monks, Music-Hall Artiste, on the telephone. But what should I find? A fat, plump, little woman, probably drinking whisky and water with her jockey husband, in a room smelling of chops and cigars, lace curtains and paper fans pinned against the wall.

Now it is too late. She has left the stage of this life, but she will not fade from the memory of any who heard her. She did not sing her songs in vain. Her fine vitality and human genius singing the eternal feelings of "The People" made her one of those wonderful and dear artists that England gives birth to.

Mr. Birrell understood and enjoyed himself, I think, for he sent me a copy of the *Vita Nuova* in memory of the new life that I had led him into.

As I sat at my desk at the Gladstone League, opening and chronicling letters, the back chambers of my mind would ponder and endeavour to explore the contradictions that I was beginning to be aware of in my new friend, Henry Lamb.

On the surface so angelic, so enchanting; but as one knew him more intimately shadows of dark storms within would sweep across that fair face. I had not hitherto met anyone like him and I was intensely interested and attracted by him, for he had the rare combination of intellectual activity and the experience of artistic bohemian life. I was much older than he, and I had the instinct that I had something in me which would supply what he needed, some ingredient in which he was lacking. It was perhaps a half-maternal instinct that pushed me towards this twisted and interesting creature. He seemed to have surrounded himself with an entanglement of barbed wire to prevent anyone from knowing the real self, also to protect his own self-esteem.

He came to stay with us at our cottage at Peppard, and it was then I began to know him better. We went on expeditions and picnics in the beech woods. It was with reluctance that I admitted my companion into these woods, for they had been my refuge and I had spent hours here alone. I had my favourite groves, where I would sit alone on the trunk of a tree reading poetry or meditating on life. I felt companionship in these tall antique trees. They had known the world so long, and had withstood its storms. I loved the feel of the grey, solid trunks, that had grown out of the earth from such strong roots, and were minute by minute growing, so patient in the damp darkness of winter, and so gay with new life in spring. In the silence I could hear their groanings and creakings as they swayed to and fro bending to each other. Sitting here I lost myself and felt that I was imbibing some of their strength and calmness.

Thus I did not wholeheartedly welcome any companion in these woods, for my hours alone here were so full of happiness and ecstasy, and I lived in a realm of my own thoughts so calm and strengthening that I dreaded anyone tramping by my side, bringing perhaps an alien atmosphere of controversy and disagreement. I felt I should have to pass by my loved companions and talk to the human bundle of nerves at my side.

I know that when I took Henry Lamb there I carefully chose ways that I did not usually frequent.

But the drives that we went on were full of delight, passing beyond the beech woods to the lovely soft open down country, with long folds sculptured so subtly out of the grey chalk—so free from the frills and *passementerie* of hedges that cut up most English country in dull, monotonous squares. How I longed to dwell in these open lovely spaces, great shining ploughed fields—with patches of bright yellow mustard and purple-red sainfoin fading into the tenderest green, changing every moment, for on those lands the sky and the clouds caress and mingle their fleeting beauty, casting phantom garments over the earth. Rushing shadows sweep on with silent haste over the land, on, on, to their endless journey across the world.

Hardly a sign of human habitation was to be seen except an inn, The White Horse. It always seemed to be under a spell, so isolated and unfrequented.

When we returned to London, Philip had a visit from the chairman of the Burnley Liberal Association, inviting him to stand for Burnley. When he was interviewing them, he showed them a photograph of me saying, "That is my wife." They looked at it and said, "Yes, she will suit the Burnley Democrats all right."

We went up there and were soon engulfed in political work of all sorts—meetings, visits and social parties in the evenings. The excitement and enthusiasm of the Burnley people was astonishing. They are so much more alive, vigorous and intelligent than the southerners. But the dreariness of life there in the damp and darkness of Lancashire—the air impregnated with smoke—is terribly depressing. It seems impossible to experience any ecstasy or joy there, but they are gay and full of wit and humour, wonderful people.

In May we returned to Peppard from London. I had to remain in bed for some time as I was ill, mostly from overdoing myself in London and Burnley. Those were very happy weeks. My bed was near the window. The enervating beauty of the spring was beginning. I could see the fruit trees covered with blossom, and the faint haze of spring across the common. The window open and the scent of the fresh mown grass, and the young daisies floated in.

Philip came and went to London and the House of Commons. I heard from Lamb that John's wife Dorelia was very ill in the south of France, having had a baby girl. He went down to see her at Martigues, and wrote me delightful letters. I remember reading them as I lay in bed.

"I am so glad to be here," I wrote in my journal, "worn out and peaceful, for I have tried to give too much, 'Myself often faithless to myself,' becoming entangled with other people's lives, with the foolish frantic desire to give. It seemed to me so essential to give, to pour out of all that one possesses, but I obviously do it with too little measurement. It exhausts me, and makes me suffer too much. I thought I did not look for any return, but in this one often deceives oneself, for the subconscious desire to receive is too strong, although one's reason brushes it aside."

Now as I re-read Lamb's letters to me during those years, I am overwhelmed with sadness that I was not wiser in dealing with him, for I do not believe these letters then awoke in me the same appreciation that I now feel when I read them. How could I ever have felt annoyed with him? I can only imagine that his behaviour was constantly so hurting that it put me into a state of nerves in which I was unable to suck "the honey of his music vows" that are in his letters, and yet as I read them I find that sentences and passages are as familiar to me as lines from Shakespeare. They have sunk into my life, and have lived there, giving it warmth and richness. No words of mine could describe this demi-angel as his letters do.

I find entries in my journal that give my thoughts at this time:

173

"Julian runs in the garden; she is well and beautiful and dictatorial; and enjoys games with her father and the maids, but is autocratic to me; and whenever I make advances to her she turns from me and pushes me away. She is entrancing to those she likes, highly strung, capricious and self-willed . . .

"As I lie here too weak to move or to read much, I look back on the hectic weeks in London, the Gladstone League, friends, Thursday evenings . . . I am so thankful to be away from everyone and to lie still, and read and read and think, and to try to learn how to live. Recollections of happy days float across my mind—Gluck's *Orfeo,* that Philip and I and Henry Lamb went to hear. I hear still those heavenly airs. They vibrate in my memory.

"Long walks with Henry Lamb on Putney Common, walking miles and miles, through lovely silver birch trees, past dark pools, and out across Richmond Park. Especially one windy evening when I was wearing a long red dress. I felt as if I was a spirit with red sails being blown along. Lamb was in a good mood, and enjoyed the country, the trees, the clouds. It made him expansive and genial. He can certainly be an enchanting companion when he is in *bonne humeur.*"

Then there float to me stray remembered lines from *Richard II* and *Antony and Cleopatra* that Philip has been reading to me, transplanting me into a world of poetic life where I am happy and at home, for it is that life that I am always reaching out to, to draw it into my own life. Life lived on the same plane as poetry and as music is my instinctive desire and standard. It is the failure to accomplish this which makes me discontented with myself. After all, it isn't the buses and the Tubes, and the noise and bustle or the egotism of others that prevent it. It is my own inability to tune myself to the hidden orchestra of life. My ears are not listening to catch the strains of heavenly music that ought to be my inspiration and guide. It isn't the facts of outward life that need a change, it is my vision and imagination that needs a "sea change into something rich and strange" —to be washed from the artificial inherited conventions with which I am caked and plastered; to be bathed in a purifying sea which would dissolve the film of self that encases and blinds one from seeing life in its true reality, and shuts one off from realizing that one is an infinitesimal figure in a great rhythm where fortune and fate are weaving their purpose.

"These beautiful days are almost too much for me. They seem to make my heart break with their beauty. This evening it is bright like day, and very hot, with a pale blue light. The Halley Comet has appeared, a faint golden blue, without a tail. Philip and I walked across the common, covered with golden gorse. The pink evening light tinting the roads, and the white chalk pits, the birds singing with fullness of joy. My spirit seems like a separate self within me. I am certainly not an intellectual for I can only really live when the spirit in me is active. Indeed, I sometimes feel I am only truly happy when I am alone, and can think and commune with the unseen. I do not know what gives me the instinct that there is a personal spirit behind life. Certainly one has to live independently of human companionship and to grow from a life within oneself, to rely on one's own source of life, to be courageous and walk alone through life, with the remembrance of this unseen companion, whose presence is more real to me and more faithful than any human being, although I often drift away from the consciousness of it, into the rush of the world."

On one of my visits to London I went with Henry Lamb to see Rembrandt's picture "The Polish Rider," which was exhibited on its way to America. It had been brought from its original impoverished home in Poland. The gay rider with a fur cap and lovely coat, sitting rather loosely on his horse, is starting off into the unknown. His face is turned round to one and has the charm that youth in its sensitive bravery has—gallantry enough to meet all life's perils. "Childe Roland to the Dark Tower Came," off on his journey through life: gallantry easily equal to whatever obstacles life may provide.

In July 1910 we went to La Bourboule, where I had to take the waters. The life that one lives at these places is made of infinitely small things—a pocket-book stolen with forty pounds in notes, expeditions to various tea places, listening to music, conversations with other guests in the hotel—which in after-years fade away and become woven into the pattern of life's tapestry, or are like characters in a book that one has read many years ago. A young French writer, Du Fresnois, nervous and clever, who was killed in the war—it was to him that I owe the knowledge of two French writers—Jules Renard and Colette. There was also a charming, tall, dark girl, with short hair, who wore a long white coat and who with her long legs and charming white face might have been one of Turgenev's heroines—for *On the Eve*—she was called Marthe.

When my cure was ended, we travelled on to join Augustus John and Dorelia at Aix in Provence, halting on the way at Marseilles as I wanted to see the frescoes by Puvis de Chavannes. I don't remember them very vividly, not as I do the narrow streets and *Le Vieux Port* where the *filles de joie* live. It was a hot day, and they sat or stood at the doors of their houses, talking to each other across the narrow street—they were all but nude—wearing only a short pink or white laced chemise, or a minute frilled petticoat, paste combs ornamenting their elaborately pomaded hair, their faces rouged and powdered, ready for customers even at midday. As they leaned against their door-posts, some of them looked very lovely with their naked limbs in the sunlight. One young girl with red hair, exquisite and thin and gentle, was talking to a sailor whose face was eaten away by disease. I was fascinated by the teeming life of this *Vieux Port*. Life bare and stripped of clothes and decorum, a chaotic emporium of East and West. African soldiers in acid yellow khaki and bright red caps, oriental sailors mounting up through the winding streets to the Old Town. It has the chaotic intensity of life that must have existed in Carthage, or Alexandria. Then to sit at one of the huge cafés on the Cannebière. How well one could imagine Conrad here in his reckless youth, drinking black coffee at a little table outside, or sitting among the draught-players in the big inner halls. If once one has mingled in these crowds, one always has the desire to return. Project one's imagination to its limit into this packed, intense corner of the globe. It still remains fascinating and unknown, for as one sits at one of those little round tables sipping coffee, one realizes it would be impossible to shed the mantle of one's past and one's own inherited code of morals sufficiently to enter into this strange world. One would be always left outside, watching the gamble, with its seasons of waiting and boredom and its swift unseen ruthless twist of hand, gay, harsh and sinister. The door is shut on one's experience, one can only sit and look at it through the glass window. It is tilted round the corner where one could not walk steadily.

On arriving at Aix we found John and Dorelia sitting outside a café, Dorelia dressed in a striped cotton skirt and a yellow scarf over her head, looking beautiful in a gypsy way. They had come over from Martigues in their donkey-cart. John had cut his square beard and wore it in the pointed French style, which made him look like a dissipated Frenchman as his eyes were bloodshot and yellow from brandy and rum.

177

We went to see Cézanne's house, which is on the outskirts of Aix. A small chateau, with an oblong Provençal basin of water, a little statue at one end, and an ilex grove and avenue leading down into vineyards. The two ladies who live there, mother and daughter, showed us over the house. There were some decorations by Cézanne on the walls of the drawing-room. One of Christ and four of the seasons, which he painted when he was quite young and signed "Ingres." These have now been removed and sold to a Paris dealer. The two ladies were very upset to see Dorelia wearing sandals. *"Pauvre femme,"* they exclaimed, shaking their heads in pity, evidently thinking that she was too poor to afford shoes and stockings.

Next day we wandered round the town with John and Dorelia looking at churches, and the tomb of Joseph Sec which was erected in the year 4 of the Revolution.

John was a bored and weary sightseer. In the afternoon when we returned we found him sitting outside a café drinking happily with the little untidy waiter from the hotel and a drunken box-maker from the street nearby. In his companions he requires only a reflecting glass for himself, and thus he generally chooses them from such inferiors. He seems curiously unaware of the world, too heavily laden and oppressed with boredom to break through and to realize life. He who had the capacity to become one of the very greatest of English painters has now taken the easy path of being a portrait painter. What a hard thing it is to be an artist—or rather to keep the talent strong and untainted. To see and to grip, to wrestle with the vision, to form and mould it into a whole, which alone can be accomplished by clearing away distractions. No mistress, no lover is more exacting than the creative instinct. It must absorb and drive on, scattering out of the path extraneous pleasures, if it is to develop into greatness such as Michelangelo, Cézanne or Van Gogh.

178

*Lady Ottoline
and Julian at
Peppard Cottage*

Peppard Cottage. The Morrell home for about five years from 1907

v

Lady Ottoline at Mells Manor,
Somerset, with Edward Horner

Garsington Manor, the terrace door

We left Aix regretfully. The old Hôtel des Thermes, its long dark corridors, its old furniture, were so sympathetic that we always wanted to return there. In 1929 we did so, but, alas, the hotel that we knew was no more. It had become an uncomfortable and expensive *hôtel de luxe*. Aix itself appeared even more beautiful on this second visit. Is it that as one grows older things appear more beautiful? The understanding and the eyes are more enlightened and educated. Perceptions and sensibilities are keener to appreciate beauty that perhaps years before was ignorantly passed over.

The lovely town of Aix, which still retains the air of a capital city with its wide streets and plane tree avenues, and its lovely fountains, appeared to me far more beautiful and interesting in 1929 than it had done twenty years before. Greek and Roman influences still seem to permeate Provence—its antique language still retaining the poetry and romance that does not exist in other parts of France. The beauty of the land that inspired Cézanne and that gave up to him its secret and its magic, and which he again formed into a new creation, seemed to me doubly beautiful. Beautiful in itself and beautiful by having been revealed by him.

On our return to England we were again at our cottage at Peppard, quiet and happy. I read a great deal; Tolstoy's *A Life* was what I remember most vividly. *A Life* has always had a great attraction for me, for in spite of his fanaticism and exaggeration he seemed to know what things really mattered and to see through the absurd shams of life. He, perhaps, is one of the few great writers whose personal life is as interesting and important as his art, for it seems as if he had so much vitality and genius that he had enough for a great life as well as for a great artist. He not only felt his own reactions but had the creative imagination of feeling and understanding the experiences of those he saw or met in life. I can never forget the

179

story of when he and Turgenev were out walking they came upon an old horse, and as Tolstoy patted it he began to tell Turgenev its history as a young and beautiful mare, its pride and its vanity, and its decay. Turgenev interrupted him, saying, "Tolstoy, I believe you have *been* a horse."

That indeed was the secret of Tolstoy's life, that around and united to his actual personality there seemed to be an unlimited capacity for becoming other Tolstoys, and indeed for entering in imagination into the experience of alien lives from his own. In youth he plunged hither and thither and was first one Tolstoy and then another, always reacting back to his own centre with remorse and new resolutions, only to dash out again into life in a new form, and so on until he reached the period after his marriage when for some years he was absorbed and unified by family life and by writing his great novels. But peace and calm was never to last in that great character. The storms of his genius and of his passionate search for the right life tore him up from this happiness and drove him on and on like Lear in the storm into the wild and lonely night.

Such are the jottings that I find in my journal of these days, and again thinking of him and feeling how lovable and fine he was makes me feel that the men one knows are poor and meagre in heart and character. They do not even seem to desire to expand their hearts, imaginations. They mincingly say it would be *incommode*. They pretend to have no heart and put sensation and excitement in its place. They do not even seem to desire the wisdom of the heart, which, as Tolstoy said, is more valuable than the wisdom of the head.

About this time we went to Cambridge for a week-end on a visit to Lowes Dickinson. I know that I did not enjoy it very much as it was wet and cold all the time, and it seemed dreary paddling about in the wet. Goldie collected his friends to luncheons and dinners, and did his utmost to amuse us. There was Bertrand Russell, E. M. Forster, Roger Fry, the Whiteheads, and I remember a delightful talk with Mr. Whitehead about Tolstoy. It ought to have been all delightful, but I felt constrained and shy, and I was not at my ease. The circulation of my being seemed arrested, feet so cold and head so hot. On Sunday I went alone to tea with Jane Harrison, who had a tea-party, and there among others I met Lytton Strachey. I half-laughingly suggested that he should come and stay with us at Peppard. He pondered it very seriously, drifted away, but after a few moments he came back to me and said, "Do you really mean me to come to Peppard?" and I said, "Of course I do," with the usual fear and dread inside me that I could not make him happy.

Passing through London on our way back to Peppard, we were to meet Henry Lamb. He was waiting for us in Philip's library at Bedford Square in a state of nervous tension. He was coming down to Peppard with us to install himself into a studio that we had found and done up for him, and was bringing large quantities of luggage with him. When Philip suggested that his luggage should go on ahead and that we could follow in a taxi, he asked, "Why do you object to driving with my luggage overhead?" It was not an easy journey down. However, it was managed without any quarrel. He stayed the night with us and next day installed himself in his studio and in his lodgings at the Dog Inn.

In a few days the visit from Lytton Strachey that I had feared came about. I felt he came more to see Henry Lamb than to see me. In my journal I say that "he terrified me" at first, but I found him more sympathetic than I had imagined, but there is something wanting in him, and something wrong with him: a perfect Epicurean without large or generous instincts, but from his exceedingly fine brain he sees light and has appreciation of nobility, but shrinks back, partly from pose, and from prejudice and nervousness. He is indeed delicate in his health and that helps to encourage self-indulgence. He too is one of those in whom feminine characteristics are strong.

He and Lamb sat up until very late at night in the little sitting-room underneath my bedroom, and I heard the duet of their voices underneath, laughing and joking, Lytton playing with him like a cat with a mouse, enjoying having his own sensations tickled by Lamb's beauty, while his contrariness adds spice to the contact. I call him the Polish count, for he seemed to me as if he was a character out of a Russian novel.

It was just before the General Election and Philip was already at Burnley, hard at work. I joined him soon after Lytton's visit, but I invited him to come and stay at our cottage while we were at Burnley, which he did for two or three weeks. I travelled up to Burnley with my dear maid Brentie—we missed trains, were delayed in fogs and arrived very late, and I had at once to go off to a dance. The next weeks were spent in a continual rush—excitements and nervous tension. The blackness and ugliness of Burnley appalled me and seemed to enter into me, but soon I grew accustomed to it, and found the people very wonderful, intelligent, electric and full of humour, and free from the pomposity of the south. I was pleased and cheered by receiving delightful letters almost every day from Lamb and Lytton Strachey at Peppard.

At last the Election Day arrived. I write:

"It was perfectly awful waiting three hours in the coffee room of the inn, for the result. Old Mr. and Mrs. Collinge and their son and daughters-in-law and the Keys were there, and were all so kind and thoughtful, but I longed to be alone and nearly went mad. Then at last I heard the cheering far away, and I thought that meant it was all against us. No cheering near the hotel, and sure enough the Boots brought word that 'Arbuthnot was in by nineteen' . . . My only thought was 'Nineteen, nineteen.' 'Why didn't we work harder?' But then he returned to say he was 'not sure' and in a few minutes Philip himself rushed in, excited and happy. The cheering was so great that I could not hear him and had to ask him to shout the result in my ear. He was in by a hundred and seventy-three. The crowd outside was like a sea, and the shouting and cheering indescribable . . ."

We returned to Peppard after the Election and had some visitors to stay with us: Roger Fry, with whom at this time we were very intimate, and who used to come and stay with us constantly. He had been arranging the Post-Impressionist Exhibition and was full of excitement and enthusiasm for the modern French painters. Indeed, it was due to him that they were brought to England.

Lamb's friend, Boris von Anrep, arrived from Paris, clever, fat, good-hearted, sensual, but full of youthful vitality and Russian gaiety. The following weeks seem to have been a mixture of talk and week-end visits from the Clive Bells and Virginia Stephen, and Desmond MacCarthy. A journey to London to see pictures there. Another visit from Roger Fry to meet Boris Anrep and Helen Maitland. I wonder if these three ever remember their first meeting, for the whirligig of time has brought about strange shiftings. Helen Maitland became first Anrep's wife. After some years she left him to live with Roger Fry.

Our cottage was too small to have people to stay in. It seemed as if we were entertaining in a bathing-box. Their personalities seem pressed too closely upon one.

I wrote in my journal:

"I shall never forget the eclipse of the moon that took place at this time. It was blood-orange red across the moon like a Van Gogh picture, flaming and terrible. We stood out on the common. Shooting stars too were flying across the sky, the orange flame over the moon. The heavens seemed aflame and it woke up all one's imagination to realize the possibilities of existence. I see that gorgeous tremendous things exist if one only looks for them, is awake to see them. But one goes through life with a bandage of stupidity over one's perceptions.

"This eclipse and Van Gogh seemed very akin. He with his super-penetrating vision saw the marvels of life, nature, the passionate beauty behind the banalities of life. The veils were rent away from before his eyes, and he saw the soul of the world, as we can only see it in rare moments of ecstasy.

"Virginia Stephen came for a week-end and I had long talks with her on all kinds of subjects.

"She feels artists are 'rather brutes,' that literature and poetry are much finer. I thought Virginia wonderful, and much more natural and full-blooded and human than when I saw her last. Her lovely intellectual imagination is like a bird—a swallow flying over life with sword-like wings.

"How hard it is to accept people as they are, not as one wants them to be.

"That is my great fault that I always want the people I love and am interested in to be 'my wished-for person,' to be perfect in my way. I must learn to accept their moods as I accept my own.

"The mauve-pink sunlight on the fallow field is a rapture to me.

"Desire seems to make one batter one's wings against other people's cages, they look so lovely inside, so variegated and attractive, as if they held such lovely treasures, and then when one approaches them with dainties in one's hand, one is wounded by their beaks that dart through the cage and tear one's offered hand. Just a few people let one inside, but how few, and if they do they want to keep one inside as their private property.

"I get very weary and tired of living for people, and enjoy more and more being alone, but I suppose by following one's foolish desires one learns a good deal of one's own weakness and selfishness, and of the madness and foolishness of the world, and of the infinite unsolved problems that trip one up at all the steps in life. One's face is smacked and one's heart is torn and one cries out in agony.

"But the joy of personal contacts is the greatest excitement one can have in life, and is never satisfied.

"But it is only by work that one finds happiness. I would turn from personal contacts and give it up if I didn't feel within me that my power of loving people was a sincere thing—in fact the only touch of genius that I possess.

"But I get very weary and worn out."

When Desmond MacCarthy was with us we amused ourselves one evening making up maxims. I don't think any of them are exceptionally good, but these are a few that I remember:

"If you always choose, you will never possess."

"If you always differentiate, you will never understand."

"If you want to know yourself, you must let others know you."

"When God spoke, He said 'Thou shalt have no other gods but me, but others may.'"

Desmond is so good-natured, affable and generous in his talk, full of human kindness and understanding. How I enjoy a large character in which I can move about, turn round and not fear to hurt myself against angles and corners and sharp nails that stick out and tear one's flesh.

On February 12th 1911, Ethel Sands came for a week-end and I found I could talk to her more freely than I could before, keep hold of a thread and work it out. "It is a great joy in life," I wrote, "to be sure of anyone that one can plunge into them and get out their inward thoughts. Friendship is after all the chief joy of this life—all the other excitements wear and tear and worry one beyond their worth."

I find as I re-read these entries that it is just twenty years ago. Do I still say that friendship is the chief joy of this life? Yes, but intimacy is rare and dangerous. Perhaps there are times of ebb and times of flow in all friendships. The tide comes in strong and enveloping, stimulating round the lonely bit of rock on which one sits, and then it retreats.

On February 22nd Brentie and I started off to Studland in Dorsetshire. I had been ill and tired and went there to recover. I was depressed and weary.

"It is all because I have no definite work to do in the world. All my 'work' is so intangible and vague and floating.

"How shall I ever teach Julian? I may be able to form her and direct her. I only hope she doesn't feel antagonistic to me. I must try and keep open and young and understanding, and to be in love with each moment of life, as I hope she will be, and not become as most middle-aged people who look on the present bright, silly, gay moments, full of folly as they may be, as if they were dim events miles away. They seem to look on people's present passions as we do on events that have taken place years ago, and like a horse trotting along a road far away. We may feel them so after a few years have blurred them, but at the moment they are vivid and gay.

"It is lovely here—a long stretch of warm sea-sand, a rough

gorse country with dark fir woods. The colours are pale like Conder's pictures, and I find iridescent shells lying on the sands, shining in the sun like butterflies' wings. I am very happy and enjoy the freedom and solitude very much. Of course I long for Philip to come, but I am so tired that I am glad to rest and be alone.

"I am reading Colette Willy's *Vagabonde* and I find it most sympathetic. Few women can write, but when they are good I find it refreshing to be in contact with a woman's mind and experiences. No man writer really knows what we feel, they don't understand the tender ideal passions we have. Men can write of their psychology, and their own feelings, which generally are tolerant friendliness, or else are really the outcome of sex, or very soon tend that way. But women can love apart from the physical side, or if that comes in, it comes as a meeting of two souls.

"Men say that sex is always in a woman's eye, but I don't believe it is. They certainly desire love and tenderness and consideration. Men always want to be the masters of the women they love.

"Colette has that love of beauty in nature, that intimate almost physical love of some corners of the earth, which make one leave something of oneself behind at certain spots, and in return one carries the vivid memory and impression of them with one on one's journey. Does this come from the instinctive desire to escape from one's own imprisonment, to fly off and dwell in a land that demands nothing?

"Love in such people's lives is never a happy, careless thing. It is a painful dragging of oneself away from the world of solitude where one is happy and calm. It is distracting and makes too great an impression. Is it *la volupté* that tempts one out of one's Eden, or is there such a thing as mutual attraction without *volupté* that makes it possible for two creatures to help each other and yet keep their separate lives sane and uninebriated? I am sure that this is possible, and one must guard against casting oneself away, casting down all that has been built up in one's inner life with such effort. Guard against *mésalliance*. One can give to these inferior souls largely, generously, sympathetically, affection and tenderness, but not one's inner freedom. One can be their comrade but not their subject. If there is *volupté,* a woman is enthralled, and she ought to be enthralled only by someone she is proud to call master.

"But it is easy to write all this, but how difficult it is to be careful of oneself, to be economical with oneself."

¶ *February 24*

"I met Philip at Swanage—he was tired from the House of Commons and from his journey.

"We drove back in the sunshine and had tea and then went down to the sea, and walked along the sands, nearly to Poole Harbour, finding lovely iridescent shells. Philip was as excited as I was about them. The sun blew all the cobwebs away. He is so satisfying and the only person in the world that I can talk to, and turn upside down in, and discuss my thoughts without fear of being misunderstood. He is the only man I desire to call master."

¶ *February 27*

"Philip went back today. I drove into Swanage with him. It seems very sad without him. We had two blissful days walking about and talking, gay and happy, like old days. I am much happier when I am free from other friendships and devote myself to him, but I learn and gain understanding from excursions. For I am still inexperienced like a child, and so unsure, and simple; but am I, I wonder?"

188

¶ *March 1st*

"I miss Philip very much and it seems lonely without him now that he has been here. '*C'est lui qui est vraiment mon camarade.*'

"I am reading the life of Ferdinand Lassalle by Brandes. He was an amazing man, and I find his life very thrilling. Such great courage, fire.

"Genius does not often give much to those near them. They are too self-absorbed, but still they give their personality and greatness. Lassalle's personality and richness of thought must have been overwhelming, even though he didn't overwhelm with love and affection.

"If a man doesn't give affection or tenderness in friendship, he must have other riches at his bank that one can draw on. Carlyle had, although he gave the minimum household affection, and even, I feel, is great and rich enough to warrant his heartlessness.

"I feel upset getting to London. All my lovely peace and calm washed away by the flood of life and people here. They are all so interesting and thrilling, but very exhausting."

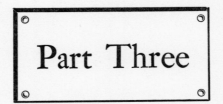

Part Three

Bedford Square: Peace and War

CHAPTER I

An Ever-Widening Circle

IN MARCH (1911) Philip and I went down to Guildford for a week-end to stay with Roger Fry in order to look for a house, as he was very anxious that we should live near him. We motored round the country, and saw several nice houses, but I suppose they were too expensive or not suitable, for we didn't take one. There was, perhaps, an instinctive sense of caution that held us off.

Junia Anrep arrived from Paris to stay with me on March 9th. She was a charming, fair, childlike creature, very Russian, gay and clever, and we made great friends. She was much more understanding and intelligent than most Englishwomen, and from having more belief in the perfectibility of human beings she saw one through simpler and truer eyes. Most English-women, if they were of the worldly or conventional order, looked on me as affected or irreligious or immoral, from know-ing such people as Augustus John; or if they were of the intellectual and advanced group, were perhaps even more puz-zled; I was in their eyes a sentimental and romantic dressed-up worldling—an endless source of amusement and wonder.

I took Junia Anrep down to Peppard with me, as I had promised to go there to sit to Henry Lamb. He wanted to finish

193

a portrait that he was doing of me. I was glad to have her with me, as she acted as a shield against his irritability. If he found a strand of hair in a different position to what it was the day before he would make me feel that I had committed a most grievous offense against Art, and I was grateful to Junia when she told him not to be so silly.

In April, Philip, Julian and I went to Studland (where we had taken a house for a few weeks). It was lovely spring weather, the leaves just opening and the birds singing, the evening light on the sea and yellow sands was tender and beautiful. I was happy with Philip and Julian—who was then seven years old and ran along the sands in a little blue kilt and jersey, or galloped on a little rough Shetland pony we had hired for her.

The day I was leaving Studland, Oliver Strachey arrived and begged me to come and see Lytton who was ill at Corfe, with mumps. I stopped on the way to London and had an amusing interview with Lytton—leaning out of the window of a small inn. I was not allowed to see him indoors for fear of infection. He looked so well with a beard that he had grown that I begged him to keep it, which he has done. I went on a delightful walk with Oliver, who was just engaged to be married to Ray Costello. He was much surprised and amused at the way I was able to fling my legs over the stiles, but somehow I felt very gay and happy that day.

On May 18th I find in my journal:

"Winston Churchill dined with us, also Massingham, Desmond MacCarthy and his wife, Virginia Stephen, Roger Fry, J. Wedgwood and his wife, Noel Buxton and Humphrey Paul. Winston was on his way to a Court Ball and was in full dress uniform, looking like a mock Napoleon. He talked high politics, which sounded to me almost like high Mathematics,

194

for he is very rhetorical, and has a volcanic, complicated way of talking which is difficult to listen to, or to gather what he really thinks."

He was immensely taken with two Picasso etchings that hung on the stairs.

On May 20th I had a surprising visit from Roger Fry. We were in the habit of seeing him very often and considered him one of our most intimate friends. He stayed with us in London and at Peppard whenever he desired. His wife had for some years been mad and one of my most painful duties was to go and see her. I never knew why Roger exacted this from me, but as I was always willing to help him I did it and suffered terribly from sympathy with her, and from the strain of adapting myself to talk to her and to avoid anything that would excite her. Roger himself was most devoted and kind to her, but it is never good for anyone who is sensitive to live with even the slightly insane, for it tends to make them deal with other people as if they were also insane. However, our friendship with him was unclouded and intimate.

When he suggested coming to see me, I was expecting one of our usual happy and interesting intimate talks—news about a visit he had paid to Constantinople. I had been out in the morning with Bertie, choosing a table for his room in Cambridge as a birthday present. I think I was feeling happy and holiday-like, as it was a Saturday afternoon, which is a favourite day with me. I do not remember if I had seen him since his return from Constantinople, where he had been with Vanessa and Clive Bell and Norton—but I expected to hear of the things he had seen and done. Perhaps we started at Constantinople, but very soon he travelled from there, for he suddenly turned on me with a fierce and accusing expression, commanding me to explain why I had spread abroad that he was in love with me. I was so utterly dumbfounded, for this thought had never entered my head—and I had certainly not uttered such an absurd thing to anyone. Denial was useless. Roger was eloquently accusing and whatever I said in denial I was only told "were lies." After nearly two hours of expostulation on my side and insistence on his, I felt shattered and hopeless and was reduced to tears—a very rare thing in my life. To battle any longer was useless. Whatever I said, his only answer was, "You know that you are not facing the truth." He refused to tell me from whom he had heard this absurd story, indeed his behaviour seemed to me quite unbalanced and he paid no attention to what I said to him.

Whatever the cause, one of my most intimate and delightful friendships crumbled to dust that Saturday. It had obviously been built on a quicksand. I had never understood the real cause of this sudden fit of destruction. It was probably some bruise on the large area of his vanity. I had never before realized what mischief a slander could do.

Since that day I have never had any intercourse with Roger. We speak when we meet at a Gallery or at another house, but even his face has a veil torn from it and it always now appears to me to resemble that of an untrustworthy dog, who softly pads up to one, fawns on one and licks one's hand, but who will nearly always turn and bite. Since this time he has never failed to speak ill of me, and I am told that he describes me as someone who delights in cruelty. But such things I have learnt to ignore, although in past days such malicious inventions caused me much pain.

We spent some part of that summer (1911) at our cottage at Peppard. These were the last months that we were to be there as we had already sold it. Lytton Strachey came and we had good talks together, as we had become more intimate. He was franker with me than he used to be, and I was less timid and nervous with him than I had been. I found my friendship with Bertie Russell was giving me more assurance as I felt that if he could care for me and like to talk to me it meant that I was not so very stupid and dull. Also my intimacy with him was leading me back into a more natural and serious world of thought than I had drifted into by my attempts to adapt myself to ————, who had been mocking and jealous of my efforts to develop my intellectual side, for he liked to keep intellectual superiority over his female friends. Also ———— was entirely lacking in the instinct of responsibility for the welfare of the nation—an instinct which both Bertie and I have, probably inherited, as each of us had come out of many generations of an historical family. Lytton talked about his writing and his shrinking from the worry and the "business of it." He had but a trembling and intermittent creative power, partly I suppose from his lack of physical vitality, and his health, about which he is nervous. He makes many excuses, such as "That it is egotistical to burden the world with one's own ideas," but this is obviously but an excuse for his own laziness—he is self-indulgent. His mind is so good, naturally, that he does not need to bestir or to exert it to keep on ahead, above ordinary men.

It is hard to realize that this tall, solemn, lanky, cadaverous man, with his rather unpleasant appearance, looking indeed far older than he is, is a combination of frivolity, love of indecency, mixed up with rigid intellectual integrity. He is, I think, frivolous about personal life, and serious about history. In these days he took a great interest in politics, but I do not see much sign of it now, beyond occasionally signing a protest in favour of free speech, for he is always intolerant of intolerance. I fancy that now it is only the politics of the past that interest him.

The steeds that draw the chariot of his life seem to be curiously ill-matched: one so dignified and serious, and so high-stepping, and of the old English breed, so well versed in the manners and traditions of the last four centuries; the other so feminine, nervous, hysterical, shying at imaginary obstacles, de-lighting in being patted and flattered and fed with sugar.

In general conversation he takes little part, rather lying in wait than giving himself away—only occasionally interrupting, throwing in a rational and often surprisingly witty remark. But *tête-à-tête* he is a charming companion—his feminine quality making him sympathetic and interested in the small things of life, and with those who know him well he is very affectionate. He may often not take any trouble to see one, but if he does he is a delightful and intimate companion, with that rare gift of remembering the past. Apart from his ordinary friendships he has attracted round him many young men and young women, whose company he apparently enjoys—partly from the pleasure he feels in instructing and enlightening youth. For he who is ordinarily severe and critical and intolerant will spend the delicate riches of his mind upon some quite unworthy and fool-ish young man or young woman, who is for the time being attractive. He will endow them with fine imaginary characteris-tics and possibilities. He who is intolerant of enthusiasms or ro-mantic ideals in his old friends is himself often carried away on his rosy clouds of romance. At this time his devotion to Henry Lamb was very great, and tossing him about on a sea of emo-tion. Lamb enjoyed leading him forth into new fields of ex-perience. They would sit in pubs and mix with "the lower orders," as Lytton called them, picking up strange friends. And so great is the imitative instinct in the human breast that he even altered his appearance to please Lamb, wearing his hair very long, like Augustus John, and having his ears pierced and wearing ear-rings. He discarded collars and wore only a rich purple silk scarf round his neck, fastened with an intaglio pin. They were a surprising pair as they walked the streets of London, as Lamb wore clothes of the 1860 period with a square brown hat, Lytton a large black Carlyle felt hat and a black Italian cape.

At the beginning of June he left us and went to Cambridge to lie in a boat and talk to his young friends on the bank as they passed by.

We returned to London when I had to prepare for an evening party for the Contemporary Art Society that we had promised to give. It was a great crowd and went off very well and was a good advertisement for the Contemporary Art Society. We had on show some of the pictures that had been bought. At that time few people took any interest in English modern art and it was amusing to see their reaction to the pictures.

The evening before, Ethel Sands, who was staying with us, went with me to the House of Commons to hear Philip speak. He was moving an amendment in order to get the proposed new St. Paul's Bridge built by a good architect, instead of merely an ordinary engineer. My brother Henry seconded the amendment. It was intensely exciting to me hearing Philip speak, for it was the first time that I had done so in the House. His speech was excellent, and his voice beautiful; he carried his amendment.

Philip and I stayed up for the Coronation. We were with the House of Commons—seats very high up, and the ceremony below looked very small and far away, and not very impressive. The little pages in red and gold, and the tall ladies-in-waiting all in gold dresses, looked beautiful, but I don't remember much else. I wore a white taffeta dress and a white lace mantilla on my head.

I really preferred the visit of a troupe of Spanish dancers

who were then in London. Augustine Birrell knew them. They were dancing at a music-hall without very much success, as the stage was too large for them. He begged me to ask them to tea to cheer them up, which I did and asked W. B. Yeats, Augustus John and a few other friends to meet them. I had not expected them to dance, but immediately they arrived they sat round the yellow rug that lay on the drawing-room floor. The little man who had brought his guitar placed a chair at one corner, and bent over his instrument and began to twang. The tall girls and another man at once jumped up and swayed and stamped and danced and clanckled the castanets madly with all the ease and inherited knowledge of centuries.

The remainder of this summer was spent at Peppard. It was one of the few English summers that are day after day hot and cloudless. Bertie was staying in lodgings at Ipsden and came over every day to see me. The beauty of his mind, the pure fire of his soul, began to affect me and attract me. We took tea out into the woods, and sat and read such things as Plato and Spinoza and Shelley, and talked of life, politics and things to come.[1] Bertie's mind travelled ahead, winding itself into the future, and speculating on what would be possible developments in life. Many of these talks that seemed so fantastic and far-reaching then are but commonplaces of life now.

A short time ago, as we were looking back at the past together Bertie and I both remembered once sitting in the woods leaning against a fallen tree talking of Rupert Brooke and a charming girl we knew with whom he had had a love affair— they had been abroad together and he had apparently tired of her, for they had parted, leaving her sad, but still the same

[1] In her journal she wrote: "I cannot remember details of this summer—great heat—B.R. at Ipsden. Coming over every day and we take tea out in the woods and read Gilbert Murray, Spinoza, Plato. . . . Why, oh why am I never happy?"   P.M.

quiet, "respectable," middle-class, sedate young woman that she had always been. From her case we speculated as to what the ideal future could be for such young people, which indeed worked itself out as what is probably now the ordinary way of life of youth—to have free intercourse with those they love, but to avoid children until they are sure of each other.

The one thing we did not discuss, strangely enough, was war. It never appeared on the horizon of our minds.

It was exhausting but delightful to me to have my mind kept in such strict order, to have to drive it on to the end of a subject, through tangled bushes and swamps, out to open ground. I often wriggled and rebelled, and wanted to hide under shady, sentimental willow trees, but this I was not allowed. Bertie would take me metaphorically by the hand and pull me up, and would perhaps take me roughly by the shoulders and shake me, telling me that I was not being honest, and that I must face the truth. Together we seemed, as we sat in those beech woods, to be on a journey through tangled and perplexing forest in search of lights, of truth, tearing down old dusty growths in my mind and opening dark windows that had been locked up in the lower depths of his being.

We soared on through space,
Voyaging through strange seas of thought alone.

In August I went off to Marienbad, leaving Philip at Peppard with Julian. When Philip joined me we remained on about a fortnight together. We made our way home by Prague and Vienna and Milan, and spent a few heavenly days in Italy, which did my spirits more good than my "cure."[2]

[2] In her journal she writes: "Yes, outside things like that do make one better. How happy we were! Then a week in Paris. Lamb and the Anreps—P. and I—and we had lovely expeditions to Versailles and St.

In October (1911) we were back in London again (44 Bedford Square). I helped Bertie furnish his flat in Bury Street near the British Museum. I enjoyed making it pretty and nice for him; he was happy to have these rooms and a few of his old family possessions in them, such as his mother's portrait and his grandfather's desk.

My life, too, was so full at home. I had Julian to attend to; she was very delicate, and needed great care. Indeed, at this time I was waiting with great anxiety to know if an operation was necessary. Philip's political life was full just then; he was working with great ardour for the welfare of Persia, seeing and interviewing many people: Professor Browne, the Persian Minister and many others. We had a large luncheon party to meet Morgan Schuster who had been recalled from Persia most unjustly, as he had been organizing the country most splendidly, but Sir Edward Grey did it at the dictation of Russia.

It was about this time that Philip and I dined at the House of Commons with Jos. Wedgwood to meet Arnold Bennett. I sat next· to him and liked him very much, he was so direct, frank, and sincere. We talked about the Potteries towns and his writing, and then about Dostoevsky. I always read his articles in *The New Age* which he wrote under the name of Jacob Tonson, mostly about life and literature in Paris, and it pleased him to hear that I read and liked them. His wife, who was French, was with him—a large, vain, silly woman. Not very long after this they parted. She was older than he was and I believe had nursed him when he was ill and lonely in Paris. A friend of hers told me that she must have been a *corsetière,* as she was the only woman that she knew who made her own

---

Germain. Trees turned to autumn colours—all gold. Saw Vollard's pictures and Salon; bought a green hat at Georgette's." P.M.

corset! Arnold Bennett came to tea with us soon after this; Desmond and Molly MacCarthy came to meet him. They got on very well, talking about Frank Harris. I believe this was the first time they had met. Molly MacCarthy always laughs at the charming little vain gestures Bennett made when I admired his very elaborate flowered silk tie, fastened with an ornate gold pin. He looked down, flicked it with his little finger, and said in his nasal rather deprecating voice, "I am pleased you like it. It *is* rather nice." His ties and his elaborate pleated and embroidered shirts were always a pleasure to me, and I am sure to himself. He told me that he got them from "The Five Towns."[3] I remember telling him how much I admired his story *The Death of Simon Fugus,* and asking him if it had been suggested to him by Conder's life. He was well aware that many of his books were not very great, for he said *The Old Wives' Tale* was a terrible effort, and that he had to write easier, less good books to rest himself. As he was telling me this I somehow felt that he could hardly face such an effort again. With odd little jerks of his head and with his short, snappy way of speaking I can hear him say, "Ah! You don't know what it means to write a book like that, very exhausting, one cannot keep it up *always.*"

We saw him fairly often after this first meeting as he came to our Tuesday evenings—indeed, I remember that Bertie Russell took such a violent dislike to him that he said he couldn't be in the room with him. I never understood why,

[3] Ottoline told me of a similar occasion during the 1920s when, at a dinner party, she was sitting next to Bennett who had on an elegantly frilled shirt.

"What a beautiful shirt, Mr. Bennett," she said. "Where did you get it? Paris?"

"The F-f-f-f-f-five Towns," stammered Bennett in answer.

except that he said he was "so vulgar," which was not accurate. He was superficially showy, but not vulgar, indeed he had a very great sense of delicacy in his life, and an exquisite love of his craftsmanship. In 1927 the two writers that he thought most important were James Joyce and D. H. Lawrence. Novel-writing, he said, ought to have force and vulgarity of the right sort.

After his second marriage he drifted more into fashionable, smart, intellectual society, but from time to time we lunched or dined with him to meet interesting people, such as Paul Valéry, Max Beerbohm or Thornton Wilder. I always enjoyed it up to a point, but latterly I felt shy and nervous with him as he said sharp and irritable things to me. I believe he thought that we were what he most disliked, "highbrows," and perhaps he imagined that I needed snubbing, whereas I was really very nervous and timid of talking to him. He had become ac-customed to the easy flattering flow of talk that society women practise so skilfully, and I would go away from his house feel-ing hurt and humiliated, which I feel sure would have dis-tressed him if he had known, for he was a most kind and tender-hearted man. He probably felt tired, as he worked very hard and woke early, often going out on long walks through the streets before breakfast. Also his stammer prevented him from talking easily; in the middle of a sentence he would remain with his mouth open for almost a minute, in an agonized strug-gle to get the word out. I wish we had known him intimately, but these last five or six years of his life I think his curiosity was dimmed, probably satiated, or directed to a life that he knew I had no dealings with, for he had to direct his social energies more to people that his wife found useful and interest-ing. She had been an actress, young and pretty, and was ambitious to continue her acting career. Whenever I went to a play or a concert I was almost sure to find him either just in front of me or just behind, when he would always be most cordial and affectionate. I know that whenever I go to a modern play I shall always feel Arnold Bennett's ghost near me.

His heart was always kind but he directed his social activities towards the successful, the fashionable and the rich. But even here there were those that he couldn't bear. Amongst these was Lady ———. He was regretting that he had ever gone to a party in her house, as he would then have to ask her back. This was more than he could face. I laughingly said that I didn't like her, and that once she had asked me after my "sweet girlie." He said, "If she had said that to me I should have said . . . (a stammer—pause) . . . Rats!"

He had a very great antipathy to anyone who drank, and perhaps was inclined to exaggerate this weakness in his fellow-craftsmen, for he was himself so well regulated, so balanced, that despair, tragedy, passion and recklessness were not part of the colouring of his existence. I should not have said that he had any appreciation of poetry, but one day when we were dining there I was arguing with Max Beerbohm about Yeats. Max was pooh-poohing him and denying that he had talent or wrote good poetry, and Arnold Bennett came out with great emphasis in praise of his work, and trotted off to his library to fetch a volume of Yeats's poems to show Max. I see them now with their heads bent over the volume held under a lamp.

And it was thus that I liked to remember him. As we stood amongst his friends and his old Fleet Street fellow-workers in St. Clement Danes Church on March 31st 1931, singing the hymn that he was supposed to have loved—"Jesu, Lover of my soul"—I could believe that he was himself standing amongst us and looking up at that lovely church with its delicate green and gold ornamented roof and its purely English character. I didn't feel we were mourning a very great man, but a very fine English writer, one in the tradition of the best, who did not soar but kept his feet well planted on pavements of cities, and who also directed his imaginative insight into the lives of human beings well lubricated with kindness and with the salty ingredients of good-humoured justice.

In February 1912 I went out with my maid to Lausanne to consult Dr. Combe, as I was feeling ill. In my Journal I find one of the usual *cris de cœur*:

"I am so glad, oh so glad, to get away alone and to have time to think and read, to store my mind with thoughts and to rest my emotions and nerves and to get away and stand off and view the past year. I am miserable all the same at leaving Philip. I depend on him so much and love him more and more. How often I regret the intrusion of anyone else into our life and yet it is selfish to feel that. I am *happier* without others, happier with only Philip, but I feel I have more in me than he needs, more to give—and if I can give it that would help others, to be complete . . . but I shrink from all it entails. I seem to have grown old and all my emotions are dead and the only human being I crave for is Philip. The question that is always torturing me is how can I go on. I love my freedom so much. My friendships certainly don't give me much happiness beyond the feeling that I am being of use to my friends, and of my passionate desire that they should fulfil their work. If only they would not entangle me, not touch me, body or soul, but let the interchange be only of intellect, imagination and sympathy. I love them, yes, of course I do, but I cannot be possessed. I gave myself to Philip, and he is the only man I want to be possessed by, for he loves me unselfishly."

¶ *March 9. Lausanne*

"I have been here a fortnight now alone. I am greedy of reading and love the long free hours, but this place is towny and conventional, and the doctor and the diet are a worry and very depressing, and my head aches a great deal, which prevents my spirits moving along freely.

"I wonder what it is in a place that makes the ingredients that draw one to love any special spot? Why is there nearly always some great sadness as one looks back on a place? I suppose it is in oneself, in one's own mismanagement of life and in not adequately controlling one's emotions. I know I am only happy if my spirit can soar up and get free from petty things.

"I am reading Spinoza. He gives one a great deal. The abstract intellectual life which is eternal, but I feel I personally learn and take in so much by my *senses*—by sight, by feelings which are not purely intellectual but are of the human and imaginative quality. If they are disciplined they ought to be as important as "Reason." I have read Bertie's paper on Religion, too, and like it very much, except that it does not include and draw into itself the ordinary life of men which after all cannot be left outside religion. Why do they all elaborate philosophies and religions outside the real life we live? Why not fuse them with our life on earth? Life, life is what we are here for and to live it well, not to go into a room and think about it all. Pure intellectual conceptions influence such men as Bertie and Moore and McTaggart, but they are almost worthless to the peasant or the clerk, and it is hard that such men should not be "eternal" in Spinoza's sense. Spinoza says that one must still all passions, know them and connect them as one knows one's body and put them away from one, divert the mind from them; only by developing the intellectual life can one attain God. Yes, that is happiness for those who have time and capacity for it, but it would be useless for the ordinary man."

When I was sitting out on the terrace under the trees, thinking of all these questions and of a letter I had had from Bertie about it, I was watching the Lausannais eat their mid-day lunch and reading their newspapers, and a young man who was carrying his child while the wife pushed along another in a pram. I found myself swept with indignation at the intellectuals who elaborate such aloof theories about life and religion and who seem to ignore the everyday lives and needs of such people, who surely need a religion or philosophy that can be interpenetrated and fused with their ordinary lives.

What is it that Shelley and all the fine spirits longed for and never found? We all strive and batter our wings against the cage of this life, passionately longing for some golden clime, some elixir that is seldom found. Passionate after something and few know exactly what.

"I love Shelley's poems now, for I feel all that he felt from Nature; winds blow through me, there is a 'something' unearthly that I am conscious of, that comes and fans my imagination. The veil between myself and that 'something' seems at moments transparent, and I almost catch sight of the beyond. Is life only material laws or is there a spirit in it? What is the vague fantasy that haunts one, the surprises, the intentions at the back of the imaginative and creative thought? Is creative imagination only a form of madness?"

¶ *March 14*

"I am sitting out in the valley that I am fond of, the grass covered with primroses, the trees still dead and hard and bony as if no sap had come up into them yet. It is very lovely, though. I love the wind blowing through me. I learn from my senses when my brain is tired and dead. I see something beautiful and that fills my soul with happiness. Those who cannot drink of this fountain become dry. It is like wine to me. How I love flowers—my one bunch is a poignant joy to me.

"I wish I had more subtlety of brain, to write well, and talk well. I have such a slow, calm brain, without charm or brilliancy. I wish I could collect people in London and make a more complete compact society of intellectuals. Perhaps I can when I am older.

"I have beautiful letters from Philip every day, full of interest and intimate delights to me.

"There is no one that I have ever met that approaches my darling Philip. I cannot imagine myself married to any other man. I often wonder what his influence on me has been, somehow he is so near me that it is difficult to put him far enough away from me to see myself apart from him. When I married him I was very earnest, full of potentialities, large and unfinished, rather Michelangelesque. I don't think I was stupid, for after all I had stepped out from my old surroundings and had gone to St. Andrews and to Oxford to educate myself, but I was, I am sure, still very indefinite. I had not had the critical training such as any man who has been to a university. This is what Philip has given me. He has chiselled me, chipped off sentimentality, made me more definite. He has such a remarkably *fine* good mind, combined with the best character in a man that I have ever known. He is entirely devoid of pettiness and self-seeking, indeed he has spent his energies, his powers, over and over again in politics and other things, and has devoted time and energy to help causes and people for which he has received no recognition or thanks. I should say that the centre of his life is a generous response to all that is noble and most beautiful in life—in politics, good causes, history, literature and music. I think that what may have deterred him from having a worldly success is that he lacks the 'drive' that comes from passion and concentration on one cause. It is indeed odd that in this we are both very much alike. Indeed, in many ways we resemble each other, only that I am always an amateur and he has so much ability that he is easily a professional."

The above note in my journal of 1912 is indeed what I feel true today in 1932, just twenty years later. He has a curious mixture of kindness and public spirit which he inherits from his father's family—one of those admirable well-established professional families who have been devoted for generations to support of Church and State; to helping on education and the building of churches and supporting all good causes—with a fine artistic and critical faculty which he gets from his mother, for she was in some ways a brilliant woman, from whom he gets most of his cleverness. The Morrells of Oxford, though endowed with a great deal of force and virtue, were perhaps never very brilliant, and yet how important to me is that unself-seeking, serious side of him, for one gets weary of mere self-indulgent cleverness.

He has not perhaps achieved great worldly success, but I feel that he himself has developed a great deal; he has much more ease and mastery now. Perhaps when he was younger he accomplished work too easily, and this may have deterred him from arduous labour. But behind him there is so much to be proud of. All the work that he did in Parliament—for he was always with the advanced courageous group of young Liberals who brought about land reform and foreign policy. And then at the debate on the declaration of the war, August 4th 1914, he alone in the House had the great courage to make a speech protesting against the declaration of war. During all those dreadful years of the war he gave his time, his energies, to help

Garsington Manor, the Green Room

Garsington Manor, the Red Room

Lady Ottoline, about 1912

Lady Ottoline, 1912

the conscientious objectors, speaking for them at tribunals, and employing them on the farm at Garsington, a difficult and thankless task.

If one could have seen more clearly and judged his capacities more accurately, I think it would have been better and more natural to him if he had devoted himself to literature and history and had not entered politics, or spent time and money on farming. But we, like many, many others have had our lives blown up by the war.

But to return to 1912.

When I arrived home from Lausanne, I was met at the station by Philip and little Julian, who I thought looked very fragile. She had had pain and an operation was decided on. It was dreadful waiting and imagining all the horrors of it; I am glad to say the operation was successful. *"Mais il faut avoir du courage,"* I wrote in my journal.

Philip and I tried to divert our minds by going on expeditions round London, such as to Hampstead Heath on Easter Monday. There were crowds of holidaymakers from the East End of London, poor, pale, red-eyed people, and factory girls too tired to be very gay, except those who were dancing to the barrel-organs. They linked themselves together arm in arm, or arms round the neck of their young men partners, and danced in two rows facing each other. The girls had coloured paper feathers in their hats, and short skirts and thick heavy boots, but their feet tripped about nimbly and exquisitely in intricate steps. The feet so gay, the faces of both girls and men almost somnambulistic.

Another day we went down to St. Ann's Hill, Chertsey, where I had lived with my mother during the last years of her life. It was full of poignant memories—which revived and carried me back to relive again that old life. It was there that my spiritual life awoke, accompanied by intense asceticism; it was there that I read and followed *The Imitation of Christ*. As I wandered over the house the thoughts and emotions that I had had in each room floated back to me—they seemed to live and speak to me again. It was not an unhappy time, except that the extreme self-denial was very hard. But I remember happy days with my mother, shut off from the fashionable world, writing for her and serving her in every way, and listening to her talk about history and politics as I sat in the window doing some fine needlework, or sometimes making a dress for myself: and the long, long expeditions with her sitting beside me as I drove the pair of black cobs in the phaeton. I was then so ravished and moved by the beauty of the trees and the roads and Chobham Common and Virginia Water and Windsor Park, the impression upon me was so strong that even now, forty years later, I can feel myself driving, perched up in the beautiful old-fashioned phaeton with the reins in my hands, driving along creamy pearl-coloured roads that turned pink in the evening light, and I see again the trees in spring, or smell the autumn and see smoke from cottage chimneys. Perhaps we went to choose rose trees at Waterers's at Bagshot, or over wild Chobham Common, where a group of gaunt fir trees grew.

I don't think I ever, as most girls of today would do, looked ahead or thought of marrying. Religious thoughts inspired me and carried me out into mystic experiences and filled me with a desire to immolate self; and then, too, my whole time, thoughts and love, apart from spiritual things, were concentrated on my mother. There was not a moment of the day or night that I was not at her service—all my love, all my devotion, were poured out upon her.

Perhaps it was not very gay—or very suited to a young girl,

but as I look back, I feel it was very happy, with the happiness that I was fulfilling the life that existed for me at the moment, filling up to the limit the frame around that moment of existence. It was the "prelude" to the fugue of my life, and it will still persist in my existence until the end.[4]

In June 1912 I again went to Lausanne for more treatment from Dr. Combe. Bertie came out there. Bertie was staying at the Old Hotel where Gibbon had lived and in the mornings he would sit out in the garden there writing. The afternoons we spent together, talking and reading and going on expeditions until dinner. Leopardi's poems were a great inspiration to him then; we read them together. He grew, indeed, most gentle, more imaginative and less logically definite, more open to spiritual ideas. On my birthday we spent an enchanting day at Geneva, going there by lake—and from there we went to Ferney and peered in through the gates at Voltaire's house and chapel, and walked in the alleys among the poplars in the Park. Bertie loved to feel he was treading the paths Voltaire trod.

Fate and chance seem to draw one to certain spots, as if they are the stages where one has to play one's little part. Only the partners are changed—the emotions are so varied. It was here that a year before I had sat with ———, and it was here that I was to sit again, far more happily, with Philip. And it is here in my thoughts that I often return.

At the end of June I was back in London. Bertie kept urging me to write. As I sat in my little closet off the large, grey drawing-room in Bedford Square, I would indeed gladly have obeyed him, but how could I attain detachment and peace?

[4] In her journal she writes: "How much I used to worship Nature: how beautiful I thought the trees and roads and Chobham Common! But it was all lonely and one longed incessantly for companionship." P.M.

With Lytton Strachey desiring to pour out his troubles to me: and —— alternating between being an angel and a devil, sometimes with angels' wings flying to me for help and sympathy and affection, and then as swiftly turning into a cruel and unkind, pathetic child (He was having a love affair at this time with a young lady who was angelically kind to him). And then my own excitable, vibrating nervous temperament tormenting me with desires and curiosity about life and about the interesting people that were around me: Henry James, Augustine Birrell and many others.

Nijinsky was at that time dancing in the Russian Ballet, and as I had met him in Paris while I was staying with Mrs. Chadbourne, he came to see me fairly often. Lytton and most of my friends were such enthusiastic admirers of him, that I, from contrariness, had rather pooh-poohed him, but when I saw him dance I was completely converted, for I saw that anyone who so completely lost himself and embodied an idea was not just a good ballet dancer—he seemed no longer to be Nijinsky, but became the idea which he was representing.

In ordinary life he was very quiet and rather ugly, but one at once recognized that the flame of genius burned within him.

He was very nervous and highly-strung, and his guardian and jailer, Diaghilev, did not allow him to go out into society as it tired and upset him, and I was one of the few people that he was allowed to come and see, as at my house he could be quiet and only meet other artists. "He is like a jockey," I laughingly told Lytton, but really I grew very fond of the little figure with long, muscular neck and pale Kalmuk face, and the hands so expressive and nervous. He always seemed lost in the world outside, and as if he looked on as a visitor from another world, although his powers of observation were intensely rapid. For on entering a room he would see all the pictures hanging in it before he had been there but a few minutes. It was not easy to talk to him as he didn't speak English and his French was very vague, but we managed to understand each other, and he was glad, I think, of real understanding and appreciation of his serious work. I was lamenting one day that I was not able to create anything myself and he quickly answered, "Oh, but you do create, Madame, for you help us young artists to create."

There were at this time fantastic fables about him: that he was very debauched, that he had girdles of emeralds and diamonds given him by an Indian prince; but on the contrary, I found that he disliked any possessions or anything that hampered him or diverted him from his art. He was incessantly thinking out new ballets, new steps; also he was absorbed by the ideas of the old Russian myths and religions which he wanted to express in his ballets as he did in *Le Sacre du Printemps*.[5] Such ballets as *Le Spectre de la Rose* did not interest him; he said it was *trop joli* and was rather annoyed when people admired it. He gave me a photograph of himself as he was in ordinary life and another to put by its side, as he was in *Petrouchka*. He said that he made up in this part as an old traditional Russian figure—"the mythical outcast in whom is concentrated the pathos and suffering of life, one who beats his hands against the walls, but always is cheated and despised and left outside alone." Perhaps the same myth Dostoevsky turned into *The Idiot*. Many years later I found in Charlie Chaplin something of the same intense poignancy as there was in Nijinsky.

A few years later Nijinsky became an ardent Tolstoyan in his own life and his consistency in putting the doctrines into practice caused dreadful trouble amongst the *corps de ballet*, as

[5] In her journal she wrote: "It is really *terrible* and intense. Too much of Idea in it to please the public. Too little grace."   P.M.

he told them that they should not work for money, and that the
women should do all their own laundry and cooking. The
strain of his life, and the over-sensibility of his temperament,
and also a family tendency, drove him mad. I saw him in 1924
in Paris where he was living with his wife. He had grown fat,
and remained almost always silent, but I had the impression
that he knew what was going on, but was unable to break down
his prison walls—*Petrouchka* again. His hands were unaltered
and had the same nervous movement of clutching the thumbs
inside the other fingers, and the dark eyes were also not much
changed, only more haunted. I thought he knew me, but was
not sure. The life of these dancers is strenuous and hard and
entails a terrible nervous strain. Diaghilev once told me the
Russian Ballet leaves a trail of madness behind it; indeed,
several of their best dancers went mad. A Spaniard left the
Ballet one evening and got into the big church in Drury Lane
and in the darkness and moonlight danced in front of the altar.

But at this time Nijinsky was still well and creating his best
ballets. He and Bakst (who also went mad) came one afternoon when Duncan Grant and some others were playing
tennis in Bedford Square garden—they were so entranced by
the tall trees against the houses and the figures flitting about
playing tennis that they exclaimed with delight: *"Quel décor!"*

He admired Julian, who was very lovely and slim and fairy-
like. I remember how she flitted into the drawing-room and as
she came dancing in he caught her up as he would a ballerina.

This July was a happy month: every week I had my usual
parties and interesting people came—Henry James, Lytton
Strachey, the MacCarthys, Virginia Stephen and her brother
Adrian, Duncan Grant, the Aranyis. We had become more
established in Bedford Square and our house was a centre
where artists of all sorts and of all nations used to meet. Indeed,

I believe these evenings were interesting; having two large rooms, it was easy to keep the gay in one room and the sedate talkers like Henry James, Augustine Birrell and Asquith in the other—carefully mixing them when there were signs of stagnation and boredom. These evenings indeed grew fuller and fuller, but I rigidly did not invite the smart or fashionable world. When one or two stray ones crept in, having asked to come, I always found that they upset the harmony and unselfconscious gaiety of the others. I remember Lady Cynthia Charteris came one evening—tall, elegant, very clever and beautifully dressed. I see her now sitting stiffly on a chair looking at everyone with a critical and obviously contemptuous eye. I took all my most interesting guests up to her, but nothing moved her from her attitude of superiority over these "untidy riffraff." Lytton Strachey was not then a success in the fashionable world; people who ten years later would entreat him to lunch or dine with them used to say, "I wonder how Ottoline can have that man in her house. I cannot stay in the same room with him!"

These evenings were exhausting as I was naturally anxiously on the watch all the time to see that everyone was talking and as happy as I could make them. How I would torture myself afterwards as I went over the evening in my thoughts, thinking of someone that I might have introduced to another and feeling that perhaps a lifelong friendship between these two might in consequence have come about.

I felt that it was of importance that young artists should meet each other and older men and interesting people from abroad and different kinds of people. My desire for other people to know each other and be friends is an instinctive, unreasoning passion with me. My double nature often makes me laugh at myself—for with the one half of me I desire so ardently a life of retirement, contemplation, solitude, reading and mediating asceticism (but even here I should need to stretch out and serve others), and on the other side there lives such a chaos of interests that when I review them they seem to pour out like an erupted stream. For here I stretch out so instinctively towards contact with fellow-creatures—loving talk, discussion, friendship, warmth and humour, endlessly interested in other people's lives, and indeed at times feeling their troubles too intensely.

I love to walk the streets and to observe the life that goes by, imagining and sympathizing with the common life around, and loving to catch a sight of the many kind, good-humoured actions that are so naturally done every day in London streets.

Sometimes I believe politics is what I care for above all else and then at another time I know that art and poetry are equally important to me. When I see old Italian or Flemish pictures, or modern French or English ones, I know that what they express to me is some individual vision of the world, an intense blending of the external with the artist's imagination, the marriage of which is a new creation that only that hand and that vision could accomplish, and what for me is an opening into understanding of life.

Trees and woods and wild heaths are a passionate joy to me, not a mere optical pleasure, but as of a revelation of something, some beauty behind life which satisfies my soul, as if the world and all its beauty were perhaps an expression of divinity—the outer edge of its garment.

To think of Italy, to speak of Rome, is to hand out before my eyes golden apricot walls and light and statues, Michelangelo buildings with white statues against a dark night sky, long and narrow brown streets, fountains and *piazzas*—the Appian Way and Tivoli beyond. So much does this vision burn me that I have to turn away, but there it is, absorbed into me by greedy love—yes, greedy love. It is that which I am consumed by in my life. I don't want simply to look and admire, to be a mere spectator; I want to absorb, have such complete contact and union with what moves me that I should for ever possess it within my being. Passionate curiosity to see, to know and to understand more and more of life is what leads me on—and to help when possible—on and away from the peaceful land of pure contemplation; but between these two lands there is a bridge upon which a temple stands, where the child that is my poor self faithfully worships. In the inner shrine there is the Divine whose will alone I desire to fulfil in worship and in life, and around that mystic rose there is the path of fire and the fountain of eternal life, and over this hovers that spirit whose wings are as "the wings of a dove that is covered with silver wings and her feathers like gold." In my heart I say—"Here is the well of light, and in Thy light shall we see light."

In the outer court there stands my darling Philip and all the poetry and music I love—Shakespeare and Milton and Keats, and Mozart and Bach. For it is through such things that I have felt the most perfect and far-reaching ecstasies in this life. The ecstasies which one shares with most human beings are seldom perfect, as they are hedged around with self-questionings and torments and do not detach one from earth or solve life's problems as music and poetry do, but again and again I knew that no Nirvana could be permanent bliss to me if it separated me from those I love.

I was very puzzled and worried at this time whether we should go and live at a country house that belonged to Philip, Broughton Grange, near Banbury. He was very anxious to go, as he had recollections of having spent enchanting days there in his childhood. We settled to go there for a month as a trial and find out if we liked it. Unfortunately, it rained nearly all the time and the place, charming as it was in many ways, filled me with gloom. Mrs. Morrell (my mother-in-law) came on a visit and as I was very tired and longed for a complete rest her presence made everything very difficult. She was critical of me, she spoilt Julian and made her very naughty. The rain poured down outside and I felt in tortured nerves indoors. I wrote in my journal:

"I am nearly addled in my mind as to whether to live here or not. It is secure and quiet, but deadly, grey and dreary; the country round seems to me very unsympathetic, the sort of English country that takes all joy out of my life—purely hunting country."

How unhappy I was there! It was all augmented by feeling that there, for the first time, was a real division between Philip and myself. He loved the place, for it was all gilded over with happy memories in his mind; I, who at the moment was suffering from the very wet, cold summer, clay surroundings, and my mother-in-law's intolerance and Julian's naughtiness, felt no glamour. I tried bravely to hypnotize myself into liking it and pretending that we should be very happy there; but it was all useless, and I knew it was a hollow sham on my part. Things were made perhaps more difficult by receiving this telegram from Lytton:

Shall arrive tomorrow. Wire train later. In need of your coraggio as well as my own.

August 19th.   Waterside, Londonderry.
                                                        LYTTON.

He had been in Ireland with Henry Lamb. I knew that their time together was not being a great success. He arrived soon after the telegram and fell into my arms, an emotional, nervous and physical wreck, ill and bruised in spirit, haunted and shocked. I comforted him and diverted him as much as I could. It was difficult to contend with the appalling weather; we gave him a sitting-room to write in, and he stayed some time. I had many an enchanting talk with him and we grew very intimate. He read aloud to me, poetry—Shakespeare, Racine and Crashaw (who carried me away by his intense passion). We took long walks together and went to see Broughton Castle where Lady Algernon Lennox was living. She had made it and the garden very beautiful, like an enchanted castle, but had just been told she must leave, as the owner, Lord Saye and Seal, wished to return. I remember when we went there I saw her eighteenth-century face resting on her hands at the window, looking out over the garden and moat; that brilliant, gay, worldly, much-loved lady was looking down on one of the vanishing chapters of her life.

At night Lytton would become gay and we would laugh and giggle and be foolish; sometimes he would put on a pair of my smart high-heeled shoes, which made him look like an Aubrey Beardsley drawing, very wicked. I love to see him in my memory tottering and pirouetting round the room with feet looking so absurdly small, peeping in and out of his trousers, both of us so excited and happy, getting more fantastic and gay.

Bertie also came to see me here, but I remember little of his visit except a melancholy walk ending in the churchyard.

I left Broughton with great relief. No decision was made as yet as to whether we should live there permanently for I shrank from hurting Philip. It had, of course, to be done; he was very disappointed at the time. I certainly have had no turning back or regrets.

From Broughton we went to a little farmhouse at Churn on the Berkshire downs which my brother Henry had lent me. It was like a farm on the African veldt, far from a village and with only a cart-track up to the house. A little branch train used to puff by twice a day and if we wanted it to stop to take us to Oxford we had to stand and wave a handkerchief. The house was very primitive, and seemed but a speck on the waves of the downs which stretched away far on either side, wild and golden, covered with those tight little purple flowers that cling to the earth. I was very happy here. I find in my journal:

"Philip and I are so happy together. He reads me Gibbon, and Shakespeare, and Catullus, he rides on the downs which I delight in, and I enjoy the freedom and simplicity and fresh air, but really underneath I hunger for sunshine and warmth and Italy, and yet these downs have such a hold on one, for they are antique and seem untouched since the Romans camped here."

I little thought that in three years' time these empty downs would be covered by a vast camp of English soldiers.

¶ *September 21st 1912*

"How odd the feeling is which rises up in me so often, almost physical and yet apparently of the soul, of pouring itself out to some imaginary creature. I had it so strongly yesterday, as if my whole being longs to embrace someone, and yet no one person that I knew—on the contrary, I shrink and would dislike to kiss anyone I know. What a curious tragic place life is with these emotional laws running through it and underneath us.

"Why cannot I give myself away with all the rush of my being to anyone who wants it and longs for it—but it is not possible. A law like the tide of the sea comes into the flowings of my soul and turns it all back, and yet there still is that sea of love and wealth of poetry ready to flow out. The religious passion of Crashaw is most like it."

222

¶ *September 28th*

"Lytton arrived from Wantage with a huge pack on his back, young and gay and debonair, after two or three days' walking. He was as excited as a boy, for he had had his ears pierced and was wearing gold ear-rings, which he kept hid under his long hair, and he was wearing his new suit of corduroys, which were very short in the legs. What squeals of laughter and giggles and fun we had about it all."

He seemed very happy here, delighted in the country; and certainly the tawny downs were lovely, with the play of clouds and shadows over them, and a great stillness over it all. Lytton stayed some days and fell so much in love with the little house that he wanted to take it. I was sad when he left, he was so well and full of fun and life and youth, adorable; and he and I and Philip had such delightful talks together. I watched his tall, thin back striding off with its rather quick nervous walk, vanishing into the distance. What a solitary figure he seemed then, seeking rather timidly and nervously for human adventures. I stood and waved to him and felt hurt that he didn't look back.

The doctor had ordered Julian to be as much as possible in the country, so we took a house of Philip's sister—Margaret Warren—Breach House, at Cholsey. It was not very far from Cholsey, very lovely country but windy and bleak in the winter. We went there in November 1912 till March 1913. When I think of the house I find I have two quite separate impressions and recollections of it. One is of a light, rather French, house with a charming drawing-room, parquet floors and a wood fire, pretty old furniture and potpourri in bowls, where I sat endlessly embroidering petit-point, with my mauve reels of silks arranged on a tray by my side, and books on the other side. Here I was very happy, and I often return to that fireside and feel again the charm of living a sequestered, industrious, monotonous life, cut off from outside tumult. There I wove, with a happy fancy, many colour pictures in silks, most of which I gave away, while Philip read to me, or he and I talked.

Then the other Breach House is a room upstairs where I used to see ———— when he came and where I tried to read history and philosophy. To that room I do not desire to return. It is dark and melancholy in my memory.

I copy out some entries in my journal:

¶ *February 8th*

"We kept our wedding-day today. Julian dressed up as a fairy snowdrop and as Philip and I came home from our walk she flew out to meet us, just like a fairy. She looked quite lovely and ethereal with a wreath of snowdrops round her head and a bunch in her sash and one on a wand. She sang little songs that she had herself made up, and some other spring songs. It was too poignant and made me feel agonized that this pure loveliness should ever fade. It seemed so fragile.

"She and I have become much nearer each other here. She is very nice to me now, which gives me great joy. It was an agony to me before when she was so cold.

"Bertie came for two days on the 15th of February.

"Captain Scott's death returning from the South Pole is fine. He wrote in his diary: 'Forces were against us, and we were beaten—but not really beaten.'

"Philip has been reading me Lord Byron's Letters and *Don Juan,* also I am reading his life by Miss Colburn Mayne. He revolts me by his inordinate vanity and selfishness, and a sort of caddishness, but he had obviously great charm and a lovely voice; as a companion one would have delighted in him, as one does in his letters, but his vulgar rudeness to anyone that he thought below him in rank would have been insupportable.

"But one is refreshed by Byron's dash and reckless courage. Lytton admires him and says that Augustus John is like him—I don't agree, as John is not cruel or sophisticated, as Byron obviously was. To men of such charm as Byron it is easy to become contemptuous of those that succumb to them. I do not know how sensitive Byron was, how much artistic sensibility he had—his vanity, his snobbishness were so great that they twisted him awry."

¶ *January 24th 1913*

"I had a long talk with Lytton last night as I was on my way to bed. I sat on my bed and he stood beside me, looking so dejected and despondent, for he seems to feel baulked in his life, doubtful about his writing; he says that he is no good at conversation so that he could never be a social success, that his small voice would prevent his going into politics, which he would rather like to do, but how could he ever make speeches with his thin tiny voice? I did my best to encourage him with his writing, as I am sure that is his real *métier*. Poor Lytton, how dejected he becomes, and yet he is really very ambitious.

"What a mistake it is to have one's visual powers so developed and sensitive and fastidious, for it makes intimacy with anything that does not satisfy them most repulsive, it becomes a sort of mania. I have to exercise all my will and goodness of heart to overcome it, but then it seems only in abeyance, never quite mortified.

"What a contest life is between inner abnegation, the tossing aside and knocking on the head of one's own little self, dying to oneself, and the instinct one has to expand and enrich and fulfil the self in its own proper development. How can one ever weigh the scales equally and get the balance right?

"If I instinctively train my senses to be fine and delicate and allow my 'sensibilities' to develop, it makes me fastidious and cruel, but I believe I could permeate it all by my wisdom and understanding, and become sensitive to my own cruel criticisms and eliminate them. But sometimes one seems to develop and develop and then to have to summon unselfish love to come and knock it all down again to become a decent individual."

¶ *March 7th*

"The great thing seems to me in dealing with people is to find the *centre* of a human being, their core, to get into touch with that, and from that to radiate out in understanding, to all the other parts and ramifications. I get obsessed by small trivial excrescences in people's characters, which quite blinds me to their central quality. Of course, the centre may be quite antipathetic. Then one can leave them alone; but if one is able to be in communication with their core, outer differences can be left alone, one can switch the light of understanding on to them.

"Understanding and wisdom are the great things, and with love one can attain them, and it is a great happiness in life to feel other personalities touching one's own, feeling one's love going out to them. This feeling is happy contact with one's fellow-beings.

"Bertie says he knows people and their concerns by his intellect, but seldom *feels* them. Now I don't see them intellectually, but feel them *demi physiquement*—really *feel* them and that is the only gift I have. I want to alter people, develop them, and I expect this is a mistake, but one can open up for them new light and understanding; if one cannot rebuild them, one could help them open more windows in their buildings.

"Love is the great thing that makes one soul flow to another, which is the ultimate good in this life, I believe."

226

On March 15th 1913 there first definitely appeared on the horizon of our lives the house that was to be our home from 1915 to 1927. In the days when Philip and I drove out to political meetings from Oxford, we used to pass an old grey stone Tudor house, set back from the road in the very high yew hedges forming a forecourt. The vision of this house as we passed it one night touched some spot of desire, and I exclaimed, "That is the only country house that I could live in." It had wonderful beauty and mystery. Curiously enough it was in the village of Garsington where Philip's father owned a good deal of property, so that my wilful desire to possess this house did not seem unreasonable. When the doctors told us that Julian must live in the country and we were searching for a house, I remembered this one. It was occupied by an old farmer of ninety who gave every sign of living on for ever. However, in 1913 he died as he sat on his horse in the stable-yard, and after some months it was put up for sale by auction. What agonies of desire, hesitation and uncertainty we went through beforehand, but on March 15th Philip went off to the sale at Oxford. It was held in a room at the Golden Cross. Julian and I waited that day with beating hearts for the telegram to arrive. Dear little Julian said to Billy, her nurse, "We must be very kind to Mummy today, for she will be very anxious." The telegram at last came to say that Philip had bought it. We were not to take possession of the house until 1915—the farm Philip could have sooner. So this day the die was cast—for better or worse. That which had been a misty castle was now a solid possession. It is lucky one cannot see the intensity of experiences that lie in store for one as one enters into a house. That was hidden; the chief anxiety now was how we could afford it.

In May 1913 we took Julian to Lausanne to see Dr. Combe as I was not satisfied with her health. He ordered her to go the following autumn to Dr. Rolier's Sun Cure Sanatorium, Les Frênes, at Leysin. We went there and arranged that she should be taken with Billy in October. We saw all the little children running about without any clothes, looking like bronze statues. Meanwhile we had a very happy time all together at Lausanne. It was lovely spring weather, and we went on expeditions on the lake. Philip remained with us for some time, until he had to return to the House of Commons. Before he went he and I went by steamer to Geneva and then to Ferney. I say in my journal:

"It was a dream of beauty—the coast of Savoy, hearing the nightingales singing, and on our return journey the sunset on the lake, and at all the little villages we stopped at the little children running down in the evening sunshine to bathe."

After Philip left us, Julian and her nurse and I went up to see Ethel Sands above Les Avants. The whole mountain sides were white with narcissus, as white as if covered with snow. It was like walking in fairyland, and the scent heavenly. Julian was very happy, running amongst the narcissus. We climbed down a steep mountain side to find some gentians, which seemed like an untold treasure as one saw them below us, a tight little bunch of pure blue. I can see them now as I pointed them out to little Julian.

I was then having treatment from Dr. Vittoz, who was a very remarkable man. He taught his patients a system of mental control and concentration, and a kind of organization of the mind, which had a great effect on steadying and developing me. I found it an enormous help then and always. The man himself impressed me by his extraordinary poise and goodness. Part of the treatment was the formation of the habit of eliminating unnecessary thoughts and worries from one's mind, and to do this one had to practise eliminating letters from words, or one number from a set of numbers. Julian would laugh at me when, perhaps in the tram, she would see me gazing into space—"There is Mummy eliminating." I stayed on alone at a little *pension* to finish my course with Dr. Vittoz, and this was a very happy time for me.

"These few days alone here are infinitely precious, they are a little island in my life, and looking out to the sea of the future, beautiful or rough, whatever it may be, I am trying to form good habits and to read and to be calm and *actif* in mind.

"This dear book [the yellow journal] is nearly done. It has seen me through one of the most troubled times of my life—so far. I have written but little of them; indeed only bare sticks and shreds—not because there was nothing to say but too much, and too complicated to express. When I am old I must take it up again when I see all the threads clearly.

"Yes, this really is the great thing in life, to risk censure and failure, and to step out with courage. I have been through two years of great doubt, great trial and worry, and hardly any happiness, but I feel for the time being that I am coming out of it, much older."

I wrote the last pages of my yellow volume, full of a contentment and happiness that I had gained from inward discipline and a uniting of myself and elimination of restless desires.

The journey back from Lausanne was most lovely, passing through rocks and green fields and wild flowers and distant hills. Everything seemed terribly painfully alive and poignant to me, all my senses were alive, and I felt as if the body was too thin to shield the soul.

This summer seems to have been a wonderful one. I was feeling better in health and not so tired, and so was more able to enjoy seeing people, and looking on at the gay and rather sympathetic, artistic and intellectual life that existed in 1913 and 1914 in London.

Simon Bussy, the French painter, a brother-in-law of Lytton Strachey, came to do a pastel sketch of me. Unfortunately, he found it impossible to accomplish and had to give it up. But we both enjoyed the sittings—he is an acute, rather mordant observer of life, with a queer subterranean mocking laugh. I don't know if it was this summer or earlier that I also sat to Duncan Grant for a portrait. He had a studio in Brunswick Square. I enjoyed these sittings immensely, for Duncan had more charm and humour, more childish enjoyment of life than anyone I knew, and we had endless jokes and fun together. Indeed, I still feel that he is one of the rarest of human beings —a possessor of a naturally delightful character, combined with being a lyrical painter. Most people with charm seem to be possessed of a dangerous and corrupting gift, but Duncan's charm apparently comes from having a childlike and lovable character, for his charm has never corrupted him. He remains apparently one of the most ideal characters. I don't know what has become of the portrait.

The Russian Ballet was again in London and Lady Ripon, whom I had met at Lausanne, asked me down to Kingston to luncheon to meet Nijinsky and Diaghilev. She sent her motor-car to fetch me and I had to pick up Maurice Baring on the way. I felt very shy sitting by his side—he was outside my group of friends, smarter and more worldly, and, I imagined, expected one to talk in the exaggerated, epigrammatic style in which such men as he are so confident and competent. However, I squeezed myself and plunged along the endless mossy walk of discussing Desmond—Desmond always runs on ahead;

and so it occupied the half-hour that it took to motor down. I found a large luncheon party of the smart artistic set: Lady Lavery, Bakst, Knoblock, Stravinsky, Diaghilev and Nijinsky are all I remember. I sat next to Nijinsky and found him as interesting as I had done the year before. He was so different from all the smart people at luncheon, for he was such a pure artist, a drop of the essence of art, and quite impersonal; he was charming to me. After this he came to tea with me several times. I asked Anrep to meet him and he stayed for hours talking about Russian myths and religion. He said he would like to meet the young artists that I knew, so the next time he came I had several of them ready for him: Duncan Grant, Lytton Strachey, Simon Bussy, Granville Barker, the Aranyis and others, young painters. He was much happier when he was with that sort of people and he enjoyed their appreciation. The next time only Duncan Grant came. Last year (1931) when Charlie Chaplin came to tea with me, he also asked to meet some of the young artists, and I again called in, amongst others, Lytton Strachey and Duncan Grant to meet him. Nijinsky and Charlie Chaplin certainly have much in common, much of the same intensity of passion and absorption in the ideas that they express, but Nijinsky was far more impersonal than Charlie Chaplin, freer from temperament and freer from himself. Nijinsky talked a good deal about his new ballet *Le Sacre du Printemps,* in which he expressed the idea of pagan worship, the religious instinct in primitive nature, fear, ecstasy, developing into frenzy and utter self-oblation. It was too intense and terrible, too much an expression of ideas to please the public who are accustomed to graceful toe-dancing or voluptuous Eastern scenes. Nijinsky's reaction to this lavish display was a conversion to Tolstoyism; Charlie Chaplin's reaction to his own wealth and the luxury of Hollywood is a conversion to

Major Douglas's scheme of finance, the abolition of capital-
ism and the substitution of vouchers for money.

The next really interesting event was my visit to Joseph
Conrad at Ashford in Kent. At this time Henry James came to
see us fairly often, and as I knew that Conrad was a friend of
his I timidly said that I should very much like to see him, as
I much admired his writings. Henry James held up his hands
in horror, and was so perturbed that he paced up and down
the grey drawing-room. I remember best some of his exclama-
tions and expostulations: "But, dear lady . . . but dear lady . . .
He has lived his life at sea—dear lady, he has never met 'civilized' women. Yes, he is interesting, but he would not understand you. His wife, she is a good cook. She is a Catholic as he
is, but . . . No, dear lady, he has lived a rough life, and is not
used to talk to—" an upward movement of the arms had to
describe who—and it was, of course, myself. This was not encouraging, but it was not the sort of discouragement that would
turn me aside from what I had so set my heart upon. I think
Henry James must have written to Conrad to prepare him for
the visit of the lady that Henry James thought so grand, for I
received a letter of welcome and went down to Ashford, reading that wonderful book of his reminiscences in the train, or
rather trying to keep my attention fixed on it, for I was so excited and nervous that it was difficult.

When I had told Desmond MacCarthy of my projected
visit, he had given me elaborate meandering advice—especially
was I to wear a smart and rather elaborate dress, as he was sure
anyone like Conrad who saw few ladies from London would
appreciate the note of fantasy in his guest. This was not difficult for me to supply, for my trouble was always to appear
conventional and discreet. Conrad's eldest son, John, met me
in a motor, and I found Conrad himself standing at the door

of the house ready to receive me. How different from the picture Henry James had evoked, for Conrad's appearance was really that of a Polish nobleman. His manner was perfect, almost too elaborate; so nervous and sympathetic that every fibre of him seemed electric, which gave him the air of a highly-polished and well-bred man.

He talked English with a strong accent, as if he tasted his words in his mouth before pronouncing them; but he talked extremely well, though he had always the talk and manner of a foreigner. It seemed difficult to believe that this charming gentleman with high square shoulders, which he shrugged now and again so lightly, and the unmistakably foreign look, had been a captain in the English Merchant Service, and was, too, such a master of English prose. He was dressed very carefully in a blue double-breasted jacket. He talked on apparently with great freedom about his life—more ease and freedom indeed than an Englishman would have allowed himself. He spoke of the horrors of the Congo, from the moral and physical shock of which he said he had never recovered, the impression had been so deep that he felt he would never lose it—but that out of this experience had come *The Heart of Darkness* and *The Outpost of Duty*, which he wrote on his honeymoon in Brittany, as he also did *The Idiots*; but of this story he obviously didn't think very highly—it was too much derived from Guy de Maupassant. I wondered what his wife thought of these strange and haunting companions of their honeymoon! But she seemed a nice and good-looking fat creature, an excellent cook, as Henry James said, and was indeed a good and reposeful mattress for this hypersensitive, nerve-wrecked man, who did not ask from his wife high intelligence, only an assuagement of life's vibrations.

He complained with a great deal of movement and manner

233

that writing was a most painful effort, and that he did not feel the need of expression, but obviously he would never have made the first attempt if he had not felt the gnawing and discomfort of the creator. As I sat there I could hardly believe that I was really talking to the man whose work had haunted me for years, and about whom I had thought and wondered with such intensity. He made me feel so natural and very much myself, that I was almost afraid of losing the thrill and wonder of being there, although I was vibrating with intense excitement inside; and even now, as I write this, I feel almost the same excitement, the same thrill of having been in the presence of one of the most remarkable men I have known. His eyes under their pent-house lids revealed the suffering and the intensity of his experiences; when he spoke of his work, there came over them a sort of misty, sensuous, dreamy look, but they seemed to hold deep down the ghosts of old adventures and experiences—once or twice there was something in them one almost suspected of being wicked. I was amused some years later when I was talking to a dear old Canterbury canon's wife—the mother of Mrs. Inge—who had known Conrad and who was obviously fascinated by him, to hear her say, "But I am afraid he might drag me down to Hell and I don't want to go there." To which I laughingly replied, "I would willingly go with Conrad." But then I believe whatever strange wickedness would tempt this super-subtle Pole, he would be held in restraint by an equally delicate sense of honour.

He talked with great admiration of Henry James. I, unfortunately, said that sometimes Henry James's very exaggerated and perfunctory and rather false worldly humour annoyed me. This Conrad, I felt, did not like, and I was sorry I had said such a stupid thing, which was so open to misunderstanding.

Yes, it was a tangled, tortured, and very complex soul that

looked out through those mysterious eyes, sensitive and understanding—one who had gone down in his imagination and experience into the hell which others had contrived to make of
their lives. He had never sat on the bank and watched coldly;
that one could see at once, for he was so obviously battered by
the journeys he had taken through the souls of the men whom
he had known. The sea with its calm, its storms, to him was but
a mirror of the restless motion of the souls of men. His prose
that has such a magic and vibrating beauty seems the outcome
of these mysterious experiences upon an instrument so sensitively tuned.

In his talk he led me along many paths of his life, but I felt
that he did not wish to explore the jungle of emotions that lay
dense on either side, and that his apparent frankness had a
great reserve. This may perhaps be characteristic of Poles as it
is of the Irish. I find in an article of an unknown writer in a
review of Conrad's letters, this sentence, which I have kept
by me:

"In *A Personal Record* the public were taken into the Park
but were kept to the broad paths, no intimacies there. We
were eluded still by the impalpable suggestion of huge conflicts of good and evil, of beauty and ugliness, in which the
things of good report in a faithful world were trampled under
the hoofs of infamy and ignorance."

I myself thought the central mystery consisted of the bruised
ideals of a sensitive idealist combined with the courage of a
man of action who was also an artist, that he had to face truth
at all costs.[6]

---

[6] In her journal she wrote: "He came with me to the station, and altogether it was a wonderful day. I found I couldn't help desiring that
he should like me, and believing also that he was quite indifferent."
P.M.

235

A short time after this first visit I took Bertie Russell down to see him. It was, indeed, he that had recommended me to read Conrad's books. They understood each other immediately and even as they walked together in Conrad's garden had a moment of intense intimacy, some spell caught them and made them look deep down into each other's eyes. Such things happen rarely, it was obviously the recognition that both these souls belonged to the kingdom of the sufferers, and the passionate and the unreconcilable.

He told Bertie Russell that he found it difficult to talk to his boys or to young people, as he disliked being insincere, and at the same time he shrank from burdening them with his own experience and knowledge of life.

I visited him again once or twice, but as he was very patriotic I did not dare go during the war, as I felt sure he would disapprove of my views, but in 1923 while Philip and I were staying with Bernard Holland not far from Conrad's new home in Kent we all went over to see him (he had not met Philip before). It was a perfectly happy day. We found him in a pleasant country house on the edge of a park, an old-fashioned house with large low rooms, which he had furnished with great distinction and with something of the air, it seemed to me, of a Polish château. It was the sort of garden that you might find described, with its view over the rather monotonous landscape of the Park, in a Henry James novel, and Conrad with his polished air was, you might have supposed, very well set there. But the view was too narrow for his taste. He missed, as he said, one thing: "It has no horizon."

As we sat round a large table at tea he talked with even more freedom, and I felt easier than before. He sat by me and he told me of his early love of England, and the sea, and his longing to get upon an English ship. His first sight of the

sea had been at Venice. He was then a boy travelling with a
tutor and he described to us in his swift way some of the emotion that he felt. But it was later at Marseilles that his life at
sea began. The Carlists were then a power in the Mediterra-
nean, which made the life more exciting; and looking down with
a smile, he murmured—with what strange memories in him,
which also flitted across his face—"It was here that I sowed
my wild oats." When at last he got taken upon an English ship
and came to England, he did not know anything of the language, and it was in a little inn at Lowestoft, frequented by
sailors, at which he stayed between his voyages, that he puzzled
out in the articles of *The Standard*—the only English literature
to be found there—his first lessons in English. Frequently in
his talk this love of England and the English would recur. He
specially liked simple young men who went into the Army and
the Navy; clear, true and direct; he delighted in their fairness
of mind. They were the people, he said, with whom he got on
most easily—"Not the learned or the intellectuals." It was the
simple adventurous Englishman that he liked, but as a rule
Conrad's talk was gay and witty. He liked to surprise you by
some slight, swift sentence. I remember how, when we happened to talk of poetry and I was urging him to read T. S.
Eliot's poetry, he professed that he never read it—"Oh, I'm
not caught by poetry," he said, "not I." He also spoke again of
the Congo. Knowing that he had met Casement there I asked
about him. All that I now remember of what he said was that
he met him emerging from one of the densest and most perilous
jungles in a white linen jacket and white tennis shoes, and for
arms and protection a walking-stick and a native boy. As he
described it I felt that in spite of disapproving of what Casement did in the war he bowed before such quixotic and aristocratic behaviour and nonchalant courage.

And again when he was describing his adventures in Poland where he and his wife and children, after many years of voluntary exile, had gone to show his ancestral home to his boys, the war was declared the day of their arrival, and it was with great difficulty that they were able to return to England—"Oh, it was a circus, a perfect circus," he kept saying, "with my wife and two boys there."

When we first arrived Conrad brought up a little chair and sat down to talk to me about all this, but his wife at once came and sat on my other side and showed me page by page of a little book of snapshots of this journey—dull, ill-focused, conventional little photographs—and it was only with the greatest difficulty that I made myself polite to her. But I knew he was very exacting that she should be treated with proper respect.

After tea we walked in the garden, on brick-paved paths, roses and flowers of all sorts around us. I had remembered Desmond's advice of old, and had put on a very lovely blue Persian jacket, over a lavender silk dress. Mrs. Conrad and I walked on ahead, while he and Philip followed. It was a lovely early autumn evening, with a mellow sunset light. On turning back from our slow pacing (Mrs. Conrad was lame), I saw the two men looking at us, and I knew that Conrad had been pleased with the touch of fantasy that I had been able to add to his garden. I asked Philip afterwards and found that Conrad had said, "How beautiful your wife looks in her colours against the green." Philip said, "Yes, that coat came from Persia."

Before leaving he took me into his own little room where he worked—small and simple, books round the walls, a photograph of his youngest boy with himself stuck up against the books. He found a book that had lately been privately printed —*The Ship's Mate*—which he wished to give me. He sat

down at the large writing-table and with a fat pen wrote my
name and his own in a book. As I stood opposite him he
looked up, and I caught with my eyes one of his surprising
and exciting glances—it was one that I had not seen before. I
received it and carried it with me, precious and unforgettable.
But one can only remember such things, not write of them.
How may a stranger to these imperial looks know them from
eyes of other mortals?

I cannot trace in the dark tunnels of my memory how I first
knew Gilbert Cannan and his wife. That rather charming and
gifted, but conceited novelist of whom we saw a great deal,
and who was the forerunner and introducer of other people
who played important parts in our life.

I believe I must have written to him about one of his first
books, *Round the Corner,* which I thought original and interesting. He had recently run off with Sir James Barrie's wife, and
perhaps I felt that people would be prejudiced against him on
this account, and certainly on the outside it did not appear very
honourable, as he had been one of Barrie's protégés. I believe
Mary Cannan, however, had not found Barrie very satisfactory
as a husband and she became entranced with this young man,
who had indeed the appearance of a rather vacant Sir Galahad,
and whose mind was prolific, poetic and romantic. I never understood how he could have been tempted to run away with
this lady, for she was double his age, and devoid of any atmosphere of romance, and certainly unable to run very far or fast.
But how can one divine the reasons for such foolish acts? It
was probably prompted by quixotic pity on Gilbert's part, but
it was doomed to be a failure, and this doom ahead already
cast its shadow backward. She was, poor woman, so determined
to keep herself young and sprightly when they came together
to see us—she so solid with thin lips and a carefully preserved

complexion, like a very competent lady house-decorator and upholsteress (this was, in fact, her chief interest), he, thin and tall, towering above her, always looking with his pale, romantic eyes into space, and shaking his fair hair and tilting his large thin nose in the air, while she vigorously chatted in a loud, harsh voice about what she and Gillie had done. It made one raise one's hands like Henry James, in horror.

But still one admired anyone who could cast off luxury and a comfortable home and devote herself in poverty to a young and as yet unknown novelist. I suppose on her side it was the maternal instinct. She always said that she would retire from his life if he fell in love with anyone his own age. But this is easy to say. It was often pathetic, and I fear rather comical, to see this gallant little woman, determinedly marshalling all her powers to keep herself erect, brisk and youthful. At times she would almost convince one that she was what she desired to appear, until suddenly, while hurrying along, she would fall down, exclaiming "Oh, Gillie," and then one realized that the effort to walk by the side of her Gillie, who always strode ahead of her and took no notice of her or even of her fall, had been too much even for resolute limbs, and she had collapsed.

They both came fairly often to tea and to our Thursday evenings, obviously enjoying being "received." Sometimes he would come and stay a night or two in our spare room, and I would immensely enjoy his talk, which was a mixture of the ideas of Blake and Plato and Goethe. Indeed, I still believe it was good—he was quite impersonal and seemed as if he were talking his thoughts aloud, but as the thoughts were sympathetic and stimulating to me I enjoyed it. He consumed a vast number of cigarettes while he mused and held forth. He also amused us all very much by sending me a sonnet which he addressed to me, on the "pleasure and delight and beauty of a lady in Bedford Square," but I soon found that he had also sent one to Mrs. Raymond Asquith to whom I had introduced him, and who lived a few doors from us in Bedford Square. On comparing them, we found we had shared the same sonnet.

In August we spent some time at Black Hall, Oxford, Philip's home. We took it from his mother for some weeks. Julian was with us and a young Swiss lady, Marion Colomb, whom, while we were at Lausanne, I had engaged to come and look after Julian and teach her French. She had great charm with rather an old-fashioned air about her, long, lanky legs, and a small, very lovely head and a ruminating expression. At first she suffered terribly, poor girl, from homesickness, but gradually she grew very fond of us, and only once did the Swiss nostalgia overcome her. It was when I said that I didn't like snow-covered mountains. She told me afterwards that she fled upstairs and remained in her room crying for hours. How could anyone she liked say such a terrible thing? She was particularly intelligent and clever, and I enjoyed her company very much, as she was also very amusing about her views of England. Her beauty and simplicity and shyness were very attractive, and she had a very romantic air. I had hoped that a friend of ours would have married her, but he could not make up his mind, and when they corresponded he found her letters so clever and accomplished, that he could not bear, he said, to marry anyone who wrote such much better letters than himself.

I find this entry in my journal:

"I enjoy the quiet days here very much. They help me collect myself, and to follow out Vittoz's rules and advice, for I see that they are good and really help one. I want to go on and become more and more conscious, and to sort out my instincts. It is there that character seems to tell: the judgment as to what instincts are good to cultivate, and which ought to be eliminated. One's character is like a casket of jewels, full of false or real stones, some to be worn and polished, some to be thrown away as rubbish. Characters are wrecked by undisciplined instincts, they never seem to know that they are deluding themselves. As Plato says: "An unexamined life is not worth living."

"Rachel Varhagen's *Life* has interested me as it shows what a woman can do who flings her whole personality into what she does, but with her it is more passion than attention.

"I wish I could write, that is what I would rather do than anything else, but I have no confidence in myself, and the only thing I can do now is to write letters, letters, and they are so ephemeral, and are probably very stupid. How difficult it is to know what are real opinions, one's own or other people's—they are so often only impressions of emotions, convincing at the moment but impossible to build on, and I find men's opinions—Bertie's and Philip's—are often only the outcome of passing emotions, and they say and do things in emotion that they don't fundamentally mean. It is no use paying too much attention to them.

"I believe women are much more cunning and reserved than men, and control and hide passing emotions, or perhaps it is that they don't intellectualize them, and that they work them off and express them in side issues, frivolity, shopping and suchlike things. Men take their emotions more seriously. I know I do not wish to speak of mine but deal with them in my secret life. I wonder if everyone has a secret companion, a second self, with whom they discuss their thoughts and emotions—a 'secret sharer.' I cannot imagine anyone existing without this secret companion. We wear each other out by our discussions."

¶ *Oxford. August 25th*

"The more I see of life the more difficult it seems to me to live it well. It is like walking a tight-rope or, as Butler says, like playing a violin in public without having learnt to play the violin. One can never expect life to be all plain sailing but must be ready to courageously play one's instrument through the difficult passages. It would be very insipid if it were all very easy. Of course, some difficulties are interesting and exciting but the test comes when they are homely and banal—it is here that the effort comes in, for if not they block the way to a creative life. Bertie says I am very selfish because I mind all the trivial fussings of life so much—perhaps I have very little power of eliminating creases but I want to make a harmony out of life, not a fretful discord of false notes.

"So many young women seem either drowsy and half-awake like puppies or else run wild like young colts careering round green fields in the spring. Perhaps it is nature protecting the nerves of the young. I expect I wore myself out by being too strenuous and anxious, and by feeling every moment was precious."

Oxford in August had great charm, it was almost like one of the old Italian towns, deserted, beautiful and romantic. The sedate, pedantic dons and their wives were all scattered; we had a very happy time, for there remained a few interesting people, such as Sir Walter Raleigh and the Prices, who lived at the lovely old house The Judges' Lodgings, a few doors from Black Hall; Madame Duclos and Vernon Lee were staying with Miss Price. Madame Duclos was Mary Robinson and writes well. She was one of a group of clever and intellectual women, Vernon Lee being another. I found her sitting in the hall at the Prices's house one day that I called. She struck me

243

as being rather artificial and French (she lives in Paris) and she has an exceedingly high, penetrating voice, but she is a good talker.

We dined with Mabel Price and had a very gay dinner— Vernon Lee, Mary Robinson, the Walter Raleighs—they all talked hard against each other, but Mary Robinson's penetrating tones trumpeted across the table with great insistence, drowning even Vernon's uninterruptable voice. Walter Raleigh watched with amusement, as he had backed Mary Robinson to talk everyone down. He was in a gay, delightful, witty mood, and said many good things, and did not seem to be overstraining himself as he often did. I remember he said, "One never can care for another person unless one wants *something* back. One may pretend that one doesn't, but really one always desires them to give one some affection back, otherwise it is mawkish. It must have reciprocity." He said that he liked to contemplate George Moore. It interested him, but he knew George Moore would have no earthly use for him.

I also remember that we were discussing if one could tell another of his or her faults. Raleigh said if one really loved anyone you can do it a few times in their life, but it can only be done in an impulse of real affection, and he suddenly stretched forward with a kind, affectionate movement, and put his hand on the knee of someone there to show how he would do it. What a strange, haunted man he was!

This little time in Oxford when we all met fairly often— the Raleighs, Vernon Lee, Eugenie Strong, the Prices, Anne Sedgwick, Ethel Sands and Harry Norton, who was staying with us—gave me an idea of what a circle of friends could be. They all knew each other well, and struck sparks from each other. Of course, Raleigh was a very good leader and conductor of conversation. Vernon was very amusing about "The

Younger Generation." She said—which was true—that they lacked "ardour." Vernon herself and all her contemporaries were "dyspeptic," but however much they were hampered they had so much desire and ardour that it kept them going, and she pointed to Madame Duclos and said, *"She* has it still." Modern youth is so discontented and dissatisfied that it prevents them from being a force in the world.

Philip was still Member for Burnley, and in September of this year (1913) we went for a month to a house just outside Burnley that had been lent to us by Lady O'Hagan. It stood on the edge of the beautiful wild, rocky country that surrounds Burnley, and it seemed just on the verge of being already tainted by the blackness of that city which boasts more chimneys than any other town of the same size. The first few days we were there was the time of the annual holiday and the fires in all the factories had been extinguished. The town without smoke, noise or the red flames at night looked unreal, ghostly and arrested, but soon again the clang and the smoke and the hooters and the noisy hard life started. I would watch this place which might almost be a town of Dante's Inferno and wonder and wonder how life was possible here—the grey stone houses in the long, black, slimy streets and the general air of dirt and monotony. No colour could be seen, for even a patch of grass was covered with slimy soot. The people are pale and small, but very lively and excitable and very good-hearted and full of humour and wit. But I could not see what they lived for—politics and football were the only things that interested them.

On Saturdays we went to the football match. About 14,000 people there, all packed together in the usual drizzle and veil of fog. It was mostly men who were there, their coat collars turned up against their white intense faces. They make one

245

great solid dark circle of human beings round the stadium, the only touch of colour being the red-and-white advertisement of Oxo on the hoarding, and the striped jerseys of the footballers as they rushed over the black ground. I found it intensely exciting, sitting in the cold, draughty stand with 14,000 intensely excited human beings around shouting and gesticulating wildly, so intoxicated that they had ceased to exist except as a mass, vicariously participating in the game. One was caught up into the storm of passion and found oneself contorted and wriggling with excitement, breathlessly urging on one's favourite player. One very neat, delicate little fellow with red hair called Mosscrop, who was a schoolteacher, was a pleasure to watch, so agile, so clever and precise in his movements (I heard afterwards that he was one of the few conscientious objectors from Burnley). Julian's favourite was a slim youth in a green jersey, Burnley's goalkeeper, called Jerry, who was a blacksmith. It was almost frightening at the end of the match when the great torrent of black-coated men poured forth into the road, rough, pushing, jostling, to get . . . where? That was what I asked. After such intoxicating excitement, what was there to be done? For one was in that unsatisfactory state of having the emotions and nerves exhausted and the body unused, and one instinctively exclaimed, "What can we do now?" For it was obviously the team alone who felt decently and wholly tired.

I remember this rush of strong violent men excited but rather frightened me, but still I always enjoy being in the midst of a crowd. Drink, violence, murder, seemed to be the inevitable reaction. Apart from their work in factories the men and women at a place like Burnley have but little mental development. There was certainly one small technical school, but to advance out into the world of science and art was very rare.

But interesting as life on the edge of Burnley was, I found it intensely depressing; my spirit seemed to roam over that gloomy town and found no foothold, nowhere where I could rest, and I felt so intensely sorry for and sympathetic with these delightful, kind, enthusiastic and emotional people, bereft of what was to me so essential: ecstasy and all enjoyment of art and beauty. I find in my journal pages of questioning as to what their lives were really filled with, and what could be done to enrich them. But so much has happened since these days! It seems useless to recall it now.

As I remember visits to great weaving-sheds, or gatherings of any sort that we attended, I have vivid recollections of excitable floods of enthusiastic affection poured out upon us. As I went through the weaving-sheds the noise was so great that I could not hear what was said to me even when it was shouted quite close to my ear. Sometimes the girls, despairing of making me hear by words, would kiss me instead! They used to understand each other by lip-reading.

In October 1913 Julian went to Leysin with her nurse, "Billy" (Miss Townshend). Philip and I went out to see her and found her far stronger, beautifully firm and brown, lying out on her veranda. Philip and I went to Rome for about a fortnight, and returned to her at Leysin again. I stayed behind with her and I went out to her later on and looked after her to give her nurse a rest. How I suffered from the cold!

In February 1914 I find this in my journal:

"Thoughts come to me and fly away and if I don't catch them here they will fade altogether. They are not of great worth except as inward resolutions. A soul seems as if it were a child within one, growing and moving and living a life curiously apart from one's ordinary life.

"For many months I have felt a dire loneliness that nothing

247

will ever relieve. I seem to have tried everyone and found them all wanting, and yet I know the fault is my own. It is as if I were condemned to walk through life quite detached; quite apart from others, and not to enter into their lives, never to arouse in others feelings of sympathy or affection, or a desire to give to me.

"At one time I seem to have plunged into others' lives—Roger Fry, Lamb, Lytton—but from some cause they all seem to have come to an end. So for ever and for ever must I float on with a passionate sense of the tragedy of life inside me. But so it must be, the only thing that I dread to lose is the power of feeling that I am on the edge of an unknown life. Just now and then one gets on tip-toe and peeps over into the unknown land, and unless one does life is drab and ghastly.

"I have just returned from a week-end at Oxford which wasn't a success. I get very irritable there. I have a feeling that if I could take my inward life in my hands and turn the understanding, good-tempered side round to the top it would be all right, turn the dial round so as to be in harmony with the electric current of life. Then one would cease to be personal, or one's person would be as current for good."

These spring months of 1914 were more than usually gay and interesting. Everything seemed to move with an odd ease and brilliance. London seemed indeed to be having a season such as it had not known for many years. Distinguished foreigners flocked here. New Russian ballets were being performed; lovely operas were sung at Covent Garden, and our little *salon* in Bedford Square shared in the gaiety and glory, for it was beginning to be known as a centre for artists and some of the foreign visitors found their way to us. It all made a very delightful summer.

Count Harry Kessler, a German, interested in art and printing, came to see us very often, and the author of the ballet *Potiphar's Wife* and *The Miracle,* Vollmöller, and the very beautiful woman who was acting in it, Maria Carmi. And besides these, Nijinsky and all our old English friends, Lytton Strachey, the Desmond MacCarthys, the Asquiths, etc., and the Gilbert Cannans. The last came, as I have said, and stayed with us from time to time, and he and I had endless conversations about life. He was very anxious that we should know a friend of his, Mark Gertler, a young Jewish painter who lived in Whitechapel with his family, fur-sewers. Gilbert Cannan was then writing a novel based on Gertler's life, which he called *Mendel.* His people were extremely poor, indeed always living on the verge of starvation. The only paintings that he had ever seen were those done by pavement artists, but somehow he had been made known to William Rothenstein through some Jewish Society, which enabled him to go to the Slade where naturally he met other young artists. Hence there began a life of intense excitement, emotion and romance for this youth who, with his small delicate frame and shock of dark curly hair looked almost like a girl, but who was in reality passionate and ambitious and exceedingly observant and sensitive.

The Cannans saw a great deal of him—he had been sent to stay with them to get some country air—and they arranged that I should go down and see him in Spitalfields. I went off to Liverpool Street station and found my way from there to the mean, hot, stuffy, smelly little street where he lived. I found the house and felt very tall and large walking up the creaky little stairs. Gertler always says that the first sight that he had of me was the crest of a purple feather: nearer and nearer it ascended, and at last the hat itself and then me, as if a large and odd bird had arrived. Indeed, I hardly believe that I was able to stand upright in the room, so tall and erect was this feather, so low was his room. I found the Cannans, and Gertler showed me his pictures. One of a fruit stall with pyramids of oranges and apples was very interesting, and another of the birth of Eve made a great impression on me. They had the intense, tangible, ruthless, hot quality that most of his work always has, but in those early days there was still the Jewish tradition, the Jewish mark, which gave them a fine, intense, almost archaic quality. I asked him to bring the "Fruit Stall" to Bedford Square as we could show it on a Thursday evening. This was done and I managed to get people to come that evening who would be interested in it—Walter Sickert and Mr. Jasper Ridley. I see little Mark Gertler now, standing by his picture, thin, erect and trembling internally, if not externally, at the excitement of having his work looked at and discussed by anyone like Sickert, whom he so respected.

What fun it all was, that summer. Everything seemed easy and light, as if the atmosphere had something electric and gay in it, imbuing anything that was done with a lovely gay, easy quality, absorbing from it the worry and care and fret, and gilding it with possibilities of growth.

I was interested in Gertler and admired the persistence and resolution that dwelt in this apparently fragile body. He came to tea with me and I tried to find out what he was really like, for although I knew about his early struggles and his internal life I felt I knew very little about what he was like in character. All that I remember from our conversation was that he told me more of his life and I asked him if he didn't find it hard reconciling his home life with the life he lived at the Slade, and with Mr. Eddie Marsh, with whom he often stayed and went into London society. He confessed that he could not but feel antagonistic to the smart and the worldly, while at the same time he felt depressed by the want of cultivation of his own people. I saw how intensely difficult it is to understand each other's experiences and how little we ever do it, when I thought of this little boy being fed on any little herring that could be bought cheap of an evening, and of the life in that dark, hot East End street. It was not, indeed, until after he went to the Slade that he knew what it was to go to the country or to see horses and cows grazing in the fields. Such a limited, almost walled-in youth may give great intensity of vision, but does not enlarge the imagination.

It was this summer that we got to know the two Spencers—Stanley and Gilbert—who were still living with their parents in a little semi-detached house at Cookham. They had as yet shown but little of their work, but what I had seen was, I thought, extremely good—especially a picture by Stanley of fruit gatherers. I had been appointed buyer for the Contemporary Art Society for six months, and with the money entrusted to me I bought a large picture of a farmyard by Gilbert Spencer, also the "Fruit Stall" by Mark Gertler. The Spencers were passionately devoted to music as well as painting. Their old father had been an organist and taught music to young ladies in the neighbourhood of Cookham. On a lovely hot Saturday afternoon we went down to Cookham to see them, and found the old father and mother in their little house. A disused bedroom upstairs was used by the two artist brothers as a studio. They had more the appearance of two healthy, red-faced farm labourers, with their rough shocks of hair and teeth protruding in all directions. But in spite of their odd appearance one couldn't talk to them without realizing how remarkable they were. I felt that they had sprung from the soil and were, what is very rare in England, two real painters.[7] Stanley, the elder one, who was smaller in stature, was the more re-

[7] She means, no doubt, that they were painters naturally and by force of instinct: not merely by training and profession.   P.M.

markable of the two, more of a genius, more intense. Besides these two brothers there are several others, one who before the war was Professor of Music at Cologne Conservatoire, another a conjurer. It was a delightful day—a hot old-fashioned summer's day—and we walked by the river with the old father and three of the sons, the two wild rubicund-faced figures from their own pictures, and a neat dapper brother who was afterwards killed in the war. We talked of their painting and of Mozart and Handel, and when the time came for us to return we discovered that we should miss the train. So Philip, in a fit of recklessness, hailed a London taxi that happened to be passing through the village street and we returned to London in it, leaving the Spencer group so astonished and amazed at our reckless extravagance that they all three nearly fell backward with their canvas shoes in air. I carried back with me two drawings, one by Stanley and one by Gilbert, which we bought.

A few days later Lady Ripon[8] offered me the use of her grand box at Covent Garden for the night that *Don Giovanni* was being given. Immediately the thought came to me—"I must take the Spencer family," as I knew they loved Mozart. And so I entered into communication with them. They were delighted, but a great difficulty arose, because no one was allowed into the sacred precincts of Covent Garden except in evening dress, and an evening suit was a thing which neither of them possessed. Old Mr. Spencer had indeed a frock coat which would pass, but how were we to dress these two very odd-looking little men, who in appearance were so very like farm

[8] The Marchioness of Ripon, tall, handsome, and devoted to music, was a conspicuous figure in the London society of that day and one of the principal patrons and supporters of the opera at Covent Garden. She had known Ottoline from childhood, having been a friend of her mother, Lady Bolsover. There is a description of her earlier in this book, when she was Lady Lonsdale.   P.M.

labourers that a smock was what would have really suited their figures? I was determined not to be daunted, so telephoned to several young men I knew asking them if they would lend an evening suit. Philip's naturally were useless, as he is well over six feet, and Stanley Spencer is little over four feet and Gilbert five. I gathered together a choice of trousers, waistcoats and swallow-tails, and with safety-pins they appeared for dinner.[9] I laugh now when I see in my memory their strange appearance, Stanley's coat-tails nearly touching the ground, the sleeves hanging down, the trousers like long concertinas on his legs. A doubt arose in my mind whether the officials would allow such oddities up the stairs to the grand tier. However, I had a very full black silk cloak, which I wore, and on arriving spread it as much as possible to act as a screen to my two odd companions. I felt like a great hen moving about with a brood of unfledged chickens under my wing. From the front I think they were fairly well hidden; what the back view was like I didn't mind. Once in the grand box we were safe, and I breathed happily. Their two ruddy faces and unkempt heads of hair first arose over the front, and their old father's with his long white beard, and the mother, neat and trim in black with a white silk crochet collar, made I expect a comic picture—but nothing mattered. The music was divine, the performance the best I have ever seen or heard, and we were all perfectly happy.

The two brothers often came to see us, and Stanley stayed with us now and then in London. He was very odd and had very remarkable religious views. I feel he was more like Blake than anyone I knew.

On June 1st 1914 I find in my journal:

[9] Mr. Gilbert Spencer, in his book *Stanley Spencer*, describes, and confirms, this incident, enriching it with a drawing which comprises an unmistakable view of Millie, the Morrells's parlourmaid, from the back.

"I have seen masses of people lately, and it has all been tremendously interesting and wonderful. I wish I could keep rested and fresh and able to expand as I feel I have it in me to do. But still I am better and less nervous than I used to be, and I hope that what I so much desire to do can be accomplished, to give real friendship, and to gather people together who have something 'real' in them. I should like this house to become a centre where the contact is sincere, and free from foolish gossip and spite, that seems to be the chief topic of most London drawing-rooms. This sounds all very priggish—perhaps I am catching it from Bertie."

I am astonished as I look back at the amount that I did in those days. People were always coming to luncheon and tea, very often to dinner; Philip's politics were all-important, and entailed constant visits to Burnley for meetings and social gatherings. Julian was a constant anxiety as she was very delicate, and my own health was wretched (I had constant headaches) which made life a great effort, but I suppose I was gifted with vitality and, what is more important, an impulse and natural interest in others, stimulated with curiosity about life, which made me squeeze as much into my day as I possibly could. I generally kept the mornings to myself and sat writing in the little closet off the drawing-room, where I was hidden and alone.

Bertie had been away from March to June in America, as he had been appointed as a temporary professor in philosophy at Harvard. He wrote very often. He had large classes of enthusiastic pupils, but none that appeared to him of much promise, except two—one a Greek called Demos, and a young man called Eliot, who, Bertie feared, was too cultivated and polished to be very creative. This is what he said (he wrote on March 27th 1914):

"This morning two of my pupils came together to ask me a question about work—one named Eliot is very well-dressed and polished with manners of the finest Etonian type. The other, an unshaven Greek appropriately named Demos, who earns the money for his fees by being a waiter in a restaurant. The two were obviously friends and had on neither side the slightest consciousness of social difference.

"I found they were not nearly so well grounded as I had thought. They were absolutely candid and quite intelligent, but obviously had not been taught with the minute thoroughness that we practise in England—window-dressing seems inevitable to Americans."

Again in May 1914:

"I have been spending the week-end in the country at the house of Fuller (of Plotinus). It was beautiful there, weather like mid-summer and the trees like early spring. He has a lake and woods and various agreeable things and by all the rules he ought to be agreeable himself, being good-natured and cultivated, but for some reason I am always saying to myself, 'After all, you are an ass,' though I can't quite make out what makes him one. I think it is that he is always imitating English people. He lives with his mother who is an arrant snob, he is too, though more subtly. My pupil Eliot was there—the only one who is civilized, and he is ultra-civilized, knows his classics very well, is familiar with all French literature from Villon to Vildrach, and is altogether impeccable in his taste but has no vigour or life—or enthusiasm. He is going to Oxford where I expect he will be very happy."

I imagine it was during this week-end visit or in consequence of it that T. S. Eliot wrote *Mr. Apollinax*.

Bertie told me afterwards that Eliot had made one remark that had seemed to denote an original mind. It was that Villon resembled Heraclitus. I puzzled over this but soon it became quite clear to me when I recalled what little I knew of Heraclitus and compared them together.

"If you expect not the unexpected, ye shall not find truth."

"If you do not expect the unexpected, you will not find it —for it is hard to be sought out and difficult."

With the lovely "Ballade" of Villon which begins:

Je meurs de soif auprès de la fontaine

and especially this verse:

Rien ne m'est plus sûr que la chose incertaine
Obscur fors a qui est tant évident
Donte ne fais fors en chose certaine
Science tiens à soudain accident.

During the summer there had been great excitement politically over the question of Ulster. It had loomed dark and turbulent on the horizon. Then there came the assassination of the Archduke at Sarajevo, which switched aside interest from Ulster, as everyone feared it would mean war between Austria and Serbia.

I went on a visit to the Asquiths at the Wharf on July 25th, and this is what I find in my journal after the visit:

"Just returned from the Wharf—not a large party, Edwin Montagu the most interesting, and of course Violet and the sons. Most of the talk was about the assassination of the Crown Prince. I went on a walk with Asquith along the river and into the meadows. I asked him what would happen about Austria and Serbia. He said with a laugh—'This will take the attention away from Ulster, which is a good thing.' He did not seem worried.

"Montagu seemed more disturbed as he feared it would lead

to a European War. He paced up and down the room saying, 'Of course, I suppose we shall have to go to war sooner or later with Germany about the Navy, and this may be as good a time as any other—they are probably not so well prepared now as they would be later.' Someone mentioned Belgium but he and Asquith seemed to think we were under no obligation to assist them. And amongst themselves they said, 'We have made no pledge to help them.' "

Except Montagu no one seemed to be disturbed about the situation.

Then came news of the assassination of Jean Jaurès, after the great Socialist meeting in Paris to protest against the war. He had just made a magnificent speech. This was a terrible blow, for he was the only man in Europe who would have headed a strong Peace Party.

The following week-end Philip and I spent at Black Hall —or rather we had meant to spend it there. But the news of the possibility of war, that England would join in the war, was so threatening and disturbing, and Philip became so agitated and unhappy that he said he must return to London at once (Sunday). He wanted to collect a number of M.P.'s together who would make a protest in the House against England joining in.

We arrived back in London and found excited crowds everywhere; even our own quiet Bedford Square filled with bands of youths marching round singing the "Marseillaise" and waving flags. It went on all night, for that day war had been declared between France and Germany. It was torture hearing these voices and knowing what it meant. Philip went down to the House of Commons. I wrote in my journal, Sunday night (August 2nd):

"Philip and I came back from Oxford today. He is determined to speak in the House even if no one else does. I sit here waiting and waiting, simply racked with the horror and madness of the war, and the utter folly of our joining in.

"Philip is out endeavouring to get up a protest meeting, but through want of courage and decision on the part of Grey, he has let the papers and the jingoes get the upper hand, and war madness is running wild and will force his hand. If he had come out bravely for neutrality it might have checked it."

It must have been during the previous week that I went to tea with Violet Asquith at Downing Street. I hear her now describing how undecided Sir Edward Grey was—whether to tell Germany we would come in if France were attacked, or whether to tell France that we should hold aloof and that she must not count on our help. He was, she said, undecided which course to pursue, and she felt a great sympathy for him in this difficulty.

We now know, of course, from the White Paper—what no one then knew outside the Inner Cabinet—that at this time both Germany and Russia were imploring Grey to state frankly what our position in the event of war would be—whether we should join in or stand aside—both saying that if only he would make a frank declaration, war might still be averted; but the opportunity passed, and war became inevitable.

¶ *August 3rd*

"Philip was at the House of Commons all day. I was there and heard him get up to make his protest, which he did splendidly and courageously. If he had not got up in the House there would have been no debate on the question of England joining in the war. He had to cut short his speech as a message came from the House of Lords. Thus it was adjourned to the evening at 6. I can never forget seeing him standing alone with

nearly all the House against him, shouting at him to 'Sit down!'
In the evening when he spoke some members followed him
—Ponsonby, Wedgwood, Rowntree, Hervey, etc."[1]

❡ *August 4th*

"I spent the morning walking up and down Malet Street
and all round the streets near here, with Bertie Russell, both
of us in great despair and unhappiness. I went down again to
the House of Commons and sat in the outer lobby waiting for
news, some of the most awful hours I ever spent."

Already excitement and war elation were gaining ground,
but few people seemed to realize the horror of what it meant.
I sat on the stone seat running along the wall, watching members going in, and the agitated groups of men waiting for news.
A few—Massingham and some others—looked miserable, but
the majority were flushed and excited, and then Lord Ridley
came out and told his brother Jasper that it was "all right." I
asked what that meant—"Why, of course, Sir E. Grey has sent
his ultimatum"—and I looked at his face, flushed and happy,
and marvelled that anyone could look or feel happy at such
dire news.

From that hour I can truthfully say that that pain and unhappiness never left my life, nor Philip's. Whatever one did,
there was always this black night upon me, and in one's eyes
there was always the vision of men in torture. I never understood how people could reconcile themselves to it and forget it.

---

[1] Philip once described the occasion to me. The short adjournment
gave him time to prepare his speech. "A lot of people," he told me, "said
it was the best speech I ever made." But it was the ending of his
political career. After that war, there was no liberal constituency for a
pacifist, and his integrity would not allow him to join the Labour
Party, in whose principles he did not believe.

We walked away from the House of Commons in despair. I remember a passionate force rose up in me and I felt that by my will-power I could stop it. "It must be stopped, it must be stopped," I kept saying. Alas, how futile and self-deluding! But we started immediately, gathering together all those that we knew were against war, and Philip worked very hard organizing a committee to consult and to form plans of what was best to do.

From now onwards our house was a centre for pacifist work. On looking through my little green visitors' book, I find on August 3rd and 4th the names of these three:

Ramsay MacDonald
Arthur Ponsonby
H. Granville Barker

and a day or two later the following:

Arnold Toynbee
Arthur Ponsonby
F. W. Hastie
Charles Trevelyan
E. D. Morel
Ramsay MacDonald

Bertrand Russell
Norman Angell
J. M. Keynes
Duncan Grant
Adrian Stephen

They were a brave little band, and suffered courageously—some were imprisoned, all were persecuted. I always admire Ramsay MacDonald for his firmness during those days; for such a vain man it was not easy to defy public opinion and to go against the great overwhelming stream of patriotic emotion, to feel an outcast from what, of course, appealed to one side of anyone who cared for England—self-sacrifice and work for one's country. I know I myself suffered intensely from this feeling, and yet something made me feel one couldn't join in and help in killing other human beings who were perfectly innocent of any crime or offence. I did what I could in helping an excellent society called "Friends of Foreigners." It supplied money to the wives of interned "enemy aliens," most of whom were German waiters who had been in England many years and frequently had married English wives. At first the men were simply left at home out of work, but as spy mania grew they were herded into vast concentration camps—like cattle —and their wives and children left at home.

There are many entries in my journal at this time:

"After the declaration of war I went down to Carlton House Terrace hoping to see Princess Lichnowsky[2] to say good-bye. I called at the house, now shunned, filled with ghosts of the gay people who had swarmed there, for she was a very re- markable, clever woman, and had gathered together interesting and clever people. Now all gone. It was an empty and hollow house, the tenseness and the tragedy were almost unbearable. A small group of people looking on—partly from sympathy, partly idle, scoffing curiosity."

I walked back up the Haymarket, and as I walked I had one of those odd, sudden and inexplicable visions, of what this war really meant and would entail. The men in the streets were going about as if nothing had happened, carrying parcels, and delivering meat at the Carlton Hotel, and I almost said aloud —"Don't you see that from this moment onward life will be entirely different? All life as it exists now will be swept away. The whole world will be changed, poverty, want, suffering, chaos, will sweep all this easy, happy life before it. You men

[2] Wife of the German ambassador, who used to come sometimes to our parties in Bedford Square, being herself a lover of art and interested in meeting artists.   P.M.

will be wounded, maimed, killed." My eyes seemed, oddly
enough, to travel out over Europe into the farthest edge of
Russia, and to see horror and suffering overturning everything
and transforming life in that very street. This vision was so intense I never forgot it, but bad as it was, that which came to
pass was far worse.

On August 9th I wrote:

"It amazes me how without any compunction the whole of
Europe throws aside the moral and humane code that has been
built up by years of civilized life. They all seem swallowed up
in an earthquake, and out of chaos has come a lurid light that
glorifies brutality and savagery, casting upon it a theatrical,
rosy, false light which turns its real grinning, hideous face into
that of some divine goddess.

"Why is it that yesterday we called death by another man's
hand murder or manslaughter, now it is called glorious bravery
and valour? For the sake of what is called 'national honour' our
whole nation is plunged into hatred, emotional passion, commercial chaos, anxious and willing to inflict as much suffering
and death as possible on millions of harmless people. A few
hundred miles away—the same sort of human beings as themselves, who have never done them any harm, and with whom
the English have no quarrel. To do this harm to our neighbours we shall have to undergo great suffering, but that must
be gladly and proudly borne, for it is called patriotic and fine!

"Is it patriotic to wreck the well-being of our own country,
and that of the country we are fighting, making them into bitter enemies for no reason?

"Is it patriotic to overthrow all social reform and national
progress that has been slowly and painfully built up?

"Is it patriotic to take the money of rich and poor and devote
it to killing and the spread of disease?

"Is it patriotic to shut down mills, factories that were manufacturing good and useful articles, putting out of gear the trade of the nation? Is it patriotic to ruin art and the fine civilization that is the result of international communication?

"Above all, is it patriotic to coarsen and brutalize thousands of men who go to fight, or to send mad those who are forced to go unwillingly? Is it patriotic to lie and lie, and worst of all to lie to ourselves, and say that we are fine and self-sacrificing and that we must persecute any who don't share this view?

"We are told that we must not speak against the war. It would be unpatriotic and would encourage the enemy, and so we must lie, and say it is all good when we know it is all evil. We must not criticize a government in war-time whatever they do. That is unpatriotic, and on this account we have to swallow our sense of truth or be outcast from society and probably find ourselves in prison.

"We have to read fulsome lies in every newspaper praising all that is brutal and covering up what is good, glorifying all that is vulgar and brutal in life.

"What are the Christian Churches doing—they who exist to make people followers of Christ? What did Christ say about force?

"They say that war makes very little economic difference— that must be untrue, for all bills of exchange, and all international finance, and trade, are put out of gear, shipping disarranged, international communications stopped, and we shall be taxed to death.

"What about political life? It is swept away. Reforms, education, housing, all overturned. We used to believe it was essential to work for better conditions of life for men and women, but we must now work to induce these same men to allow themselves to be used simply as machines to kill or as targets to be shot at or cruelly maimed. No one raises up a voice of protest in England, except just a handful of men—Philip, Bertie and a few others. Even Massingham and *The Nation* have gone over now, from fear. Courage is a rare thing.

"Why should we have troubled about slavery and atrocities or disease? I believe that even soldiers are beginning to realize the horror of being mown down like wheat and to ask why —they must ask themselves why all that we have striven for should be annihilated in a moment.

"Is it for some great end that will build up beauty and happiness and prosperity and moral well-being? No! Only because two distant countries have had a quarrel with each other, and strangely enough we are supporting the one which is blamed for the murder of the Austrian Archduke.

"Instead of helping to make people realize the horror and wickedness of war, clergy write to the papers, and preach and do all they can to praise it. They have lost all humanity and all realization of what man was created for, or what we in these more civilized times assumed that he was created for. It does not seem to shock them at all that man, whom they believe is made in the Divine Image, should be simply used as food for cannon. Young men leading lives of probable use and creativeness, men that might lead humanity forward and build up great things are to be mowed down and cast away. Is it good for the future to make men accustomed to kill each other? It must harden and brutalize them, and if they survive will make them violent and brutal, or nerve-shaken, degenerate men. It is inevitable if men are impregnated with the war attitude, even for a year, that they should be unable to throw it off. It must make a mark on their psychology.

"I know what the warlike would answer to all this: 'We have not sought war, it has been thrust upon us.'

"I can only answer that I am certain that wise, strong, foreseeing statesmen could easily have averted it, and most probably stopped the war between Russia and Germany.

"I find it very difficult to see my old friends who are in favour of war. It is almost impossible to talk to them without quarrelling, and I feel such a disgust for them, that they can be carried away by such a terrible false emotion, and not divine the inner horror of it all. ———— has been here several times but it is very difficult to talk to her. She came to tell me that Sir Edward Grey insists on the Asquiths sending away their old German governess, who has been with them for fifteen years. He said, 'I always knew she was a spy.' "

I find in my journal of this time:

"How curious and remote London life seems now! The people who flocked to me on Thursdays are all gone—blown away. Great division has come from our being pacifists. Of course, art, literature and politics have faded away, and now all that is left is War, War, War. Those who are pro-war and anti-war. We try and gather together all who desire peace. Ramsay MacDonald comes sometimes and Lowes Dickinson, and others of that sort. The intellectuals keep straight about the war, the emotional people go over at once."

¶ *February 1915*

"Since writing this a good deal has happened. The war goes on like an evil dance of the furies—evil spirits seem to besiege the earth like the witches in Macbeth, gaining more and more possession. They have a firm hold now, their sway is dull, monotonous, brutal and tragic. Young lives are swallowed up, thrown into the vast black cauldron. All that soldiers can say of it is that it is 'Hell'—that is the one and only word they use for it, and that, after all, is all that can be said. And yet they submit and go, and obey the mysterious will of a few cabinet ministers and military authorities who are quite callous about human suffering. The great machine turns round and round —and rolls on blind and deaf to any voice of protest or any anguish and pain. Most people seem to become partially indifferent and numb to it, or they become curiously reckless, knowing that any serious life or work apart from the war has ceased, and that they had better catch at the joy as it flies."

All these months there were constant meetings at our house of those who were against the war, the outcome of which was a society called "The Union of Democratic Control." Bertie Russell came up and down from Cambridge where he still was teaching, although for a time he was turned out of his rooms. It was proposed to make Trinity into a hospital but Belgian professors were installed there instead, who, poor men, were so lost at not having pupils to lecture to that they lectured to each other. I saw a great deal of him all these days, and I find the following paragraphs in a sketch that he wrote recalling his feelings at this time:

"On the morning of the 4th of August, I walked with Ottoline up and down the empty streets behind the British Museum, where now a tank has been placed to show what the British Government thinks of learning. We discussed the future in gloomy terms. When we spoke to others of the evils we foresaw, they thought us mad; yet it turned out that we were twittering optimists compared to the truth. On the evening of the 4th, after quarrelling with George Trevelyan along the whole length of the Strand, I attended the last meeting of a neutrality committee of which Graham Wallas was chairman. During the meeting there was a loud clap of thunder, which all the older members of the committee took to be a German bomb. This dissipated their last lingering feeling in favour of neutrality. The first days of the War were to me utterly amazing. My best friends, such as the Whiteheads, were savagely warlike. Men like J. L. Hammond, who had been writing for years against participation in a European War, were swept off their feet by Belgium. As I had long known from military friends at the Staff College that Belgium would inevitably be involved, I had not supposed important publicists so frivolous as to be ignorant on this vital matter. The *Nation* newspaper used to have a staff luncheon every Tuesday, and I attended the luncheon on the 4th of August. I found Massingham, the editor, vehemently opposed to our participation in the war. He welcomed enthusiastically my offer to write for his newspaper in that sense. Next day I got a letter from him, beginning, 'Today is not yesterday . . .' and stating that his opinion had completely changed. Nevertheless, he printed a long letter protesting against the War from me in his next issue. What changed his opinion I do not know. I know that one of Asquith's daughters saw him descending the steps of the German Embassy late on the afternoon of the 4th of August, and I have some suspicion that he was consequently warned of the unwisdom of a lack of patriotism in such a crisis.

"For the first year or so of the War he remained patriotic, but as time went on he began to forget that he had ever been so. A few pacifist M.P.s, together with two or three sympathizers, began to have meetings at the Morrells' house in Bedford Square. I used to attend these meetings, which gave rise to the Union of Democratic Control. I was interested to observe that the pacifist politicians were more concerned with the question which of them should lead the anti-war movement than with the actual work against the War. Nevertheless, they were all there was to work with, and I did my best to think well of them.

"Meanwhile I was living at the highest possible emotional tension. Although I did not foresee anything like the full disaster of the War, I foresaw a great deal more than most people did. The prospect filled me with horror, but what filled me with even more horror was the fact that the anticipation of carnage was delightful to something like 90 per cent of the population. I had to revise my views on human nature. At that time I was wholly ignorant of psycho-analysis, but I arrived for myself at a view of human passions not unlike that of the psycho-analysts. I arrived at this view in an endeavour to understand popular feeling about the War. I had supposed until that time that it was quite common for parents to love their children, but the War showed me that it is a rare exception. I had supposed that most people liked money better than almost anything else, but I discovered that they liked destruction even better. I had supposed that intellectuals frequently loved truth, but I found here again that not 10 per cent of them prefer truth to popularity. Gilbert Murray, who had been a close friend of mine since 1902, was a pro-Boer when I was not. I therefore naturally expected that he would again be on the side of peace; yet he went out of his way to write about the wickedness of the Germans, and the superhuman virtue of Sir Edward Grey. I became filled with despairing tenderness towards the young men who were to be slaughtered, and with rage against all the statesmen of Europe. For several weeks I felt that if I should happen to meet Asquith or Grey I should be unable to refrain from murder. Gradually, however, these personal feelings disappeared. They were swallowed up by the magnitude of the tragedy, and by the realization of the popular forces which the statesmen merely let loose.

"In the midst of this, I was myself tortured by patriotism. The success of the Germans before the Battle of the Marne were horrible to me. I desired the defeat of Germany as ardently as any retired colonel. Love of England is very nearly the strongest emotion I possess, and in appearing to set it aside at such a moment, I was making a very difficult renunciation. Nevertheless, I never had a moment's doubt as to what I must do. I have at times been paralysed by scepticism, at times I have felt cynical, at other times indifferent, but when War came I felt as if I heard the voice of God. I knew that it was my business to protest, however futile protest might be. My whole nature was involved. As a lover of truth the national propaganda of all the belligerent nations sickened me. As a lover of civilization, the return to barbarism appalled me. As a man of thwarted parental feeling, the massacre of the young wrung my heart. I hardly supposed that much good would come of opposing the War, but I felt that for the honour of human nature those who were not swept off their feet should show that they stood firm. After seeing troop trains departing from Waterloo, I used to have strange visions of London as a place of unreality. I used in imagination to see the bridges collapse and sink, and the whole great city vanish like a morning mist. Its inhabitants began to seem like hallucinations, and I would wonder whether the world in which I thought I had lived was a mere product of my own febrile nightmares. Such moods, however, were brief, and were put an end to by the need of work.

"Throughout the earlier phases of the War, Ottoline Morrell was a very great help and strength to me. But for her, I should have been at first completely solitary, but she never wavered either in her hatred of war, or in her refusal to accept the myths and falsehoods with which the world was inundated.

"I found a minor degree of comfort in the conversation of Santayana, who was at Cambridge at that time. He was a

269

neutral, and in any case he had not enough respect for the human race to care whether it destroyed itself or not. His calm, philosophical detachment, though I had no wish to imitate it, was soothing to me. Just before the Battle of the Marne, when it looked as if the Germans must soon take Paris, he remarked in a dreamy tone of voice, 'I think I must go over to Paris. My winter underclothes are there, and I should not like the Germans to get them. I have also another less important reason, which is that I have there a manuscript of a book on which I have been working for the last ten years, but I do not care so much about that as about the underclothes.'

"He did not, however, go to Paris because the Battle of the Marne saved him the trouble. Instead, he remarked to me one day, 'I am going to Seville tomorrow because I wish to be in a place where people do not restrain their passions.'

"With the beginning of the October Term, I had to start again lecturing on mathematical logic, but I felt it a somewhat futile occupation. So I took to organizing a branch of the Union of Democratic Control among the dons, of whom at Trinity quite a number were at first sympathetic. I also addressed meetings of undergraduates, who were quite willing to listen to me. I remember in the course of a speech saying, 'It is all nonsense to pretend the Germans are wicked,' and to my surprise the whole room applauded. But with the sinking of the *Lusitania,* a fiercer spirit began to prevail. It seemed to be supposed that I was in some way responsible for this disaster. Of the dons who had belonged to the Union of Democratic Control, many had by this time got commissions. Barnes (afterwards Bishop of Birmingham) left to become Master of the Temple. The older dons got more and more hysterical, and I began to find myself avoided at the high table.

"Every Christmas throughout the War I had a fit of black

despair, such complete despair that I could do nothing except sit idle in my chair and wonder whether the human race served any purpose. At Christmastime in 1914, by Ottoline's advice, I found a way of making despair not unendurable. I took to visiting destitute Germans on behalf of a charitable committee to investigate their circumstances and to relieve their distress if they deserved it. In the course of this work, I came upon remarkable instances of kindness in the middle of the fury of war. Not infrequently in poor neighbourhoods landladies, themselves poor, had allowed Germans to stay on without paying any rent, because they knew it was impossible for Germans to find work. That problem ceased to exist soon afterwards, as the Germans were all interned, but during the first months of the War their condition was pitiable."

As I look back on that time it seems almost too ghastly to have been lived through. It was as if one was existing in an atmosphere deprived of all blue rays. We seemed to have passed through the portal of Dante's Inferno and had lost hope. The pressure upon one of the suffering, mental and physical, that was tormenting thousands and thousands of men nearly drove one mad, and there was nothing, nothing that we could do to arrest it. Added to this, it was terribly painful going against the current of patriotic emotion that was carrying the whole nation further and further into the war. The whole world seemed intoxicated—drunk with a mysterious primitive emotion that stimulated people to deeds of noble self-sacrifice, enabled them often to endure great suffering and privations, but even acts of cruelty and intolerance were transformed in their eyes into a sacred duty. We and our friends seemed like a wretched little shivering humiliated group of people who alone remained sober, but despised, disgraced. How often I wished

I could throw myself into this great stream of emotion and be carried along with the others, and let myself indulge in this patriotic enthusiasm! Of course, if that had been possible I should probably soon have forgotten the suffering and horror in drugging myself with work in a hospital or canteen. I saw the young uniformed women so free, so gay and liberated, driving cars so competently, and looking so fresh, proud and robust. I couldn't help feeling a violent resentment against them, that they should gain their freedom and happiness by trampling on the men, by liberating them, and so sending them out to the front. In the streets one was always meeting little companies of patriotic and unsuitable-looking men being marched along, pale clerks and shopmen and town roughs and country youths, all in their own ordinary clothes with military bands round their arms,[3] some of the men obviously hating it but resolute; and then there would come a little square company of raw youths. If one hadn't seen what they were marching out to, they would have been a ludicrous spectacle. I still cannot pass Chelsea Hospital grounds without seeing, as I saw there from a bus in the King's Road, companies of young men being trained in bayonet practice by attacking sacks, themselves just food for cannon.

We felt ourselves bound to offer hospitality to refugees. The first one who came was a strong, healthy young Belgian, who obviously, as his own country was being invaded, ought to have been there fighting. It was intolerable having him sitting, talking his common French, in my drawing-room, tasting and mouthing with relish stories of German atrocities—and I soon passed him on.

[3] They had enlisted under what was called Lord Derby's scheme. So many volunteered that they could not all be taken into the army: as a sign of their status they were given arm-bands to wear.

272

We next took a French actress, whom I had seen act at the Vieux Colombier Theatre in Paris. She had acted marvellously, and had been entirely bewitching. When I heard that she was living in a wretched lodging in London, I enthusiastically offered to put her up. Expecting to see the gay and bewitching Grouschka with her lovely hat and feathers and her Russian dress arrive in the hall, I was disappointed to find that a very commonplace fair French *bourgeoise,* who was accompanied by a vast array of trunks, had arrived in her stead. Luckily we did not see very much of her, as she was teaching French in an Institute at Marble Arch, but when I had people in the evening she insisted on reciting very sentimental French poems. This was very distressing, but worse when she asked an old French woman friend to accompany her with "soft feeling music" to a long poem in the nature of an Ave Maria. Luckily she found somewhere in London a rich Frenchman. A warm, expensive fur coat appeared and a week-end in Paris ensued, where she told me she had to drive through the streets with the blinds of the motor drawn for fear that her mother or father would see her. I felt that with this comfortable and rich friend she would be happier elsewhere, so we affectionately parted and I have seen her several times in Paris, where she is now famous. She greets me still with nice *bourgeois* fervour —"*des baisers sur les deux joues.*" Indeed, she has left on me but a slight impression, except that of an amiable vain child.

About this time I had been reading some very remarkable books, *Sons and Lovers* and *The White Peacock,* by D. H. Lawrence, the scenes of which were laid in Nottinghamshire, and they had stirred up my early memories, which had lain dry and curled up. In reading these books they blossomed out as old Japanese flowers in a glass of water.

In a dumb and ignorant way I had always felt so romantic

about the great oaks and grass rides where day after day I had ridden with my brothers; or when I was quite small driven my pair of tiny Shetland ponies with their long manes and tails flying in the wind as I made them scamper along, my darling cousin Cattie by my side. Indeed, the commons and the forests were the centre of romance in my early life. I half believed that I might catch a glimpse of Robin Hood and his merry men hanging his venison up on the old tree that was called Robin Hood's Larder. And then later, when I was older and drove my black ponies out on the dark dreary roads with their black hedges, I would feel excited and even a little nervous when I met groups of colliers on their way home from the pits. These men, tall, black and mysterious, appeared rather fierce and yet full of laughter and fun, joking together as they hurried pell-mell along the dark roads to tea, the grey winter light, a gleam of setting yellow sun behind them. The Nottinghamshire winter evening light which is in my memory so soothing and enfolding after a wild, stormy day. How I wished I could talk to these men, or share their good solid tea, and so bridge the gulf that lay between us, these men whose lives were lived in a world that I knew nothing of. I knew that they went off to the pits at early morning, that they were comparatively well off, that they kept lurchers, and poached and betted, but that was all I could gather from outside. I often nearly stopped my ponies as we trotted along the black slimy road, to have a few words with them as they hurried along, but what could I say? They would only look surprised and perhaps laugh. The cords that hold us back from escaping from our own herd are very strong and take time to wear thin.

These books having excited and moved me, I felt how much I should like to know Lawrence himself, whose home had also been in Nottinghamshire, and to my surprise I found that Gilbert Cannan knew him—indeed, Lawrence and his wife

were at this time living at a cottage near them at Chesham.
Lawrence was pleased to hear that I admired his work, and one
evening in February 1915 he and his wife came to see us.
He was a slight man, lithe and delicately built, his pale face
rather overshadowed by his beard and his red hair falling over
his forehead, his eyes blue and his hands delicate and very
competent. He gave one the impression of someone who had
been under-nourished in youth, making his body fragile and
his mind too active. Soon after coming to see us, they went to
live at Greatham, near Pulborough, in a cottage lent to them
by Viola Meynell—one of a group of cottages built by old Mr.
Meynell for his children. Here I went several times to see
them, and except that one night I could not sleep on account
of the cold, I was extraordinarily happy and at ease. When we
met we at once went back to our memories of Nottinghamshire.
We talked of the lovely wild commons, of Sherwood Forest, of
the dark pit villages, of the lives of the colliers and their wives,
and of all those scenes which he has described so vividly in his
early books, scenes which were a part of his own life. He
talked to me in the Nottinghamshire dialect which I loved to
hear again. He also liked to talk of my family in Nottinghamshire, for he had a romantic feeling for them. He used to please
me by saying that the "Bentincks were always looked up to as
being disinterested."

The long bare room with its refectory table and luncheon
cooked by Lawrence himself are all vivid in my memory. It
was impossible not to feel expanded and stimulated by the
companionship of anyone so alive, so intensely interested in
everyone and everything as he was. Indeed, he seemed to
possess a magnetic gift of quickening those he talked to and of
making them blossom with new ideas, new enthusiasm, new
hopes. His whole attention seemed concentrated on them. He
who became so vehement in his writings was nearly always

—certainly with me—gentle and tender in personal contact. Indeed, I felt when I was with him as if I had really at last found a friend, that I could express myself without reserve, and without fear of being thought silly. He felt the wind and the flowers with the same vividness that I did. He seemed to open up the way into a holy land by his gospel of instinctive development.

We used to go on long walks through woods and over the downs. On one visit, when John Middleton Murry was staying with him, we climbed to the top of the Downs to look at the view towards Arundel and the sea—a view by which he said he tested the character of his friends. Murry lagged with a melancholy air behind us as we climbed. Another day in the early spring we went to the woods still bare of leaves, but he showed me the little flame-red buds of the trees not yet in leaf and said, "See, here is the little red flame in Nature." I looked at him as he was speaking and thought, "In you, too, there certainly dwells that flame." It was the central fire of his being, intermittent as nature is, and if he had been able to root himself in some soil, this flame would have lit him through the seasons.

On one of my visits to Greatham I took Bertrand Russell with me and it appeared a great success. From the first these two passionate men took to each other and Bertie Russell, as we drove away, exclaimed, "He is amazing; he sees through and through one."

"Yes. But do you think he really sees correctly?" I asked.

"Absolutely. He is infallible," was Bertie's reply. "He is like Ezekiel or some other Old Testament prophet, prophesying. Of course, the blood of his nonconformist preaching ancestors is strong in him, but he sees everything and is always right."

I reluctantly agreed. At the same time I had my doubts, which later on grew into a certainty, for he was much too impatient even then to see through all the layers and contradictions and subtleties of an English character. His insight was indeed very intense, but sometimes so bright that it distorted those it focused.

I find I wrote in my journal then:

"Lawrence is the spirit of flame. He has indeed a fire within him, a fire which flames into excitement and conviction when a subject or a controversy strikes a light. And what subjects do not strike a light? For that indeed is the rare quality that Lawrence has, he is interested in almost everything. Few subjects bore him. And by his wonderful capacity of being absolutely natural he stimulates those round him to be the same."

Many people are interested in others in a superficial way, but his interest would penetrate and lay hands on his object, breaking down barriers. No wonder that there were those that resented it, and resented what they thought was his interference in their private lives, that he would tell them that he knew better than they did what was good for them. He was not the child of an old cultivated family who inherits a natural restraint and respect for his neighbour's hidden and secluded lives; Lawrence's ancestors had never learnt the art of courtly bowing and curtsying. His old home was a small intense world where interests were passionate, direct and often violent. Poverty, hard work and an innate moral delicacy were the only restraints. Apart from that, it was a life untrammelled by middle-class conventions or decorum; kindness, curiosity, anger, were all freely and frankly expressed, and in this little world, Lawrence, young as he was, was supreme—for it was he who brought into it cultivation, excitement, intelligent talk and argument. The only one who remained outside was his father, who carried on his own hard-working, hard-drinking existence, and was often rough and abusive.

A miner's home in the Midlands is not the unlearned and

untidy home of the south, and Lawrence's mother was obviously—from what he told me—a very remarkable woman, who
had great delicacy of feeling and distinction of mind: clear,
orderly, dominating towards the children. Anyone who has
read *Sons and Lovers* and Lawrence's poems to her must have
realized how important she was to him. But what an absorbing,
troubling and agitating son Lawrence must have been to this
delicately-minded, orderly and capable mother who was the
centre of the family, but above all was dominating and pos-
sessive of this son. And upon her he concentrated himself. She
had so much in her character that satisfied him; she was sharp
in retort and had a witty resistance—proud and erect—reserved
—above all she had a complete admiration and devotion to him.
No doubt as a result of her detachment from her husband she
called forth his protective devotion and tenderness. The poems
that he wrote to her show how lovely and tender was his feeling for her.

The early habits of his home life were never shaken off. He
was quick and competent in cleaning a floor, washing up cups
and saucers, cooking, nursing: violent in argument, free in expression and abuse. Burns and Lawrence are, I suppose, almost
the only two important writers who have sprung from working-
class homes. But Lawrence, unlike Burns, was never at one with
his old companions. He could not have remained as Burns did,
one of them. If he had been only a poet it might have been
possible, but he was a seeker after life and a prophet preacher.
He had to leave, to go out to wider fields, but he never really
found a "Home."

CHAPTER II

The First World War

I N THE SPRING we at last were preparing to make our move to Garsington in May, and we had often to go up and down there to supervise the painting, decorating of the house and planting in the garden. I was, of course, anxious and worried over all this, especially as we could not afford to do very much. I don't recollect very much, except enjoying good bread-and-cheese lunches in one of the old public houses at Garsington, and endless discussions about the alterations.

In November (1914) I began my Thursday evenings again —a great many people came, though of course none of the fashionable set—they avoided us as pacifists, or as they liked to say, "Pro-German." We lent the rooms to the Aranyis for a concert; they, being Hungarian, were looked on with suspicion, and were glad to come.

These are some of the people who came to the Thursdays:

The Clive Bells, Duncan Grant, Mark Gertler, Gilbert Cannan, Irene Cooper Willis, Enid Bagnold, Barbara Hiles, Dorothy Brett, Walter Sickert, the Sangers, the MacCarthys, the Delacres, the De Bergens, Vernon Lee, Lytton Strachey, James Strachey, Marjorie Strachey, Oliver Strachey, David Garnett,

John Dodson, St. John Hutchinson, H. J. Norton, Hawtrey, Helen Dudley, the Hubrechts, Bob Trevelyan, Augustus John, Valentine Tessier, Lascelles Abercrombie, the Olivier girls, Mrs. Popham, J. M. Keynes, F. W. Hirst, Mary A. Hamilton, Bertrand Russell, Iris Tree, Nash brothers, the Bevans, Ginner, Gilman, H. Lamb, Milne, Squire, Arnold Bennett.

When I look back at these Thursday evenings during these months, I am puzzled to understand how it was that they were so gay, for nearly all those who came were people who felt the war intensely, and were certainly neither careless nor heartless about it. I believe that the pressure of unhappiness was so great that any diversion once a week was welcome, especially in the company of those who were sympathetic—just a few hours' escape from the horrors that one kept seeing in one's imagination.

Those who came often dressed themselves up in gay Persian, Turkish, and other Oriental clothes, of which I had a store. Philip played tunes of all kinds on the pianola, which was a new toy—Brahms's Hungarian Dances, Russian ballet music, *Prince Igor* or *Scheherazade,* Mozart, or even some of the good old music-hall song tunes—such as "Watch your step" or "Get out and get under" and "Dixie." These would inspire us all to dance gaily, wildly and often very beautifully, following the rhythm as the spirit moved us. It was odd to see how each one expressed his personality as he danced. Duncan Grant was almost fierce, but full of humour and grace, as he bounded about like a Russian ballet dancer, or wound in and out in some intricate dance with Vanessa Bell or Bunny Garnet, who looked really fierce and barbaric in bright oranges and reds, a gay-coloured silk handkerchief on his head. Duncan's special dance was one of Brahms's Hungarian Dances. Mark Gertler and Gil-

bert Cannan would act and dance a queer London East End
Jewish play together, the refrains of which were the cry of that
despised race, "I am only a Jew." When there was a general
mêlée, Bertie Russell would be dragged in by one of the
Aranyis. It was very comic to see him—a stiff little figure,
jumping up and down like a child, with an expression of surprised delight on his face at finding himself doing such an
ordinary human thing as dancing. It seemed to liberate him
from himself, and made him very happy for a short time at
least. Now and then Lytton Strachey exquisitely stepped out
with his brother James and his sister Marjorie, in a delicate
and courtly minuet of his own invention, his thin long legs
and his arms gracefully keeping perfect time to Mozart—the
vision of this exquisite dance always haunts me with its half-
serious, half-mocking, yet beautiful quality. I remember dancing
a Spanish dance with Augustus John.

Mark Gertler would bring with him some of his Slade
friends, a little group of girls in corduroy trousers, coloured
shirts, short hair. At their first appearance they all wore masks
and were ushered in as "mysterious strangers." There was Carrington with whom Mark was passionately in love, and Dorothy
Brett, their constant companion and "virgin aunt"—indeed,
these three were inseparable. Gertler who was then very remarkable, very full of an intense vitality, was unhappily and
passionately devoted to Carrington who looked like a wild
moorland pony, with a shock of fair hair, uncertain and elusive
eyes, rather awkward in her movements, which gave her a
certain charm. Brett was in years a good deal older, but for
some odd reason looked hardly more than a girl of seventeen,
with her peach-like complexion, *retroussé,* Joe Chamberlain
nose, small open rabbit mouth and very tiny childish hands.
She was, alas, very deaf. With them the first evening there

also came two friends who were part of their group at the Slade, Faith Bagenal and Barbara Hiles. This last was a nice springing and gay girl, in looks very like Mark himself. They all seemed fresh and interested in life, and hated the war.

Then there was Guevara, a painter who was always called Chile, who brought a wonderful Japanese dancer, Ito. Ito had a long, dark, antique type of face, like a monk, and as he danced his movements were marvellously beautiful. I shall never forget the dance that he invented to "Yip i Yaddy i Yay." He would ask Philip to play a tune through, then think about it for a few minutes, and then start his interpretation of it, wild and imaginative, with intense passion and form. I have lost sight of him entirely now. I think he went to America.

And so these dark days went grinding on. Once a week there was this outburst of gaiety and giddiness. Next day we relapsed into the weary monotony of the war.

My family, of course, disapproved of us. Philip's family, too, could never forgive him. If we went to Black Hall my mother-in-law and her friends would say the most cruel things.

Bertie Russell helped me with the work of visiting the destitute Germans. One felt at least that one was bringing some relief and kindness to those who were in need of it, and it was nice to hear of the many kindnesses they had received from their neighbours. But nothing could really make one happy, or lift the cloud of suffering.

It must have been a few months before this time that I received a letter from Edith, one of the daughters of our old coachman Ellis and his wife, who had been my mother's cook, telling me that her parents were dead and that she and her sister Mildred had had to give up their home at Bournemouth. I wrote and offered to find situations in London for them if they liked to come up. The elder, Edith, arrived and soon afterwards Millie, her sister. Edith went to some lady as maid, but was not very happy and soon returned to me, first as housemaid and then later as cook. Millie fitted into our life at once and never looked for any other post. She was for a time housemaid, then parlourmaid, which she still is, and I hope will remain so until Philip and I both pass away. It would be absurd for me to give any account of our life henceforth without Millie's presence, for she is daily entwined into it—every friend who comes to the house knows Millie and Millie knows them. Indeed, I have such confidence in Millie's power of seeing through people that I generally ask her opinion about any newcomer. I find that "these foreigners" sometimes baffle her, but generally she is infallible. Though she may criticize my brothers, she falls entirely under the ducal or lordly glamour when they come, and Millie's face of loyal adoration as she looks up at them is charming to see. We have been through much together, have seen the rise, quickening and decline of many friendships. I fear her views have veered more and more to the right, in that she doesn't believe those that are born in humble estate wear well when instances of difficulties arise. She will say, "Well, you see, my lady, honestly I must say I always think such people after a time show where they come from." But how many of these friends has she not helped, comforted and sympathized with on their visits.

The entries in my journal at this time seem very scanty, except jottings of despair about the war—"dull, grinding agony." One was told at first that modern warfare was so terrible that it *could* not go on beyond a few weeks. I hardly believed this when it was said, people get accustomed to anything, however terrible. There is one entry as follows:

"I was sitting alone last night after dinner in the drawing-room, when in came, unexpectedly, Lawrence, bringing with him Katherine Mansfield, Koteliansky,[1] Gordon and Beatrice Campbell, and some other men. I was rather taken aback to see these great figures trooping in, and felt shy and lost, and I did not know how on earth I should entertain them as, except for Lawrence, they were complete strangers to me.

"Katherine Mansfield sat very silent and Buddha-like on the big sofa—she might almost have held in her hand a lotus-flower! The men looked immensely large and solid compared with Lawrence. The talk was, as far as I can remember it, mainly political. Campbell sat on a small chair near the fire; Lawrence knows him very well and they started a violent argument—or rather it was calm and irritatingly rational on Campbell's part; Lawrence stood over him shaking his arm above his head and every two or three minutes very quickly rubbing the tips of his fingers on his scalp in rapid friction, at the same time making a face, drawing back his mouth in a sort of grin which reached up to the top of his face, his voice mounting to a shriek—'You lie, you lie,' or 'You know it is not true,' and again and again more friction of the scalp.

"Somehow I could not take it seriously, nor did Campbell, or any of us. It all seemed rather comic and rather an access of exuberance. I don't think Lawrence was really angry. It was his method of controversy."

There are a few impressions left in my memory—one of a walk I took with Bertie Russell through Regent's Park, up Primrose Hill. I think it must have been in March, for the sheep and lambs were there, and somehow I had a vivid invasion of Blake into my consciousness. I was convinced that he had lived near there or had written a poem about Primrose Hill,

[1] An associate and friend of what has come to be known as the Bloomsbury group. He published a number of translations from the Russian, some of which were done in collaboration with Virginia Woolf.

but whatever was the cause the thought of Blake dominated my mind and was lovely and assuaging to me. When we were on the top of the hill, we looked out over London, stretching far away beneath, right over to St. Paul's on the horizon, and a great anguish overtook both Bertie and myself at the sight. The vision we both had, that all this might possibly be swept away and destroyed by enemy bombs. It was these passionate moments in him that always held me to him, these moments when he became liberated from himself, when he had power to soar into visions beyond most men's. It is a pity that so little of his imaginative side is known to people, or that it has been expressed, and for this reason I hope that his letters will one day be read. I found in one of his letters afterwards that this vision had not faded from his mind.

"It was extraordinarily happy today—and on the hill it was terribly moving. The children playing, and St. Paul's and the thought of all the destruction of war. If I could really believe that the world will be less warlike after the war, it would half reconcile one, but I don't believe it. I don't believe peace can be inculcated by bayonets. I feel wonderfully near to you these days—even when you take me to task, it is only what my own conscience says more roughly. This time gives one a very great feeling of tenderness towards all living things—a wish to preserve some corner of peace and goodwill, and a terrible horror of destruction. St. Paul's seemed wonderfully strong and eternal —as if what it stands for would survive all our madness—yet all the time I was thinking of Germans battering it down with their guns. But they can't batter down love—it will spring up again through everything—it has lived and given hope in the darkest ages of the world. The Italy of St. Francis was worse than anything now. It is difficult to know what love would have one do. It seems to me the only thing one can do now is

285

to think out how wars come and how they might be avoided, and then, after the peace, do all one can to bring other people round. At the moment, public action is very little use. What might bear fruit later would be if we could get together about a dozen people to meet fairly often, and discuss together about ways of making war less likely. They need not all agree with us about England's share in this war—all that would be necessary would be that they should desire peace greatly, and that they should have some knowledge or wisdom that would make them able to throw out good suggestions. If they worked well together, they might become the nucleus of a movement after the peace. Most people seem to me to be thinking too much of the moment, in which we are powerless. It is thought for the future that we can do now."

During this time there was always a haunting fear of something dark and terrible, a fear not for one's own safety, but for the safety of all that had made England so happy and so remarkable, so poetic. When Philip and I drove through country lanes, perhaps on a lovely autumn evening, and looked out on to ploughed fields and lovely farms and old barns, already falling into disrepair—the fields tilled only by old decrepit men or boys, I could but imagine and imagine what it might be a few years hence. And then as I walked through the narrow streets of the City I remember looking up at the great buildings which I had hitherto taken so much for granted, and where I had always enjoyed the rush and the sense of importance of the life that flowed in here from all over the world and flowed out into lands where buildings were frail and pagoda-like, and where dark men and women lived in jungles—but who depended on England to send them their beads and the bright cotton that bound their loins. Indeed, I always welcomed any excuse to go into this busy world which was such a relief from the luxury shop-windows of the West End, and felt so proud of Old London dominated by Wren's dome, but which had been gay and rich and violent long before this St. Paul's had been built, when the robust and independent merchants of King Edward, and Elizabeth's adventurous traders had trodden these streets, the names of which were so charming and familiar from old plays. It was here that Donne had walked "The City's mystique Body" with a smart young gallant in grey velvet and listened to strange long-winded bores in threadbare "tufftafutti," and met "Captains, Bright parcel gilt with forty dead men's pay" or "A briske perfumed piert courtier." Even plague and fire could not kill or for long check this gay life, for sturdy, red-faced aldermen would not even wait King Charles's pleasure, and his desire to make their city beautiful with Wren's ambitious design, but hurriedly built it up as best they could and filled their new warehouses with fantastic goods from East and West, North and South, brought to satisfy the growing needs and the whims of men, timber from Scandinavian forests, imperial silks from China, furs and strong-smelling leathers from Muscovy, velvets from Genoa, and even those strange herbs tobacco and coffee that were so new and precious.

There came great ships fraught with cochineal—and myrrh; aloes and cassia too, I am sure—all brought up that same river on which Raleigh had sailed and set out on his adventures, and perhaps unloaded at Wapping Great Stairs.

As I wandered along peeping into doorways and courts—it must have been a Sunday, for it was all very still and deserted—I felt how deep would be the humiliation to us if this was no longer the centre of civilized trade, the emporium of the world. If it sunk to be past and dead, and these great buildings should become as empty and still as palaces in Rome or Florence, or as I saw them that day.

In April before leaving 44 Bedford Square, that dear and perfect house, I put on my graceful yellow silk embroidered dress on our last Thursday evening, and made my curtsy to the company, and said to myself and Philip, "This play is ended," and with a sad heart put out the lights.

CHAPTER III

Bolsover Castle

In APRIL I went by myself to the Hydro in Buxton to have some treatment for rheumatism. While I was there furniture and household were moved to Garsington and we left Bedford Square; after that time I only returned for brief periods, as we let it.

Buxton has rather faded from my memory—what I chiefly remember is reading the manuscript of *The Rainbow* which D. H. Lawrence sent me in detachments, also that he wrote me charming letters to cheer me and keep me company in my solitude.

I read *The Rainbow* sitting in my little bedroom by a smoking fire—it interested me, but I was shocked in reading it by what then seemed to me to be the slapdash amateurish style in which it was written, and the habit which he then first began of repeating the same word about ten times in a paragraph. I counted the word "fecund," I think, twelve times on one page. Reading very loose, sloppy writing gives me always a feeling of great discomfort, almost shame; but there were also passages of such intensity and such passionate beauty that they never leave one's memory. I did not know then what I know now, that it is a description of Lawrence's own life and struggles with his wife, Frieda.

Whilst I was still at Buxton, Bertie Russell came to stay for
a few days, and as the weather was fine and lovely we made
an expedition—a treat from him to me—to see Bolsover[1] Castle.
I had so often told him what a peculiar love I had for this place
that I had known so well in my childhood, going over there
with my mother from Welbeck about ten miles distant. The
day we set forth was a perfect May day, vivid, clear atmosphere
and the trees just powdered with tender green and gold. We
drove through wild Derbyshire moors and rocky valleys, and
then, suddenly, perched very high on a hill, I saw Bolsover,
lonely, proud, erect, surrounded by pale trees. I looked at Bertie
and was surprised to see that even he who seldom vibrated to
visual beauty was moved. It was so many years since I had come
here, for I had not been invited to Welbeck for a long time, on
account of our politics, that I was uncertain as to whether I
should find the place that in my youth had seemed to me so full
of beauty and romance, as lovely and magical as I had then
thought it, or whether it might only have been the idealization
of a child—who had found here liberation and escape into romantic beauty.

As we turned in through the old gateway, where I could if I
liked put out my hand and touch and trace with my fingers on
the rough golden stone the wound made by a Commonwealth
cannon-ball, trace it gently as I would an old scar inflicted on
the wrinkled cheek of a faithful servant guarding one's home,
but I felt too impatient to remain there or to worry about the
rights and wrongs of Puritan and Royalist then. On we went
into the outer circle of the garden, where old William Caven-

---

[1] In her young years, when she was first yearning to escape, Ottoline
asked if she might have some rooms done up at Bolsover, as a separate
home for her. This suggestion was—no doubt after a family conclave—
turned down.

dish's riding school and stables stand. From there I could see my darling Castle face to face. Uncertainty and doubts vanished. I held out my arms and heard myself saying, "You *are* beautiful." High, tall, fair and proud it stood, the four little pointed watch towers on the top, the old discoloured shaky glass windows, the little iron balconies supported by stone statues, and at its feet the formal garden of dark hedges and fruit trees, now a foam of white blossom, the flat topped wall encircling it all. I could hardly stop to greet the little hunchback with the pathetic face, who was so excited and glad to see me again, and, I felt, thought of me still as "His Grace's sister, with long auburn hair." I twitched at Bertie's sleeve and the little hunchback ran on to open doors and windows. Through the old gateway we went into the little garden where Venus was still bathing in her fountain, lovelier than ever, but even here I couldn't dally long, but waved to her that I would return. On into the old paved forecourt on the other side where lilac trees in the corner were in bloom. I stood and pointed up and up at the tall square castle, the lovely flights of stone steps into the house, and above them another fragile balcony supported by a stone giant and other monsters. Then up those steps and through the old empty rooms we wandered, floor upon floor, climbing up the wide winding stone stairs, with their mysterious little dungeons, which as a child I had been told were prisons, and that fair Arabella Stuart even had been kept here. On into the warm panelled rooms, painted green and bedecked with golden Chinese designs, and then the black and white marble court with the lovely roof, the two lovely rooms with painted Rubens ceilings, like the "Heavenly Room" and the "Elysian Room" which I used to be told were Heaven and Hell, but I could never distinguish which was which, as apparently the luscious and bacchic gods and goddesses were happy and ignorant of sin. Into the Star Chamber with its frieze of Caesars and its star-spangled roof, and from there into the beautiful pillar parlour, so richly and ornately panelled, painted in blue and gold, the room spreading out from a central pillar. As we stood looking down from this high perch, through the little dim discoloured diamond panes, which although so exposed had withstood rough winds and storm for four hundred years, old impressions invaded me, for here at this window I could see only the view which spreads away over many counties, through dark storm and mist with perhaps a gleam of sunlight catching Hardwick's windows.

"But, you know, Bertie, they say that Bess of Hardwick died because a great frost came and stopped the building here. She had been warned that the day she stopped building would be her last, and so she pressed on her stonemasons crying out, 'It is a matter of life and death, men; you are killing me.' But the old lady's voice was too cracked to move them, they only said to each other, 'The Crazy dame is at her scolding,' and so she died.

"Her charming son, Sir Charles Cavendish, carried on her work, but it was his son, Sir William Cavendish (afterwards Duke of Newcastle), who loved and built and adorned Bolsover, and it was in this room—I know that fireplace—that he, so courtly, so learned, sat with his children and his wife. 'That thrice noble, chaste and virtuous, if somewhat fantastical and original brain, generous Margaret Newcastle,' as Lamb called her."[2]

[2] Ottoline's little vision must not be too roughly handled. Historical truth, however, compels the statement that the baroque, fantastical Duchess was the Duke's second wife, whom he met some ten years later in Paris, at the exiled court of Queen Henrietta Maria. Being barren, she bore him no children which, as she wrote, "did never lessen his Love and Affection for me."

As I turned round I seemed to see them there, and they became so gay and merry, laughing and talking, the young ones stretching down to play with the little spaniel, and stretching up to lean against the great chimneypiece. William had a great book before him in which he with his lovely writing was adding some new ideas on *manège*, and his wife too had her notebooks. Bertie seemed to fade away, and my old forebear William Cavendish became more real and living, and I heard him telling his children that they could not possibly receive the King in this old castle when he came on his visit next year, and didn't they agree that he ought to call on Mr. Smithson immediately to bring his plans and those clever Italian workmen, that he had heard were in England—"for you know our dear King Charles delights in the art of Italy and Italians: work quickly for the time is short."

"But where will you build your new wing, William my Lord? You have already built on the best site with your great riding-house and stables, and you need the long grass terrace for your horses' *manège*."

"There is room enough there, my dear, a fine site that would be. The building would stretch along the terrace and there could be a flight of Italian steps, on top of which the good King shall sit and look out over fair Derbyshire, and I will train the cream horses to circle round and bend down and salute their King with bowed heads."

He grew quite excited at the vision he had of himself in a lovely feathered hat on his yellow curls, and a new pink velvet suit and his best point collar and a long whip in his hand, surrounded by his obedient horses with their scarlet trappings, making their obeisance to His Majesty, "And perhaps by then," he went on, "our young Prince will be ready to take his part, for he cometh on well with his horsemanship."

293

"If you bring out your horses, my Lord, I must have my players," Margaret laughed. "I shall write to burly, untidy old Ben Jonson today and order him to write us a Masque, and I shall tell him it must be gay and fantastical, and have much music and lutes and singing—not like one of his horrid coarse plays about rough St. Bartholomew Fair. It must begin with a song to welcome their Majesties, but he can put in a joke or two if he likes about Derbyshire and its good ale.

"Ah! I conceive," she exclaimed, "I conceive. Write quickly what I tell you, Henry." She turned to her stepson and began to pace the room. "It must be called *Love's Welcome*.

Let Welcome fill
Our thoughts, hearts, voices, and that one word trill
Through all our language—welcome, welcome still."

And as if she imagined herself saying it then to the King she ended by a deep curtsy, sweeping the stone floor with her rich velvet dress, and I thought how charming and gay the dear, generous, kind, eccentric lady looked against the blue and gold panelling, the red taffeta curtains trimmed with gold, the silver cloth and red velvet chairs. And through the door into the next room I saw by the light of the log fire the tapestry on the wall and her tall bed with purple velvet and gold hangings.

"Come, my dear," I heard William say, "the evening is warm, let us look and see where we can build and where my dear horses can circle and bow, and where your Masque will be best given, and don't you think we had better consult Mr. Inigo Jones about it too?" He wrapped her carefully in her sable tippet and gave her his arm, and led her down the stairs, the sons and daughters following, talking, laughing and the little dog yapping.

294

I said to Bertie, "Let us come." Down the steps into the fore-court and out into the perron, and from there on to the long green terrace, where the birds were singing their evening spring love songs. I watched this happy little company pass away, one of the daughters had taken her lute and was singing a madrigal as they went, the brothers joining in, while William and his lady planned and argued . . .

The beautiful rooms were built by his Italian workmen and are still there, lovely but roofless. I could well imagine that en-chanting scene in July 1634 when, as the old *Life* says, "The King and Queen came over from Welbeck, which William Newcastle had resigned to them for their visit." Inigo Jones designed the setting for Ben Jonson's masque, *Love's Welcome*, which was performed with lutes and tenors and basses, and nothing was spared that might add splendour to that feast. The Earl sent for all the neighbouring gentry to come and wait on their Majesties, and in short did all that ever he could imagine to render it great and worthy of their Royal acceptance.

In less than ten years a very different company were assem-bled there—probably indeed some of the same neighbouring gentry, but this time there were no gay ladies. William Caven-dish, who was lavish and generous in peace, was even more generous and lavish in adversity and war; here he assembled a regiment of 3,000 strong men, known as Newcastle's White Coats—for when he provided their liveries there was not suffi-cient red cloth to clothe so many, at which the men called out, "Let us have white, my lord."

Leaving a garrison to defend Bolsover he led his White Coats gallantly out to fight for the King, and was many times successful, but in July 1644, against Newcastle's advice, Prince Rupert insisted on fighting the battle of Marston Moor. New-castle, though strongly opposed to this battle, had to give way

295

before the impetuous Prince—all he could say was that happen what would, he would not shun to fight for he had no other ambition but to live and die a loyal subject to His Majesty. In the battle he held no command but led his troops forward. He fought bravely with his page's half-leaden sword in his hand, but his valour was of no avail and his beloved White Coats were all cut down, his hopes ruined, and he himself left broken and almost penniless. He sadly asked Prince Rupert to give a just and true report of him to His Majesty, and that he had behaved like an honest man, a gentleman and a loyal subject. There was nothing more he could do. His homes were in the hands of the enemy, so he and his wife with a few pounds in their pockets took ship to Hamburg and lived in exile for sixteen years.

Bolsover itself was besieged; shortage of food made it impossible to hold out and the castle was surrendered in August 1644. Parliament ordered that much of it should be demolished and sold as building material, but by a lucky chance William's brother, Sir Charles Cavendish, was able to buy it back; notwithstanding a great part of it was pulled down already.

Bertie and I wandered in and out of the ruined banqueting hall and the many rooms adjoining, looking up at the tall doorways, and the deep empty fireplaces, and then we sat on the steps where King Charles and the courtiers had sat and watched Ben Jonson's masque and William's cream horses. We pondered on many things, on Kings and Parliaments and Civil Wars, and Loyalty and Beauty.

"You certainly would have been a Roundhead, Bertie. There is no doubt about that! Yes, and you would then have led the prayers and called upon God to smite the enemy hip and thigh, and you would have helped the Lord in his work too, and smitten as well as prayed."

Bertie laughed one of his loud laughs, thinking of himself smiting hip-and-thigh.

"But you would have been a Roundhead too," he asked, "wouldn't you?"

"I always wonder," I replied. "I hope I should, but how hard it would have been to be disloyal, and how hard it would have been to see those strong, determined, fierce, fanatical, self-righteous men and women, battering down and destroying the fragile beauty that my ancestors had loved and built up, and to have heard them denouncing innocent beauty as wicked, fit only to be cast out and trodden underfoot with the roses from my grandparent's tomb, and they would surely have called me 'The Scarlet Woman.' But I know they were in the right, and stalwart and noble and very good, and I expect one side of me would have been quite happy singing psalms with Lady Fairfax and Cromwell's daughters, although I might have shed a tear when I thought of being parted from my charming Cavendish cousins, and of having to wear grey wool dresses instead of lovely yellow satin ones.

"*That* civil war never ends, does it, Bertie? The war between beauty and puritanism? I know I always feel those two sides fighting in myself. Sometimes I believe I have made peace, but it soon begins again. Is beauty after all but a temptress from the straight and narrow way of goodness? Is she but a wanton Circe that leads people on to wallow in luxury and selfishness and depravity? There must be something in beauty that stirs men to fury and intolerance and instigates them to have a desire to destroy. It sometimes seems to me as if it were a magnet to drive men mad."

Bertie sucked away at his pipe and silently nodded his head.

"Cannot one love goodness and beauty equally?" I went on. "Or does beauty always weaken one, and make one dally by the

297

way, chasing butterflies instead of bravely climbing the hill of life?

"Ought I always to keep my eyes from looking at king-fishers and dragonflies and peacocks, and rest them only on jackdaws and crows? And in my garden must I grow only laurels and cauliflower and cabbage, and banish gay, striped bastard tulips, Turks' head lilies and laburnums as wanton and wicked? No, no, I know that those who fear and destroy beauty and colour in life are denouncing what the Creator thought good, and that in destroying it they are envious, ignorant and irreverent.

"There must be some way of balancing beauty and goodness —of uniting them, and permeating the one with the other, of finding 'the hidden soul of harmony' that haunts those that have once known it."

"Milton and Mozart found it, Spinoza found it, Shakespeare and Michelangelo followed it, but I expect there were men who persecuted them, from envy," Bertie said. "And Mozart was buried in a pauper's grave and only one friend followed his coffin," he added.

"I have an idea that in this imperfect world great beauty can in some mysterious way exceed the balance of harmony and so turn some men astray. It may have some electric quality that tips the scales. 'Nature, fair as she seems, rests ever on grim foundations, and Pan to whose music the nymphs dance hath a cry that drives all men distracted.' "

"Perhaps if men grow purer they will be more prepared to enter into harmony with it. It may be that we have to pass through the spheres of cleansing fire, and be cleansed by the waters of abnegation before becoming fit to rejoice in great beauty. I think Milton knew something of beauty's danger and had heard the Syren's Song, for he could not have made Comus so eloquent unless he too had tasted of its dangerous draught. How convincing does Comus's rebuke to the Lady seem:

O foolishness of men! that lend their ears
To those budge doctors of the Stoic fur,
Praising the lean and sallow Abstinence!
And fetch their precepts from the Cynic tub,
Wherefore did Nature pour her bounties forth
With such a full and unwithdrawing hand,
Covering the earth with odours, fruits and flocks,
Thronging the seas with spawn innumerable,
But all to please and sate the curious taste?
And set to work millions of spinning worms,
That in their green shops weave the smooth-haired silk,
To deck her sons.

But he made the Lady resist that cup, didn't he? For it would undoubtedly have turned her into an 'ugly-headed monster.' It is a comfort to me to remember that Milton was so sensuous, so passionate, and yet so wise."

"You are more Puritan by instinct than I am, aren't you, Bertie? I don't think these things torment you as they do me. I expect your ancestors were mostly austere Puritans, weren't they?"

"Yes, perhaps they were."

"Do you think one's forefathers affect one, Bertie? I don't mean the thought of them, of feeling proud or ashamed of them, but the thing that is called continuity of race. Can one recognize their instincts and characteristics in oneself. After all, one cannot but be coloured by the sap that flows in the tree, that has given one life. In old days I didn't think about my ancestors, or perhaps I took pride in not feeling proud of them, but now when there is a lull in life and when I am more bereft of companions, the company of the dead seem to press upon me, and to assert themselves in me, and Time seems but a vapour. Just as it is easy to recognize in some old family portrait hanging at Welbeck a nose or a mouth, or the shape of a face, that one has obviously inherited, so do I recognize traits and characteristics that have come down to me."

"Yes," Bertie interrupted, "I dare say that's true, but if so it is more a loss than a gain, for you are far too disciplined and bound by tradition, and you certainly haven't the primitive free instincts which give vigour and creativeness to such men as D. H. Lawrence, for instance."

"Well, one can't have it all ways," I answered. "Coming of a long line of men and women who have enjoyed inherited wealth and so have been free to move about in the world—to travel hither and thither—and who have sunned themselves in the sunshine of art and culture and who, too, have taken part in weaving the tangle of history, have become conscious of what civilization and subtlety of thought and quickness of action mean, must influence one and make one more complex, more mature, and richer in comprehension, and must lay a foundation of quick perception and understanding. Think, too, what it must mean to a small child to be brought up in the midst of historical associations and treasures from every land, and to wander from early years in beautiful rooms filled with such things as other children only see in museums. How I loved to finger and caress the pearl drop from King Charles's ear, and to lock up and hide my first precious letters in a casket given by King William the Third, with keys that are a pattern of beauty and delicacy, and to play and act with King Henry VIII's ruby-studded dagger. It made the past vivid and interesting and perhaps endowed me with greater awareness and sensibility."

Bedford Square: Peace and War

Bertie sat on the grey stones by my side, clasping his knees,
listening to my outpouring, and I am afraid thought me very
vulgar; but at last he said, "Yes, I suppose coming from a good
stock gives one a certain standard and balance, an unconscious
assurance and courage, and one isn't so easily tilted awry as
those who come out of families who have always had to obey.
I have certainly inherited the instinct of responsibility to my
country, and it is undoubtedly an advantage to have had a first-
class education. But show me what all these privileged people
do now with their inherited sensibility and culture. You know
they despise art and cultivation as degenerate. Learning is a
thing to laugh at and avoid as too wanting in humour for ordinary life. They very seldom encourage good architects or painters or writers. You have often told me yourself how angry your
brothers were with you for reading Spenser or Chaucer, and
scolded you when they found Tolstoy in your room, and told
you to read Rudyard Kipling instead. And Augustus John's pictures were horrible and disgusting in their eyes, and such musicians as Mozart and Bach 'impossible,' 'laughable.' They only
order the most worthless flattering portraits, and music for them
is musical comedy. I am sure they wouldn't recognize a line of
Milton if they heard it. The only thing they really care for or
take seriously is sport or golf, and now the War. Why even this
old beautiful place has had its roof removed and panelling
taken away, and you say your brother talks of selling the man-
telpieces, and left to itself it will in a few years fall into complete decay. A treasure as beautiful and historical as anything
in England is entirely unappreciated. If they spent the money
they now spend on fishing and shooting for a year it could be
restored. No, no, don't talk to me of their inherited taste and
sensibility. I don't believe in it!"

I gathered up my grey cape round me and we wandered once

more round the garden and listened to the thrushes and the black-birds singing to the lovely Venus as the fountain sprayed around her. I quoted to Bertie the old ballad written by one of Bolsover's first admirers, a Dr. Andrewes, in 1620:

AN ANCIENT RHYME

Respecting Welbeck Abbey, Hardwick Hall, Bolsover Castle, and Worksop Manor. It was written about the year 1620, by a Dr. Andrewes

Hardwicke for hugeness, Worsope for height,
Welbecke for use, and Bolser for sighte;
Worsope for walks, Hardwicke for hall,
Welbecke for brewhouse, Bolser for all.
Welbecke a parish, Hardwicke a court,
Worsope a pallas, Bolser a fort;
Bolser to feast, Welbecke to ride in,
Hardwicke to thrive, and Worsope to bide in.
Hardwicke good house, Welbecke good keepinge,
Worsope good walkes, Bolser good sleepinge;
Bolser new built, Welbecke well mended,
Hardwicke concealed, and Worsope extended.
Bolser is morn, Welbecke day bright,
Hardwicke high noone, Worsope good night;
Hardwicke is now, and Welbecke will last,
Bolser will be, and Worsope is past.
Welbecke a wife, Bolser a maide,
Hardwicke a matron, Worsope decaide;
Worsope is wise, Welbecke is wittie,
Hardwicke is hard, Bolser is prettie.
Hardwicke is rich, Welbecke is fine,
Worsope is statelie, Bolser divine;

Bedford Square: Peace and War

Hardwicke a chest, Welbecke a saddle,
Worsope a throne, Bolser a cradle.
Hardwicke resembles Hampton Court much,
And Worsope Windsor, Bolser Nonesuch;
Worsope a duke, Hardwicke an earl,
Welbecke a viscount, Bolser a pearl.
The rest are jewels of the sheere,
Bolser the pendant of the eare.

Index

Note: the initials O.M. and P.M. stand for Lady Ottoline and Philip Morrell in incidental references

i

A NOTE ON THE TYPE

THE TEXT of this book was set on the Linotype in
Fairfield, a type face designed by the distinguished
American artist and engraver, RUDOLPH RUZICKA. This
type displays the sober and sane qualities of a master
craftsman whose talent has long been dedicated to
clarity. Rudolph Ruzicka was born in Bohemia in 1883
and came to America in 1894. He has designed and
illustrated many books and has created a considerable
list of individual prints in a variety of techniques.

Composed, printed, and bound by
The Haddon Craftsmen, Inc., Scranton, Pa.
Typography and binding designs by
VINCENT TORRE

		DATE DUE